BIG IDEAS
MATH.
Blue

A Common Core Curriculum

Resources by Chapter

- Family and Community Involvement

- Start Thinking! and Warm Up

- Extra Practice (A and B)

- Enrichment and Extension

- Puzzle Time

- Technology Connection

- Project with Rubric

BIG IDEAS LEARNING.

Erie, Pennsylvania

Big Ideas Learning and *Big Ideas Math* are registered trademarks of Larson Texts, Inc.

ISBN 13: 978-1-60840-476-6
ISBN 10: 1-60840-476-5

123456789-VLP-17 16 15 14 13

Contents

About the Resources by Chapter

Family and Community Involvement (English and Spanish)

The Family and Community Involvement letters provide a way to quickly communicate to family members how they can help their student with the material of the chapter. They make the mathematics less intimidating and provide suggestions for helping students see mathematical concepts in common activities.

Start Thinking! and Warm Up

Each Start Thinking! and Warm Up includes two options for getting the class started. The Start Thinking! questions provide students with an opportunity to discuss thought-provoking questions and analyze real-world situations. The Warm Up questions review prerequisite skills needed for the lesson.

Extra Practice

The Extra Practice exercises provide additional practice on the key concepts taught in the lesson. There are two levels of practice provided for each lesson: A (basic) and B (average). Chapters with Extensions also have Extra Practice.

Enrichment and Extension

Each Enrichment and Extension extends the lesson and provides a challenging application of the key concepts.

Puzzle Time

Each Puzzle Time provides additional practice in a fun format in which students use their mathematical knowledge to solve a riddle. This format allows students to self-check their work.

Technology Connection

Each Technology Connection provides opportunities for students to explore mathematical concepts using tools such as scientific and graphing calculators, spreadsheets, geometry software, and the Internet.

Project with Rubric

The Projects summarize key concepts. They require students to investigate a concept, gather and analyze data, and summarize the results. Scoring rubrics are provided.

Chapter 1

Name_____ Date _____

 Chapter 1 **Equations**

Dear Family,

The Internet has made more information available to people than ever before. Because much of this information comes from other countries, you are likely to see more metric units of measure than ever before. The dimensions for many products are often given using centimeters (cm) or meters (m). You may find a recipe online that uses milliliters (ml) and grams (g) instead of cups and ounces. How will you convert these measurements to more familiar units?

You may know some ways to approximate some familiar customary units. An inch is about the width of your thumb. A cup of flour fits in two cupped hands. "Room temperature" is about 72° Fahrenheit (°F). To develop a way to approximate metric measurements, you will need to convert an unfamiliar unit to a familiar one.

Work with your student to find some analogies for some common metric units. For example, one centimeter (cm) is about four tenths of an inch. A common approximation for a centimeter is the width of the nail on your index finger.

Figure out these analogies with your student:

- Find out what "room temperature" is on the Celsius scale. Normal body temperature is 98.6°F—what is normal body temperature on the Celsius scale?

- A mile is about 12 city blocks. Find out how many city blocks are in a kilometer (km).

- A yard is roughly the distance from your nose to your outstretched fingertips. About how long is a meter?

- About how many grams of flour fit in two cupped hands?

There may be other units you have encountered. By finding common analogies, these new units of measure may become more familiar.

A pinch of understanding is worth a pound of information!

Capítulo 1 Ecuaciones

Estimada Familia:

La Internet ha hecho posible que hoy más que nunca, las personas tengamos más información disponible. Dado que la mayoría de esta información proviene de otros países, estará viendo más unidades métricas que nunca antes. Las dimensiones de muchos productos a menudo se expresan en centímetros (cm) o metros (m). En Internet podrá encontrar una receta que use mililitros (ml) y gramos (g) en vez de tazas y onzas. ¿Cómo convertiría estas medidas a unidades más conocidas?

Pueda que conozca algunas formas de aproximar algunas unidades conocidas. Una pulgada es aproximadamente el ancho de su pulgar. Una taza de harina cabe en dos manos cóncavas. La "temperatura ambiente" es alrededor de 72° Fahrenheit (°F). Para desarrollar una forma de aproximar las medidas métricas, necesitará convertir una unidad no conocida en una conocida.

Trabaje con su estudiante para hallar algunas analogías para ciertas unidades métricas comunes. Por ejemplo, un centímetro (cm) equivale aproximadamente a cuatro décimas de pulgada. Una aproximación común para un centímetro es el ancho de la uña de su dedo índice.

Averigüe estas analogías con su estudiante:

- Averigüen cuánto es la "temperatura ambiente" en la escala de Celsius. La temperatura normal del cuerpo es 98.6°F—¿cuál es la temperatura normal del cuerpo en la escala de Celsius?

- Una milla es alrededor de 12 cuadras de la ciudad. Averigüen cuántas cuadras de la ciudad equivalen a un kilómetro (km).

- Una yarda es más o menos la distancia desde su nariz hasta las puntas estiradas de sus dedos. Aproximadamente, ¿cuánto será un metro?

- Aproximadamente, ¿cuántos gramos de harina caben en dos manos cóncavas?

Pueda ser que hayan encontrado otras unidades. Al encontrar analogías comunes, estas nuevas unidades de medida se hacen más conocidas.

¡Un poquito de comprensión equivale a una libra de información!

Start Thinking!
For use before Activity 1.1

What are some rules in your classroom
or school? How are they similar to rules
in mathematics?

Warm Up
For use before Activity 1.1

Use a protractor to find the measure of the angle.

1.

2.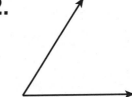

3.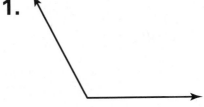

4.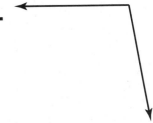

5.

6.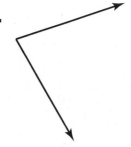

The Addition Property of Equality states that adding the same number to each side of an equation produces an equivalent equation. What do you think the Subtraction, Multiplication, and Division Properties of Equality state?

Describe a real-life situation that you can relate to one of the properties of equality.

Lesson 1.1 **Warm Up**
For use before Lesson 1.1

Find the value of x. Check the reasonableness of your answer.

1.
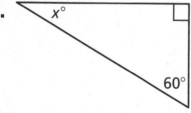

2.
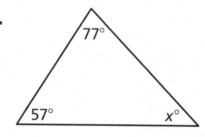

3.
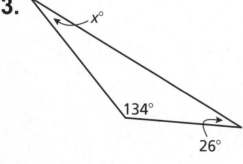

4.
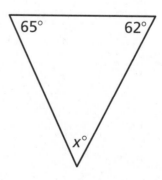

Name_____ Date_____

1.1 Practice A

Solve the equation. Check your solution.

1. $x + 4 = 11$

2. $n - 14 = 20$

3. $-6 + k = -9$

4. $2\pi + d = 5\pi$

5. $y - 1.4 = -2.7$

6. $\dfrac{2}{5} = w - \dfrac{3}{2}$

7. Your school's football team scored 49 points. Your team's score was 19 points more than the opponent's score s. Write and solve an equation to find the opponent's score.

Solve the equation. Check your solution.

8. $5y = 40$

9. $\dfrac{d}{9} = -2$

10. $1.2 = -3b$

11. $\dfrac{x}{4.1} = -2$

12. $\dfrac{2}{5}p = \dfrac{3}{5}$

13. $-4.5 = -1.2k$

14. You earn \$7.50 per hour to help your uncle in his shop. You earn \$33.75. Write and solve an equation to find how many hours you worked.

Solve the equation. Check your solution.

15. $s - \left|-4\right| = 7.3$

16. $p + 1.6 \div (-0.4) = -12$

17. Without solving, determine whether the solution of $\dfrac{1}{3}x = 21$ is *greater than* or *less than* 21. Explain.

18. The volume V of the cylinder is 65π cubic centimeters. The height h of the cylinder is 5 centimeters. Use the formula $V = Bh$ to find the area B of the base of the cylinder.

19. The total area of this shape is 44 square inches. The area of the triangle is 20 square inches. Write and solve an equation to find the area of the rectangle.

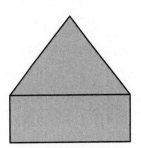

1.1 Practice B

Solve the equation. Check your solution.

1. $-13 + x = -25$

2. $h + 4\pi = 30\pi$

3. $4.5 = m + 2.75$

4. $a - \dfrac{3}{4} = \dfrac{2}{3}$

5. $\dfrac{1}{6} = \dfrac{5}{12} + p$

6. $c - 2.3 = -5.1$

7. You shopped online and found your MP3 player for $9.75 less than the store price p. The online price was $64. Write and solve an equation to find the store price.

Solve the equation. Check your solution.

8. $-1.6x = 8$

9. $\dfrac{h}{2\pi} = 4.3$

10. $\dfrac{4}{3} = \dfrac{2}{15}j$

11. $-23.6 = 5.9t$

12. $6\pi = -2\pi q$

13. $\dfrac{3}{7}w = -4$

14. The area of a rectangle is 55.8 square inches. The width of the rectangle is 4.5 inches. Write and solve an equation to find the length of the rectangle.

Solve the equation. Check your solution.

15. $5.6 \div 0.4 - r = -8$

16. $n - 5 \bullet \dfrac{2}{3} = \dfrac{3}{4}$

17. Write an addition equation and a multiplication equation that each have a solution of -5.

18. A fruit basket contains oranges and grapefruits. One-third of the oranges and one-fourth of the grapefruits were spoiled. You threw away 4 oranges and 7 grapefruits. How many pieces of fruit were in the basket?

19. You and two friends pay $40 for tickets. The cost was divided three ways in the ratio 1 : 3 : 6. How much did each person pay?

Name_____ Date_____

1.1 Enrichment and Extension

Properties of Equality

There are four properties of equality. These properties are usually used to solve equations. They can also be used to write an equivalent form of a given equation.

Determine which property of equality can be used to transform the first equation into the second equation. Then use the color key to shade the square the appropriate color.

Color Key:
Addition Property of Equality - Yellow
Subtraction Property of Equality - Green
Multiplication Property of Equality - Red
Division Property of Equality - Blue

$2x = 4$ $4x = 8$	$10x = -100$ $x = -10$	$x + 1 = 0$ $x + 6 = 5$	$7 - 2x = -2$ $14 - 2x = 5$	$15x = 45$ $x = 3$	$5x = 10$ $6x = 12$
$9x = 81$ $x = 9$	$x + 5 = 1$ $x + 9 = 5$	$x + 4 = 5$ $x = 1$	$x + 7 = 10$ $x + 2 = 5$	$x = 8$ $x + 2 = 10$	$2.2x = 22$ $x = 10$
$x = 0$ $x + 2 = 2$	$x + 3 = 3$ $x = 0$	$3x = 11$ $-3x = -11$	$12.5x = 7$ $25x = 14$	$x + 2 = 19$ $x = 17$	$3 - x = -4$ $5 - x = -2$
$x + 3 = 6$ $x + 6 = 9$	$x = 2$ $x - 1 = 1$	$4x = 5$ $20x = 25$	$2x = 10$ $5x = 25$	$x - 2 = 14$ $x - 4 = 12$	$x + 1 = 2$ $x + 6 = 7$
$-12x = 60$ $2x = -10$	$2x - 1 = 5$ $2x + 2 = 8$	$x + 13 = 15$ $x + 4 = 6$	$x = 10$ $x - 8 = 2$	$3x + 1 = -4$ $3x + 6 = 1$	$1.5x = 20$ $0.15x = 2$
$-4x = 1$ $16x = -4$	$100x = 50$ $20x = 10$	$x + 1 = 3$ $x + 8 = 10$	$x + 1.5 = 1.7$ $x + 2.8 = 3$	$-14x = 28$ $x = -2$	$x = 3$ $9x = 27$

1. Is it possible to complete the board so that there are no blue squares? Explain your reasoning.

2. Is it possible to complete the board so that there are no green squares? Explain your reasoning.

Name_____ Date _____

1.1 Puzzle Time

Did You Hear About...

A	B	C	D	E	F
G	H	I	J	K	L
M	N	O	P		

Complete each exercise. Find the answer in the answer column. Write the word under the answer in the box containing the exercise letter.

5 WHO	
7.2 HOW	
−9 MAN	
−13 SOUP	
−$\frac{4}{3}$ IT	
−14 HE	
$\frac{3}{4}$ ARE	
$\frac{7}{8}$ IN	
42 SOMETHING	
4.5 WASH	

Solve the equation.

A. $x + 9 = -12$

B. $-8 + k = -17$

C. $-0.3 + r = 4.7$

D. $f + 3\pi = 12\pi$

E. $d - 6\pi = -\pi$

F. $\frac{1}{8} = s - \frac{3}{4}$

G. $m - \frac{1}{4} = -\frac{1}{3}$

H. $-0.8b = 10.4$

I. $46.2 = 4.2p$

J. $-7\pi h = 98\pi$

K. $12.5 = \frac{t}{\pi}$

L. $3.9r = 17.55$

M. $\frac{3}{8}q = -\frac{1}{2}$

N. $-\frac{5}{6} = \frac{2}{3}w$

O. Your dog weighs 28.5 pounds more than your cat. Your dog weighs 37.8 pounds. What is your cat's weight?

P. Nathaniel's sister has $\frac{5}{6}$ as many songs on her MP3 player as he has on his MP3 player. His sister has 35 songs. How many songs does Nathaniel have?

9.3 WITH	
5π SOAP	
12.5π COULD	
8π WAS	
−$\frac{1}{12}$ HIS	
9π PUT	
−$\frac{5}{4}$ DOWN	
11 SO	
−21 THE	
−$\frac{3}{5}$ THAT	

Activity 1.2 Start Thinking!

For use before Activity 1.2

Why do you think it is important to check your answer to a math problem?

Activity 1.2 Warm Up

For use before Activity 1.2

Simplify the expression.

1. $2n + 5 + 3n$

2. $x - 7 - 4x$

3. $4f + f + 6f$

4. $(9 - m) + 4m + 7$

5. $17 + 2t - 9 + 2t$

6. $(y + 7) + (2y - 5)$

Explain why the following situation can be modeled by a multi-step equation.

A plumber charges $80 per hour for labor plus $60 for parts.

Come up with your own scenario that can be modeled by a multi-step equation.

Lesson 1.2 **Warm Up**
For use before Lesson 1.2

Find the value of _x_. Then find the angle measures of the polygon. Use a protractor to check the reasonableness of your answer.

1.

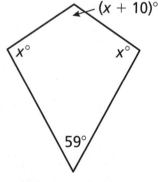

Sum of angle measures: 180°

2.

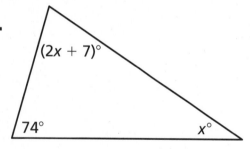

Sum of angle measures: 360°

3.

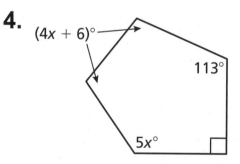

Sum of angle measures: 360°

4.

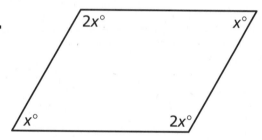

Sum of angle measures: 540°

Name_____ Date _____

1.2 Practice A

Solve the equation. Check your solution.

1. $8y - 7 = 9$

2. $14 - 3m = -1$

3. $30 + 2k + 5k = 100$

4. $z + (z - 6) - 2 = -10$

5. $3.2x - 1.7x + 5.5 = 10$

6. $\dfrac{3}{4}x - \dfrac{1}{4}x + 14 = 3$

7. The cost C (in dollars) of making n feet of cabinet is represented by $C = 18n + 45$. How many feet of cabinet are made when the cost is $441?

8. The sum of the measures of the interior angles of the parallelogram is 360°. Write and solve an equation to find the value of the variable.

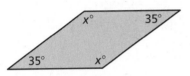

9. At the movies, you order 3 boxes of popcorn and a bottle of water. The cost of the bottle of water is $1.75. Your total cost is $9.25. Write and solve an equation to find the cost of one box of popcorn.

10. You and your friend each purchase an equal number n of magazines. Your magazines cost $1.50 each and your friend's magazines cost $2 each. The total cost for you and your friend is $10.50. Write and solve an equation to find the number of magazines you purchased.

11. A rope 25 feet long is cut into 3 pieces. The first piece is $2x$ feet long, the second piece is $5x$ feet long, and the third piece is 4 feet long.

    a. Write and solve an equation to find x.

    b. Find the lengths of the first and second pieces.

12. The average of your 3 quiz grades is 17 points. Two of your quiz grades are 14 points and 19 points. Write and solve an equation to find the third quiz grade.

13. You had $26 in your pocket. You purchased x pens at $3.50 each. You now have $8.50 in your pocket. Write and solve an equation to find the number of pens purchased.

1.2 Practice B

Solve the equation. Check your solution.

1. $4k - 1.5k = 50$

2. $\dfrac{5}{7}p - \dfrac{2}{7}p + 12 = 6$

3. $\dfrac{2}{3}y + y - 4 = 31$

4. $2.1x + 1.3x - 4.6 = 2.2$

5. $3(5 - 2h) + 9 = -30$

6. $14(x - 3) - 22x = -18$

7. The sum of the measures of the interior angles of the triangle is 180°. Write and solve an equation to find the value of the variable.

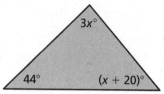

8. A rectangular field has an area of 2100 square feet. The length of the field is 50 feet.

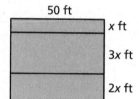

   a. How wide is the field?

   b. The field is divided into 3 rectangles, as shown. Write and solve an equation to find x.

   c. Determine the dimensions of each rectangle.

9. You are researching the price of MP3 players. You found an average price of $58.80. One MP3 player costs $56 and another costs $62. Find the price of the third MP3 player.

10. The perimeter of a triangle is 42 inches. One side measures 18 inches. The shortest side measures x inches. The longest side measures 1 inch less than four times the length of the shortest side. Write and solve an equation to find the length of the longest side.

11. You order 4 fish sandwiches and a hamburger. The cost of the hamburger is $2.50. Your total bill before tax is $14.30. Write and solve an equation to find the cost of a fish sandwich.

Name_____   Date _____

Solving Equations

Work with a partner to design a game board. Cut out each of the cards, fold them in half, and place them in a bag.

Game Rules:

Each player puts a game piece on the start square. The youngest student goes first, selects a card from the bag, and solves the equation on a separate piece of paper. If the answer is positive, the player moves forward that many spaces. If the answer is negative, the player moves backward that many spaces. If there are no spaces to move back, the player loses a turn. If a player suspects his competitor's answer is incorrect, he or she can challenge by solving the equation to check the solution. If a player challenges and wins, he or she moves forward 3 spaces. If a player challenges and loses, he or she forfeits a turn. Place the card back in the bag and it is the next person's turn. The first player to the end square wins.

$2x - 12 = 8$	$\frac{1}{2}x = 3$	$2x + 6 = 0$
$-14x + 7 = -21$	$0.75x + 0.5 = 2$	$4x + 2 = 22$
$15x + 2 = 62$	$-30x = 90$	$3x = 21$
$x + 10 = 7$	$2x - 4 = 10$	$\pi x = 6\pi$
$4x - 10 = 6$	$\frac{3}{4}x - 0.25 = 0.5$	$13x - 2x - 3 = 41$
$25x - 20 = 5$	$-\frac{2}{5}x = -2$	$4x - 11x + 32 = 4$

Puzzle Time

Where Was The Declaration Of Independence Signed?

Circle the letter of each correct answer in the boxes below. The circled letters will spell out the answer to the riddle.

Solve the equation.

1. $8 - 3x = 17$

2. $5a - 6 - 2a = 12$

3. $4.3t - 2.1t - 2.3 = 7.6$

4. $8.1 + 3.8h - 5.6h = -7.2$

5. $\frac{2}{5}c + 4 - \frac{1}{5}c = -9$

6. $2(4s - 16) - 5s = -5$

7. $3g - 6(g - 8) = 42$

8. $1.3(8 - b) + 3.7b = -5.2$

9. For the past three months, Grace used her cell phone for 43 minutes, 62 minutes, and 57 minutes. How many minutes would she have to use her cell phone this month for the average usage over the four months to be 55 minutes?

10. A triangle has one angle measuring $3x$ degrees. A second angle measures $2x + 20$ degrees and the third angle measures $4x - 20$ degrees. What is the value of x?

11. You and a friend buy two fruit smoothies and leave a tip. You split the total and your half comes to $3.60. What percent tip (in decimal form) did you and your friend leave if the fruit smoothies cost $3 each?

A	M	T	E	S	R	T	I	H	P	E	D	G	B	Y
2	60	6	8.2	0.10	5	9	0.18	8.5	55	−3	10.5	−2	0.15	−62

F	B	I	R	O	H	T	C	U	T	N	O	L	M	S
9.5	0.20	3	10	−65	15	58	90	8	20	−55	4.5	68	−6.5	12.5

Study the equation below.

The same number of 1-chips are in each box with a question mark. How many chips are in each box?

Activity 1.3 **Warm Up**
For use before Activity 1.3

Find the width of the rectangle.

1. Area = 32 m²

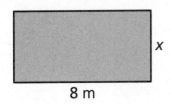

8 m

2. Area = 150 cm²

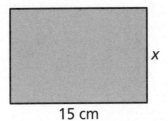

15 cm

3. Perimeter = 35 in.

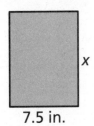

7.5 in.

4. Perimeter = 40 ft

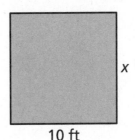

10 ft

Try solving the equation $2x + 20 = 12x$ by first subtracting 20 from each side. What property allows you to do so? Does it help you get closer to finding a solution?

What is a better first step? Explain.

The value of the solid's surface area is equal to the value of the solid's volume. Find the value of x.

1.

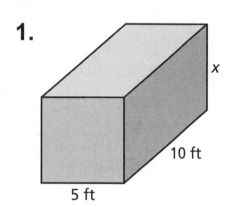

10 ft

5 ft

x

2.

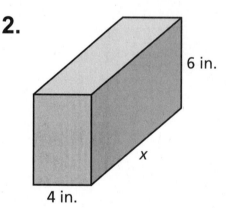

6 in.

4 in.

x

Name_____ Date_____

1.3 Practice A

The value of the perimeter of the figure is equal to the value of the area. Find the value of x.

1.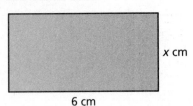

   x cm

   6 cm

2.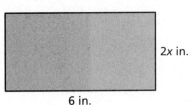

   $2x$ in.

   6 in.

Solve the equation. Check your solution.

3. $y - 12 = 4y$

4. $6n - 12 = n + 3$

5. $\dfrac{1}{5}q = 9 - \dfrac{2}{5}q$

6. $4.3d + 7.5 = 5.8d$

7. $6(h + 4) = -2h$

8. $3(b - 4) = 5b - 2$

9. Your long distance telephone provider offers two plans. Plan A has a monthly fee of $15 and $0.25 per minute. Plan B has a monthly fee of $20 and $0.05 per minute. Write and solve an equation to find the number of minutes that you must talk to have the same cost for each of the plans.

10. One-third of a number x is equal to 22 less than the number. Write and solve an equation to find the number.

11. Find the perimeter of the regular polygon.

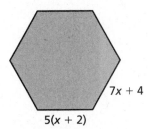

$7x + 4$

$5(x + 2)$

12. You purchase a desk for 60% of the original price p. This price is $32 less than the original price. Write and solve an equation to find the original price of the desk.

Solve the equation.

13. $8x + 3 = 8x$

14. $-25(10 - x) = 25x + 250$

15. $x + 1 = x + 1$

16. $6(2x + 4) = 4(3x + 6)$

17. $x + 2 = 5x$

18. $5x + 2 - x = -4x$

1.3 Practice B

The value of the solid's surface area is equal to the value of the solid's volume. Find the value of x.

1.

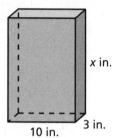

x in.

10 in.   3 in.

2.

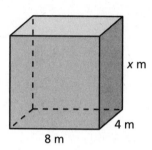

x m

4 m

8 m

Solve the equation. Check your solution.

3. $5y - 14 = 2y - 2$

4. $\dfrac{4}{7}m = 18 - \dfrac{2}{7}m$

5. $16(p - 2) = 7p + 4$

6. $4(2s - 3) = 3(s + 1)$

7. $0.3(t - 2) = 0.4t$

8. $\dfrac{2}{9}n + \dfrac{1}{2} = \dfrac{2}{3}(n + 3)$

9. Describe and correct the error in solving the equation.

$$
\begin{aligned}
0.4x &= 0.2(x - 8) \\
0.4x &= 0.2x - 8 \\
0.2x &= -8 \\
x &= -40
\end{aligned}
$$

Solve the equation.

10. $4.2x - 3 = 0.5(8.4x + 6)$

11. $\dfrac{2}{3}x + 1 = \dfrac{2}{3}x - 1$

12. $1.5(6 - 2x) = 3x - 9$

13. $\dfrac{1}{2}x - 5 = \dfrac{3}{2}x - 5$

14. $-3(x + 5) = -(3x + 15)$

15. $-\dfrac{1}{2}x + 1\dfrac{1}{2} = \dfrac{1}{2}(3 - x)$

16. The original price p for a necklace is the same at both jewelry stores. At Store A, the sale price is 60% of the original price. Last month, at Store B the sale price was $40 less than the original price. This month, Store B is selling the necklace for 80% of last month's reduced price. The current sale prices are the same for both stores. Write and solve an equation to find the original price of the necklace.

1.3 Enrichment and Extension

Where can you buy a ruler that is three feet long?

Solve the equations. Order the solutions from least to greatest. Once ordered, the variables will spell the answer to the riddle.

1. $5d - 4 = 4 - d$

2. $-10e + 15 = 95 - 30e$

3. $15t + 17 = 13t + 14$

4. $-12 - a = 4a - 7$

5. $4a - 16 = a - 15$

6. $4y + 12 = 6y + 12$

7. $0.25r - 0.25 + 0.25r = 0.5 - 0.25r$

8. $-4a + 7 = a + 32$

9. $13s - 31 = 2s - 9$

10. $a + 1.25 = 2a - 1$

11. $3\ell + 4 + \ell = 13 + \ell$

Solution			■		■				■			
Variable			■		■				■			

1.3 Puzzle Time

What Happens When A Frog Double-Parks On A Lily Pad?

Write the letter of each answer in the box containing the exercise number.

Solve the equation.

1. $x + 36 = 4x$

2. $6a + 12 = 2(3a - 8)$

3. $\frac{3}{2}p - 14 = p + 13$

4. $7 - 4.9t = 15 + 7.6t$

5. $\frac{1}{3}(12f - 3) = 4f - 1$

6. $\frac{1}{3}(b + 6) = \frac{1}{4}b + 8$

7. $\frac{3}{5}(2m - 10) = \frac{2}{3}m + 10$

8. $8.2(s + 4) = 6.7s + 5.2$

9. On Monday, you run on a treadmill for $\frac{1}{2}$ hour at x miles per hour. On Tuesday, you walk the same distance on the treadmill, at 2 miles per hour slower, and it takes you $\frac{3}{4}$ hour. How many miles did you run on the treadmill on Monday?

10. Jess spent $7x$ minutes on the computer. Her sister spent $5x + 10$ minutes on the computer, which was the same amount of time Jess spent. How many minutes was Jess on the computer?

11. A rectangle is 6 units wide and $x - 8$ units long. It has the same area as a triangle with a height of 7 units and a base of $x - 3$ units. What is the area of the rectangle?

Answers
Y. 72
A. -18.4
T. 42
O. no solution
A. 35
S. 54
A. 12
D. -0.64
W. 3
I. infinitely many solutions
T. 30

5	7		3		11	2	10	4		8	9	1	6
		,											

List all of the formulas for area and perimeter (including circumference) that you know. Draw and label a sketch for each shape.

Find the volume of the solid.

1.

2 ft
3 ft
5 ft

2.

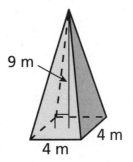

9 m
4 m
4 m

3.

7 in.
7 in.
9 in.

4.

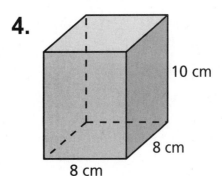

10 cm
8 cm
8 cm

How does solving the equation $5x + 4y = 14$ for x compare to solving the equation $5x + 20 = 14$ for x? Describe the steps involved in each solution.

Lesson 1.4 **Warm Up**
For use before Lesson 1.4

1. a. Write a formula for the area A of a rectangle.

b. Solve the formula for b.

c. Use the new formula to find the base of the rectangle.

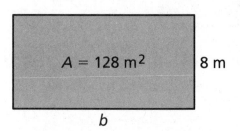

2. a. Write a formula for the volume V of a prism.

b. Solve the formula for B.

c. Use the new formula to find the area of the base of the prism.

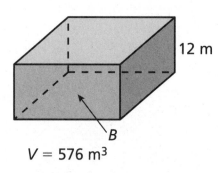

Name_____ Date_____

1.4　Practice A

Solve the equation for _y_.

1. $\dfrac{2}{5}x + y = 7$

2. $24 = 4x + 6y$

3. $5x - \dfrac{1}{2}y = 3$

4. $6\pi = x + 2y$

5. The formula $d = 2r$ can be used to find the distance _d_ traveled after 2 hours when driving at rate _r_.

    a. Solve the formula for _r_.

    b. Find the rate _r_ when the distance traveled is 130 miles.

Solve the equation for the bold variable.

6. $P = \boldsymbol{R} + C$

7. $p = \dfrac{\boldsymbol{X}}{N}$

8. $V = \dfrac{1}{3}\pi r^2 \boldsymbol{h}$

9. $A = \dfrac{1}{2}\boldsymbol{b}h$

10. The formula for the circumference of a circle with diameter _d_ is $C = \pi d$.

    a. Solve the formula for _d_.

    b. The circumference of a circle is 8 inches. What is the diameter of the circle?

    c. The circumference of a circle is 6π inches. What is the radius of the circle?

11. The formula for the area of a rhombus with diagonals of lengths _c_ and _d_ is $A = \dfrac{1}{2}cd$.

    a. Solve the formula for _c_.

    b. The area of a rhombus is 35 square feet. The length of one of the diagonals is 10 feet. What is the length of the other diagonal?

    c. In a square (which is a rhombus), the lengths of the diagonals are the same. If a square has an area of 32 square feet, then what is the length of each diagonal?

1.4 Practice B

Solve the equation for *y*.

1. $3x - \dfrac{1}{4}y = -2$

2. $5x + 8y = 6\pi$

3. $4y - 3.2x = 6$

4. $4.5x - 1.5y = 5.4$

5. The formula for the volume of a rectangular prism is $V = \ell wh$.

   a. Solve the formula for *w*.

   b. Use the new formula to find the value of *w* when $V = 210$ cubic feet, $\ell = 10$ feet, and $h = 3$ feet.

Solve the equation for the bold variable.

6. $T = hP + 2\boldsymbol{B}$

7. $C = 1000 + 80\boldsymbol{x}$

8. $S = \pi r^2 + 2\pi r\boldsymbol{h}$

9. $A = \dfrac{1}{2}\boldsymbol{P}a$

10. The formula $F = \dfrac{9}{5}C + 32$ converts temperatures from Celsius *C* to Fahrenheit *F*.

    a. Solve the formula for *C*.

    b. The boiling point of water is 212°F. What is the temperature in Celsius?

    c. If a house thermostat is set at 80°F, what is the setting in Celsius? Round your answer to the nearest tenth.

11. The formula for the area of a sector of a circle is $A = \dfrac{m}{360}\pi r^2$, given the measure *m* of the angle and the radius *r* of the circle.

    a. Solve the formula for *m*.

    b. Find the measure of the angle when the area of the sector is 5 square centimeters and the radius is 2 centimeters. Round your answer to the nearest tenth.

    c. If the area of the sector in part (b) is greater than 5 square centimeters, is the measure of the angle *greater than* or *less than* the answer to part (b)? Explain.

1.4 Enrichment and Extension

Rewriting Formulas

Neon is a gas that is used in signs. Neon is usually transported in large cylindrical tanks from laboratories to manufacturers.

The volume of neon is measured in cubic centimeters. A laboratory wishes to transport 22,222.22 cubic centimeters of neon using a cylindrical tank. The tank is 15 centimeters in diameter.

The formula for the volume of a cylinder is $V = \pi r^2 h$. In feet, how tall will the tank need to be in order to accommodate the volume of the gas? Round your answer to the nearest hundredth.

There are two methods that can be used to solve this problem. Complete each of the methods and answer the questions.

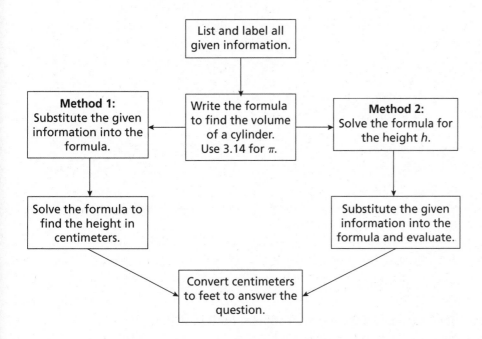

1. What is your solution using Method 1? What is your solution using Method 2?

2. Which method do you prefer? Why? Explain your reasoning.

1.4 Puzzle Time

What Can't Walk, But Can Run?

Write the letter of each answer in the box containing the exercise number.

Solve the equation for y.

1. $16 - 12x = 4y$

   A. $y = -3x + 4$ **B.** $y = 3x + 4$ **C.** $y = 3x - 4$

2. $2x + \dfrac{6}{5} = 2y$

   D. $y = 2x + \dfrac{6}{5}$ **E.** $y = x + \dfrac{3}{5}$ **F.** $y = 2x + \dfrac{3}{5}$

3. $7 = 14x - 42y$

   G. $y = -\dfrac{2}{3}x - \dfrac{1}{6}$ **H.** $y = \dfrac{1}{3}x + \dfrac{1}{6}$ **I.** $y = \dfrac{1}{3}x - \dfrac{1}{6}$

4. $8.1x - 4.5y = 5.4$

   R. $y = 1.8x - 1.2$ **S.** $y = -1.8x + 1.2$ **T.** $y = 1.8x + 1.2$

5. The formula for Body Mass Index is $BMI = \dfrac{w}{h^2} \times 703$, where w is a person's weight (in pounds) and h is a person's height (in inches). Find the weight of a 13-year-old boy that is 60 inches tall and has a BMI of 20.5.

   Q. 98 pounds   **R.** 105 pounds   **S.** 112 pounds

6. The formula $d = rt$ relates distance d to rate r and time t. Find how long it takes an airplane to fly 375 miles at 500 miles per hour.

   T. 35 minutes   **U.** 40 minutes   **V.** 45 minutes

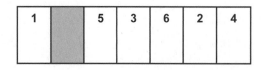

1		5	3	6	2	4

Name_____ Date _____

Using a Graphing Calculator to Solve Equations

You can use a graphing calculator to solve equations.

EXAMPLE Solve the equation $2x - 3 = x + 1$.

SOLUTION

Step 1 Use the $\boxed{Y=}$ key. Enter the left side of the equation as Y_1 and the right side of the equation as Y_2.

Step 2 Press the $\boxed{\textbf{GRAPH}}$ key. Use the STANDARD WINDOW.

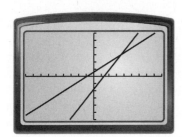
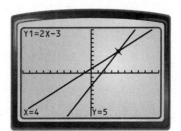

Step 3 Use the $\boxed{\textbf{TRACE}}$ key and the left and right arrow keys to find the x-value where the two lines cross. The two lines cross when $x = 4$.

Step 4 Check your answer in the equation.

$$2x - 3 = x + 1$$
$$2(4) - 3 \overset{?}{=} 4 + 1$$
$$8 - 3 \overset{?}{=} 5$$
$$5 = 5 \checkmark$$

Use a graphing calculator to solve the following equations.

1. $3x + 2 = x + 6$ **2.** $2x + 5 = 3 + x$ **3.** $5x + 4 = 3x + 7$

Chapter 2

Chapter 2 Transformations

Dear Family,

Photo albums record our most precious memories—and can last for generations. It can take a lot of creativity to make a great family album. One of the keys to designing the album is to use photos and text in a variety of sizes and positions.

You and your student may want to work together on a family album. While working, you might think about some of the following possibilities.

- Move your photos around on the page—don't position every photo in the same way. In mathematics, this is called a *translation* of the image—and it's a simple way to add interest to your pages.

- Try rotating your photos—not every photo has to be straight on the page. Rotate some photos so that they are on an angle.

- Sometimes a photo works better when you use its reflection. For example, digital photos can be "flipped" so that a person faces in another direction. This can make the composition more pleasing, but use this with care—it can make people look a bit different and any written words in the photo will appear backwards.

- Try different sizes for the text and rotate the position of the text. A good rule of thumb is to use three fonts or less on a page.

- Remember to leave some space around the photos and text. A page with too much on it will look cluttered. Try to figure out a proportion of covered to uncovered space on the page that looks good.

Computers have simplified the task of making family albums, but don't be afraid to work on paper—it's still a great way to work on a project together.

Show the album to your family and friends—they are sure to enjoy it!

Capítulo 2 Transformaciones

Estimada Familia:

Los álbumes de fotos registran nuestras memorias más preciadas—y pueden durar por generaciones. Se requiere de mucha creatividad para hacer un álbum familiar increíble. Una de las claves para diseñar el álbum es usar fotos y texto en una variedad de tamaños y posiciones.

Usted y su estudiante querrán trabajar juntos en un álbum familiar. Al trabajar, pueden pensar acerca de algunas de las siguientes posibilidades:

- Muevan las fotos por toda la página—no coloquen cada foto del mismo modo. En matemáticas, esto se conoce como *traslación* de la imagen—y es un modo simple de añadir interés a sus páginas.

- Intenten rotando las fotos—no todas las fotos tienen que estar derechas en la página. Roten algunas fotos para que queden en ángulo.

- A veces una foto funciona mejor cuando se usa su reflejo. Por ejemplo, las fotos digitales pueden voltearse para que la persona mire hacia el otro lado. Esto puede hacer que la composición sea más agradable, pero háganlo con cuidado—la gente puede verse algo distinta y cualquier palabra que aparezca en la foto se verá escrita al revés.

- Intenten con distintos tamaños para el texto y roten la posición del texto. Una regla muy importante es usar tres tipos de letra o menos en cada página.

- Recuerden dejar algo de espacio alrededor de las fotos y el texto. Una página que contenga mucho de esto se verá demasiado llena. Intenten averiguar una proporción de espacio cubierto y sin cubrir en la página que se vea bien.

Las computadoras han simplificado la tarea de hacer álbumes familiares, pero no tengan miedo de trabajar en papel—aún sigue siendo una gran manera de trabajar todos juntos en un proyecto.

Muestren el álbum a sus familiares y amigos—¡les va a encantar!

Start Thinking!

Activity 2.1 For use before Activity 2.1

Draw two triangles that are:

1. the same shape and size.

2. the same shape but *not* the same size.

3. *not* the same shape and *not* the same size.

Which pair of triangles do you think are called *congruent triangles*? Why?

Warm Up

Activity 2.1 For use before Activity 2.1

Copy the triangle and use a ruler to measure each side.

1.

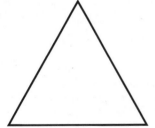

2.

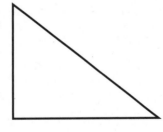

3.

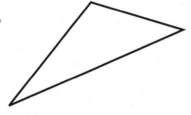

4.

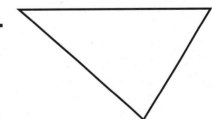

Lesson 2.1 **Start Thinking!**
For use before Lesson 2.1

With a partner, discuss the questions below. Be sure to support your answers.

1. Is it possible for two triangles to have the same angle measures but not be congruent?

2. Is it possible for two triangles to have the same side lengths but not be congruent?

Lesson 2.1 **Warm Up**
For use before Lesson 2.1

Tell whether the triangles are *congruent* or *not congruent*.

1.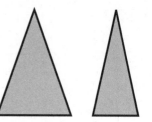

2.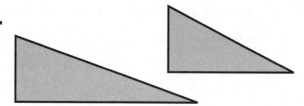

3.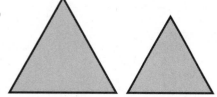

4.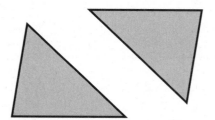

5.

6.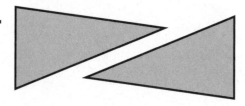

2.1 Practice A

Tell whether the triangles are *congruent* or *not congruent*.

1.

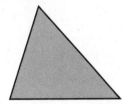

2.

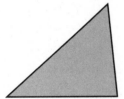

The figures are congruent. Name the corresponding angles and the corresponding sides.

3.

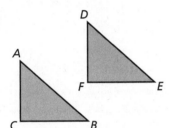

4.

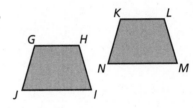

Tell whether the two figures are congruent. Explain your reasoning.

5.

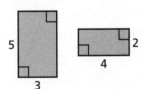

6.

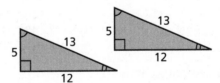

7. Describe and correct the error in telling whether the two figures are congruent.

⤫ Both figures have four sides and corresponding angle measures are equal. So, they are congruent.

8. Can two polygons be congruent if one has a right angle and the other does not? Explain.

2.1 Practice B

The figures are congruent. Name the corresponding angles and the corresponding sides.

1.

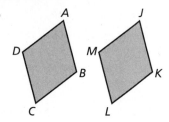

2.

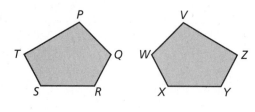

Tell whether the two figures are congruent. Explain your reasoning.

3.

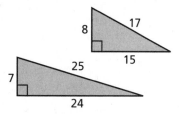

4.

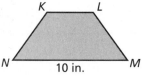

5. The figures are congruent.

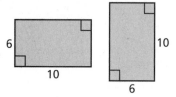

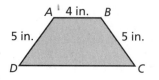

   a. What is the length of side *CD*?

   b. Which angle of *KLMN* corresponds to ∠*B*?

   c. What is the perimeter of *ABCD*?

6. The pentagons are congruent. Determine whether the statement is *true* or *false*. Explain your reasoning.

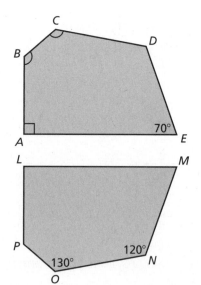

   a. ∠*B* is congruent to ∠*C*.

   b. Side *MN* is congruent to side *AE*.

   c. ∠*B* corresponds to ∠*O*.

   d. Side *BC* is congruent to side *PO*.

   e. The sum of the angle measures of *LMNOP* is 540°.

   f. The measure of ∠*B* is 120°.

Name_____ Date _____

Perimeter and Area of Similar Figures

The triangles shown are similar. Use the given information to draw conclusions about the relationship between similar figures, their areas, and their perimeters.

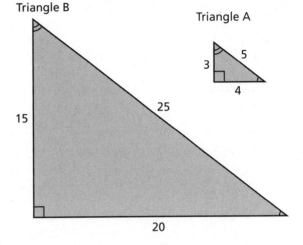

Triangle B

Triangle A

In Exercises 1–8, use the figure.

1. What is the relationship between the side lengths of Triangle A and Triangle B?

2. Find the perimeter of Triangle A.

3. Find the perimeter of Triangle B.

4. What is the relationship between the perimeter of Triangle A and the perimeter of Triangle B? How did you predict this relationship?

5. Find the area of Triangle A.

6. Find the area of Triangle B.

7. What is the relationship between the area of Triangle B and the area of Triangle A?

8. Area is a two-dimensional measurement. How did you predict this relationship?

In Exercises 9 and 10, use the relationships you discovered above.

9. Rectangle A has a width of 2 centimeters. Rectangle B has a width of 6 centimeters. Rectangle A has an area of 18 square centimeters. Rectangle A is similar to Rectangle B. What is the area of Rectangle B?

10. Would the relationship you discovered still apply if the two shapes were not similar? Explain your reasoning.

2.1 Puzzle Time

What Is A Lion's Favorite Food?

Circle the letter of each correct answer in the boxes below. The circled letters
will spell out the answer to the riddle.

In Exercises 1–5, use the figure.

1. What side of *TUV* corresponds to side *QS*?

2. What side of *QRS* corresponds to side *UV*?

3. What angle of *TUV* corresponds to ∠*R*?

4. What angle of *QRS* corresponds to ∠*V*?

5. What is the measure of ∠*U*?

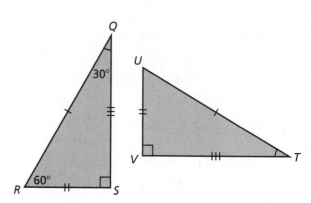

In Exercises 6–11, use the figure.

6. What side of *EFGH* corresponds to side *BC*?

7. What angle of *EFGH* corresponds to ∠*C*?

8. What is the length of side *CD*?

9. What is the length of side *EF*?

10. What is the measure of ∠*D*?

11. What is the measure of ∠*E*?

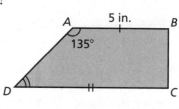

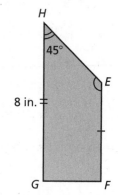

B	R	A	L	O	K	T	E	S	M	D	R
60°	13 in.	side *TV*	∠*T*	side *BC*	135°	∠*Q*	∠*U*	side *GH*	30°	side *FG*	180°
O	**B**	**T**	**E**	**W**	**C**	**I**	**H**	**N**	**G**	**P**	**S**
side *QR*	∠*S*	∠*E*	8 in.	90°	side *EF*	45°	∠*H*	side *RS*	5 in.	side *UV*	∠*G*

Discuss with a partner careers that use the concept of scale drawings.

Plot each point in a coordinate plane.

1. $N(-3, 2)$ **2.** $P(0, -2)$ **3.** $Q(1, 4)$

4. $R(2, 0)$ **5.** $S(-4, 0)$ **6.** $T(-1, -3)$

Lesson 2.2 **Start Thinking!**
For use before Lesson 2.2

Give an example of a translation you could find in your home that is also a tessellation. Explain how it is a translation.

Lesson 2.2 **Warm Up**
For use before Lesson 2.2

Tell whether the shaded figure is a translation of the nonshaded figure.

1.

2.

3.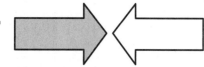

4.

Name_____ Date_____

2.2 Practice A

Tell whether the right figure is a translation of the left figure.

1.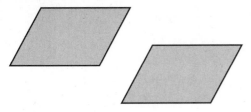

2.

3. Translate the triangle 3 units left and 2 units up. What are the coordinates of the image?

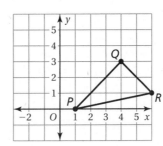

The vertices of a triangle are $A(-2, 0)$, $B(0, 3)$, **and** $C(2, 2)$. **Draw the figure and its image after the translation.**

4. 4 units down

5. 2 units right and 1 unit up

6. Describe the translation from the solid line figure to the dashed line figure.

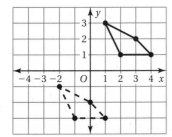

7. In Exercise 6, describe the translation from the dashed line figure to the solid line figure.

Name _____ Date _____

2.2 Practice B

Tell whether the right figure is a translation of the left figure.

1.

2.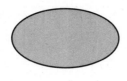

3. Translate the figure 5 units right and 1 unit up. What are the coordinates of the image?

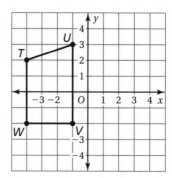

Describe the translation of the point to its image.

4. $(1, 5) \rightarrow (-1, 1)$

5. $(-2, -3) \rightarrow (-2, 4)$

6. A square is translated 3 units left and 5 units down. Then the image is translated 4 units right and 2 units down.

   a. Describe the translation of the original square to the ending position.

   b. Describe the translation of the ending position to the original square.

7. You rearrange your bedroom. Tell whether each move is an example of a translation.

   a. You slide your bed 1 foot along the wall.

   b. You move your desk and chair to the opposite wall.

   c. You move your bed stand to the other side of the bed.

Name_____ Date _____

2.2 Enrichment and Extension

Tangrams and Translations

Tangram puzzles are believed to be ancient in origin but were first published in the early 1800s in China. The goal of a tangram puzzle is to arrange seven smaller shapes, called tans, without overlapping, to form the tangram shape. Your challenge is to create the tangram shapes below by translating the tans that appear on the same coordinate plane.

Describe a translation for each tan so that they fill the tangram outline. Find both possible sets of translations for Exercise 3.

1.

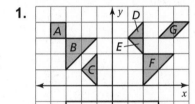

2.

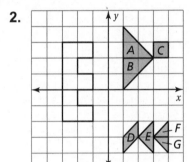

3.

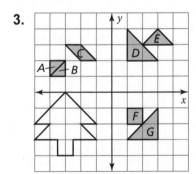

4.

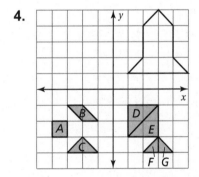

5. There are two ways to make the tangram in Exercise 4. Find the other way.

6. Make your own tangram puzzle and describe the translations necessary to create it. Then give your puzzle to a friend and compare his or her translations with yours. Are they the same? Do they give the same result? Explain.

2.2 Puzzle Time

What Is There More Of The Less You See?

Write the letter of each answer in the box containing the exercise number.

Translate the point as indicated to find its image.

1. $(1, 2)$

    2 units right and 4 units up

2. $(-1, -1)$

    3 units right and 3 units down

3. $(-4, 5)$

    4 units left and 1 unit up

4. $(4, -6)$

    8 units left and 7 units up

5. $(-2, -3)$

    6 units left and 5 units down

6. $(14, 23)$

    20 units left and 15 units down

7. $(-6, -19)$

    12 units right and 17 units up

8. $(-13, 9)$

    18 units right and 8 units down

Answers			
K. $(6, -2)$		**S.** $(3, 6)$	
D. $(5, 1)$		**E.** $(-4, 1)$	
N. $(-8, -8)$		**R.** $(2, -4)$	
A. $(-8, 6)$		**S.** $(-6, 8)$	

8	3	2	7	5	4	1	6

Start Thinking!
For use before Activity 2.3

Explain how flying in an airplane is
a translation.

Warm Up
For use before Activity 2.3

The vertices of a triangle are $A(-4, 4)$,
$B(-4, 1)$, **and** $C(-1, 1)$. **Draw the figure**
and its image after the translation.

1. 6 units right

2. 1 unit left and 3 units down

Start Thinking!
For use before Lesson 2.3

Words like "racecar" and "deed" are known as palindromes. What are some other examples of palindromes? Are palindromes reflections? Explain.

Warm Up
For use before Lesson 2.3

Tell whether the shaded figure is a reflection of the nonshaded figure.

1.

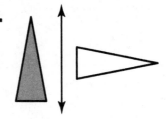

2.

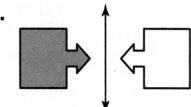

3.

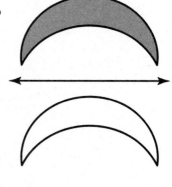

4.

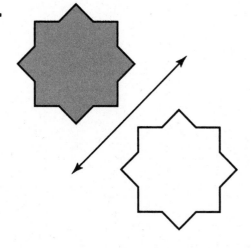

Name_____ Date_____

2.3   Practice A

Tell whether one figure is a reflection of the other figure.

1.

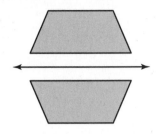

2.

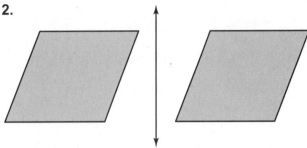

Draw the figure and its reflection in the *x*-axis. Identify the coordinates of the image.

3. $E(0, 2)$, $F(3, 1)$, $G(4, 3)$

4. $H(-3, 2)$, $I(-1, 5)$, $J(2, 1)$

Draw the figure and its reflection in the *y*-axis. Identify the coordinates of the image.

5. $X(0, -1)$, $Y(2, 3)$, $Z(4, -2)$

6. $U(-5, 1)$, $V(-4, -2)$, $W(-2, 0)$

7. What does the word MOM spell when it is reflected in a horizontal line?

The coordinates of a point and its image are given. Is the reflection in the *x*-axis or *y*-axis?

8. $(-5, 2) \rightarrow (5, 2)$

9. $(4, 3) \rightarrow (4, -3)$

10. Translate the triangle 2 units left and 1 unit up. Then reflect the image in the *x*-axis. Graph the resulting triangle.

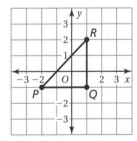

11. A figure is in Quadrant IV. The figure is reflected in the *y*-axis. In which quadrant is the image?

Name _____ Date _____

Tell whether one figure is a reflection of the other figure.

1.

2.

Draw the figure and its reflection in the *x*-axis. Identify the coordinates of the image.

3. $K(-3, 3)$, $L(-2, 1)$, $M(1, 2)$, $N(2, 5)$ **4.** $O(-2, -1)$, $P(-1, -3)$, $Q(1, -4)$, $R(3, -1)$

Draw the figure and its reflection in the *y*-axis. Identify the coordinates of the image.

5. $B(2, -3)$, $C(3, 1)$, $D(5, 3)$, $E(3, 0)$ **6.** $G(-5, -5)$, $H(-3, -1)$, $I(-2, 4)$, $J(-1, -1)$

7. What does the word "pop" spell when it is reflected in a horizontal line?

The coordinates of a point and its image are given. Is the reflection in the *x*-axis or *y*-axis?

8. $(0, 3) \rightarrow (0, -3)$ **9.** $(1, 5) \rightarrow (-1, 5)$

10. Reflect the triangle in the *x*-axis. Then reflect the image in the *y*-axis. Graph the resulting triangle.

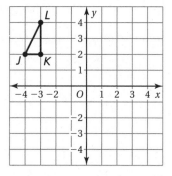

11. $\triangle ABC$ has vertices $A(-2, -1)$, $B(4, 2)$, $C(2, -2)$.

   a. Reflect $\triangle ABC$ in the *x*-axis. Then reflect $\triangle A'B'C'$ in the *y*-axis. What are the coordinates of the resulting triangle?

   b. How are the *x*- and *y*-coordinates of the resulting triangle related to the *x*- and *y*-coordinates of $\triangle ABC$?

2.3 Enrichment and Extension

Mirror Mirror On the Wall…

Some of the following figures are created by reflecting part of the Master over an imaginary line of reflection. Some of the figures cannot be created using this method. Determine whether the figures can be created using the Master. For those that can be created, draw a diagram showing the part of the Master and the imaginary line that were used. (*Hints:* The Master can be turned before being reflected. The line can go through the middle of a shape.)

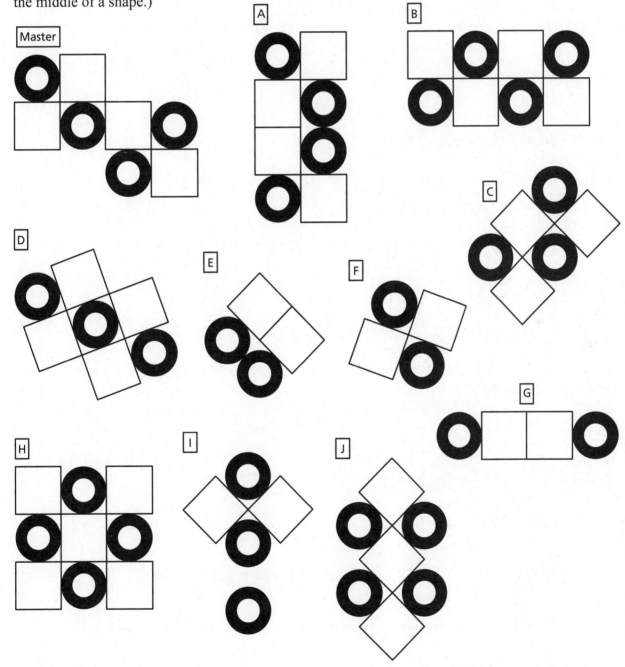

2.3 Puzzle Time

What Kind Of Coat Can You Put On Only When It's Wet?

Write the letter of each answer in the box containing the exercise number.

Reflect the point in the *x*-axis. Identify the coordinates of the image.

1. $(2, 5)$

    R. $(-2, -5)$ **S.** $(-2, 5)$ **T.** $(2, -5)$

2. $(-3, 7)$

    A. $(-3, -7)$ **B.** $(3, 7)$ **C.** $(3, -7)$

3. $(-4, -12)$

    D. $(4, -12)$ **E.** $(4, 12)$ **F.** $(-4, 12)$

4. $(13, -8)$

    M. $(-13, 8)$ **N.** $(13, 8)$ **O.** $(-13, -8)$

Reflect the point in the *y*-axis. Identify the coordinates of the image.

5. $(7, -6)$

    O. $(-7, -6)$ **P.** $(-7, 6)$ **Q.** $(7, 6)$

6. $(9, 5)$

    H. $(9, -5)$ **I.** $(-9, 5)$ **J.** $(-9, -5)$

7. $(-15, -12)$

    A. $(15, -12)$ **B.** $(15, 12)$ **C.** $(-15, 12)$

8. $(-23, 8)$

    M. $(23, -8)$ **N.** $(-23, -8)$ **O.** $(23, 8)$

The coordinates of a point and its image are given. Is the reflection in the *x*-axis, *y*-axis, or *neither*?

9. $(11, 7) \rightarrow (11, -7)$

    A. *x*-axis **B.** *y*-axis **C.** neither

10. $(-4, -5) \rightarrow (4, -5)$

    B. *x*-axis **C.** *y*-axis **D.** neither

11. $(-8, 8) \rightarrow (8, -8)$

    R. *x*-axis **S.** *y*-axis **T.** neither

12. $(53, -26) \rightarrow (-53, -26)$

    O. *x*-axis **P.** *y*-axis **Q.** neither

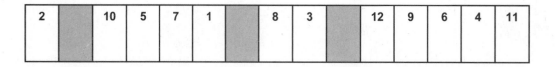

2		10	5	7	1		8	3		12	9	6	4	11

Does a football field have a line of reflection?
Explain.

Find the coordinates of the figure after reflecting in the *x*-axis.

1. $D(-5, -4)$, $E(-5, -2)$, $F(-1, -2)$, $G(-1, -4)$

2. $H(2, 1)$, $I(2, 5)$, $J(4, 4)$, $K(4, 2)$

Give an example of a translation, reflection, and rotation in a basketball game.

Identify the transformation.

1.

2.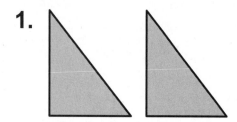

3.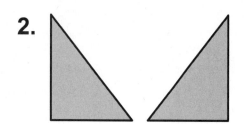

2.4 Practice A

Tell whether the dashed figure is a rotation of the solid figure about the origin. If so, give the angle and direction of rotation.

1.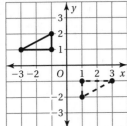

2.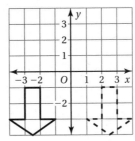

The vertices of a triangle are A(−4, 1), B(−2, 2), and C(−1, 1). Rotate the triangle as described. Find the coordinates of the image.

3. 270° clockwise about the origin

4. 90° counterclockwise about the origin

5. 90° counterclockwise about vertex A

6. 180° about vertex C

Tell whether the figure has rotational symmetry.

7.

8.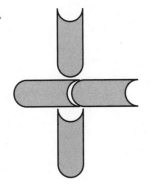

2.4 Practice B

Tell whether the dashed figure is a rotation of the solid figure about the origin. If so, give the angle and direction of rotation.

1.
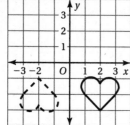

2.
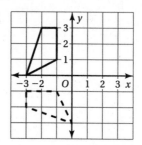

The vertices of a trapezoid are $A(1, 1)$, $B(2, 2)$, $C(4, 2)$, and $D(5, 1)$.

Rotate the trapezoid as described. Find the coordinates of the image.

3. 90° clockwise about the origin

4. 270° counterclockwise about the origin

5. 90° clockwise about vertex A

6. 180° about vertex D

Tell whether the figure has rotational symmetry.

7.
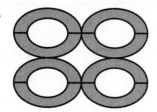

8.

2.4 Enrichment and Extension

Help Save the Lost Animals

You are part of a lost animal search and rescue team. Because of the treacherous terrain, you often have to go way out of the way and do some back-tracking in order to locate animals. Not only that, but the navigation equipment keeps mixing up the signals and getting the directions out of order. Your job is to look at the map and put the steps in order.

For each situation, the transformations will lead the rescue team to the animal, but they are not in the correct order. Find the correct order. Use each transformation exactly once. In each situation, you start out at the "x," and the animal that you are trying to rescue is located at the bull's eye.

1.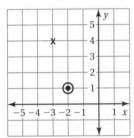

- Translate 2 units left and 2 units up.
- Rotate 90° clockwise about the origin.
- Reflect in the x-axis.
- Rotate 180° about the origin.

2.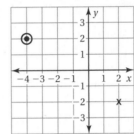

- Translate 1 unit right.
- Rotate 90° counterclockwise about the origin.
- Rotate 180° about the origin.
- Translate 3 units down.
- Reflect in the y-axis.

3.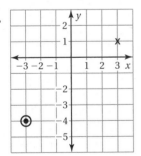

- Reflect in the x-axis.
- Translate 3 units down.
- Reflect in the y-axis.
- Rotate 90° clockwise about the origin.
- Rotate 90° counterclockwise about the origin.

4.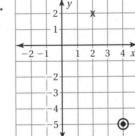

- Rotate 90° counterclockwise about the origin.
- Rotate 180° about the origin.
- Translate 3 units left.
- Translate 2 units up.
- Reflect in the x-axis.
- Reflect in the y-axis.

2.4 Puzzle Time

What Jam Can't You Eat?

Write the letter of each answer in the box containing the exercise number.

The vertices of a triangle are $A(2, 3)$, $B(7, 4)$, and $C(6, 1)$. Rotate the triangle as described. Find the coordinates of the image.

1. 90° clockwise about the origin

2. 180° about the origin

3. 90° counterclockwise about the origin

4. 180° about vertex A

The vertices of a triangle are $D(3, 4)$, $E(3, 1)$, and $F(1, 1)$. Rotate the triangle as described. Find the coordinates of the image.

5. 180° about the origin

6. 90° clockwise about vertex D

7. 90° clockwise about vertex E

8. 90° clockwise about vertex F

The vertices of a parallelogram are $W(-6, 3)$, $X(-4, 4)$, $Y(-2, 2)$, and $Z(-4, 1)$. Rotate the parallelogram as described. Find the coordinates of the image.

9. 90° clockwise about the origin

10. 90° counterclockwise about the origin

11. 180° about the origin

Answers for Exercises 1–4

A. $A'(-3, 2)$, $B'(-4, 7)$, $C'(-1, 6)$

F. $A'(3, -2)$, $B'(4, -7)$, $C'(1, -6)$

C. $A'(-2, -3)$, $B'(-7, -4)$, $C'(-6, -1)$

T. $A'(2, 3)$, $B'(-3, 2)$, $C'(-2, 5)$

Answers for Exercises 5–8

F. $D'(-3, -4)$, $E'(-3, -1)$, $F'(-1, -1)$

J. $D'(4, -1)$, $E'(1, -1)$, $F'(1, 1)$

M. $D'(3, 4)$, $E'(0, 4)$, $F'(0, 6)$

A. $D'(6, 1)$, $E'(3, 1)$, $F'(3, 3)$

Answers for Exercises 9–11

R. $W'(6, -3)$, $X'(4, -4)$, $Y'(2, -2)$, $Z'(4, -1)$

A. $W'(-3, -6)$, $X'(-4, -4)$, $Y'(-2, -2)$, $Z'(-1, -4)$

I. $W'(3, 6)$, $X'(4, 4)$, $Y'(2, 2)$, $Z'(1, 4)$

10		4	11	7	1	5	9	2		8	3	6

How can you use proportions to help plant a garden?

Tell whether the ratios form a proportion.

1. $\dfrac{2}{5}, \dfrac{10}{25}$

2. $\dfrac{7}{14}, \dfrac{21}{28}$

3. $\dfrac{12}{21}, \dfrac{15}{30}$

4. $\dfrac{15}{24}, \dfrac{35}{36}$

5. $\dfrac{6}{8}, \dfrac{15}{20}$

6. $\dfrac{36}{8}, \dfrac{63}{14}$

Explain how to determine if two figures
are similar.

**Tell whether the two figures are similar.
Explain your reasoning.**

1.

2.

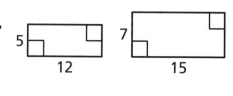

3.

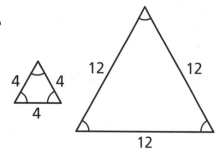

4.

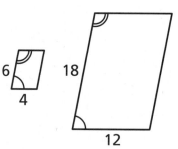

Name_____ Date _____

2.5 Practice A

1. Name the corresponding angles and the corresponding sides of the similar figures.

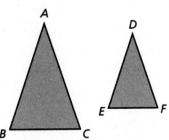

2. Tell whether the two figures are similar. Explain your reasoning.

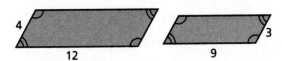

3. The rectangular traffic sign is 18 inches wide and 8 inches tall. The rectangular realtor sign is 27 inches wide and 10 inches tall. Are the signs similar?

4. The given rectangle needs to be modified.

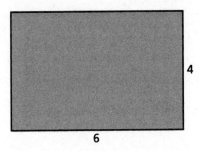

   a. Each side length is increased by 2.

   Is the new rectangle similar to the original?

   b. Each side length is increased by 50%.

   Is the new rectangle similar to the original?

5. Which of the following card dimensions are similar rectangles?

   2 in. by 5 in.   3 in. by 6 in.

   1 in. by 3 in.   1 in. by 2.5 in.

2.5 Practice B

1. In a coordinate plane, draw the figures with the given vertices. Which figures are similar? Explain your reasoning.

   Rectangle A: $(0, 0), (3, 0), (3, 2), (0, 2)$

   Rectangle B: $(0, 0), (1, 0), (1, 3), (0, 3)$

   Rectangle C: $(0, 0), (2, 0), (2, -3), (0, -3)$

2. A rectangular index card is 6 inches long and 4 inches wide. A rectangular note card is 1.5 inches long and 1 inch wide. Are the cards similar?

3. Given $\triangle PQR \sim \triangle TUV$. Name the corresponding angles and the corresponding sides.

The two parallelograms are similar. Find the degree measure of the angle.

4. $\angle A$

6. $\angle D$

5. $\angle H$

7. $\angle F$

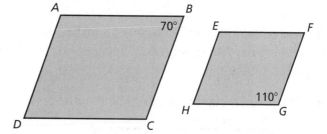

8. Is it possible for the following figures to be similar? Explain.

   a. A stop sign and a speed limit sign

   b. A cell phone and a test paper

   c. A yield sign and a home plate

   d. A laptop and a swimming pool

9. Can you draw two triangles each having two $45°$ angles and one $90°$ angle that are *not* similar? Justify your answer.

10. You have a triangle that has side lengths of 6, 9, and 12.

    a. Give the side lengths of a similar triangle that is smaller than the given triangle.

    b. Give the side lengths of a similar triangle that is larger than the given triangle.

    c. Each side length is increased by 30%. Is the new triangle similar to the original?

Name_____ Date _____

2.5   Enrichment and Extension

You Be the Video Game Designer!

Some video game designers use coordinate planes to identify the location of players and obstacles in the playing field. Imagine that you are creating a video game in which the player can use a laser to shrink and enlarge objects. Because the laser simply changes the size of the object but does not distort its shape, you will be creating similar figures.

List the coordinates of the points of the enlarged and shrunken objects. When you are enlarging an object, keep point A stationary. When you are shrinking an object, keep point B stationary. All coordinates should be listed as whole numbers or fractions. (*Hint:* You may want to graph the points and draw the objects on graph paper.)

1. Describe a situation in a video game in which a laser might be used to enlarge or shrink an object.

2. A triangle has vertices $A(1, 4)$, $B(1, 1)$, and $C(5, 1)$.

   a. Enlarge: Multiply the lengths of the sides of the original triangle by 3.

   b. Shrink: Multiply the lengths of the sides of the original triangle by $\dfrac{2}{3}$.

3. A house has vertices $A(0, 3)$, $B(3, 0)$, $C(2, 0)$, $D(2, -3)$, $E(-2, -3)$, $F(-2, 0)$, and $G(-3, 0)$.

   a. Enlarge: Multiply the lengths of the sides of the original house by $1\dfrac{1}{2}$.

   b. Shrink: Multiply the lengths of the sides of the original house by $\dfrac{1}{3}$.

4. A star has vertices $A(-2, 1)$, $B(-3, -1)$, $C(-5, -1)$, $D\left(-3\dfrac{1}{2}, -2\dfrac{1}{2}\right)$, $E(-4, -5)$, $F\left(-2, -3\dfrac{1}{2}\right)$, $G(0, -5)$, $H\left(-\dfrac{1}{2}, -2\dfrac{1}{2}\right)$, $I(1, -1)$, and $J(-1, -1)$.

   a. Enlarge: Multiply the lengths of the sides of the original star by 5.

   b. Shrink: Multiply the lengths of the sides of the original star by $\dfrac{1}{2}$.

5. How many times larger is the area of the enlarged triangle compared to the area of the original triangle? Why do you think this is the case?

2.5 Puzzle Time

Did You Hear About...

A	B	C	D	E	F
G	H	I	J	K	

Complete each exercise. Find the answer in the answer column. Write the word under the answer in the box containing the exercise letter.

side *LM* **ALWAYS**
side *YZ* **FALLING**
side *PR* **CAR**
90° **UNDER**
∠*X* **THE**
∠*L* **FLAT**
∠*M* **WHEELS**
60° **FOR**
side *XY* **KEPT**
side *PQ* **HOW**
side *VW* **TWO**
70° **IT**

In Exercises A–F, use the two similar triangles.

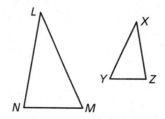

A. What is ∠*L*'s corresponding angle?

B. What is ∠*M*'s corresponding angle?

C. What is ∠*N*'s corresponding angle?

D. What is side *LM*'s corresponding side?

E. What is side *MN*'s corresponding side?

F. What is side *LN*'s corresponding side?

In Exercises G–K, use the two similar trapezoids.

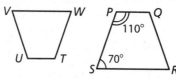

G. What is the measure of ∠*T*?

H. What is the measure of ∠*W*?

I. What is side *PQ*'s corresponding side?

J. What is side *RS*'s corresponding side?

K. What is side *QR*'s corresponding side?

80° **EVER**
∠*Y* **BICYCLE**
side *MN* **PEDALS**
∠*Z* **THAT**
side *PS* **THEY'RE**
110° **BECAUSE**
side *UV* **TIRED**
side *LN* **SO**
∠*N* **WERE**
180° **WHO**
side *XZ* **OVER**
side *TU* **WAS**

Activity 2.6

Start Thinking!

For use before Activity 2.6

You want to put new carpet in your room. How do you make sure you buy enough carpet?

Activity 2.6

Warm Up

For use before Activity 2.6

Find the perimeter and area.

1.

7 in.

9 in.

2.

15 cm

15 cm

3.

3 cm

5 cm

4 cm

4.

14 in.   13 in.

10 in.

Your neighbor wants to replace his rectangular deck with one that is double the side lengths. Use what you have learned in Activity 2.6 to explain to your neighbor what will happen to the perimeter of the deck.

Complete the following exercises.

1. How does quadrupling the side lengths of a triangle affect its perimeter?

2. How does doubling the base of a triangle affect its area?

3. How does tripling the side lengths of a rectangle affect its perimeter?

4. How does doubling the side lengths of a parallelogram affect its perimeter?

Name_____ Date_____

2.6 Practice A

The two figures are similar. Find the ratio (small to large) of the perimeters and of the areas.

1.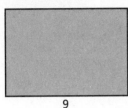

   9

2.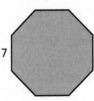

   3   7

3. How does doubling the side lengths of a triangle affect its area?

4. The ratio of the corresponding side lengths of two similar rectangular tables is 4 : 5.

   a. What is the ratio of the perimeters?

   b. What is the ratio of the areas?

   c. The perimeter of the larger table is 44 feet. What is the perimeter of the smaller table?

5. The figures are similar. The ratio of the perimeters is 5 : 9. Find x.

   30   x

6. The ratio of the area of Triangle A to Triangle B is 16 : 49. Triangle A is similar to Triangle B.

   a. Which triangle is larger, A or B?

   b. A side length of Triangle B is 3.5 inches. What is the corresponding side length of Triangle A?

   c. What is the ratio of the perimeter of Triangle A to the perimeter of Triangle B?

   d. The side lengths of Triangle A are increased by 40%. The side lengths of Triangle B do not change. What is the new ratio of the area of Triangle A to Triangle B?

2.6 Practice B

1. The two figures are similar. Find the ratio (small to large) of the perimeters and of the areas.

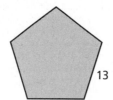

5

13

2. How does tripling the side lengths of a pentagon affect its perimeter?

3. The figures are similar. The ratio of the perimeters is 12 : 7. Find *x*.

18

x

4. The ratio of the corresponding side lengths of two similar parallelogram signs is 9 : 14.

   a. What is the ratio of the perimeters?

   b. What is the ratio of the areas?

   c. One side length of the smaller sign is 45 feet. What is the side length of the corresponding side of the larger sign?

5. A window is put in a door. The window and the door are similar rectangles. The door has a width of 4 feet. The window has a width of 30 inches.

   a. How many times greater is the area of the door than the area of the window?

   b. The area of the door is 32 square feet. What is the area of the window?

   c. What is the perimeter of the window?

6. The area of Circle P is 4π. The area of Circle Q is 25π.

   a. What is the ratio of their areas?

   b. What is the ratio of their radii?

   c. The radius of Circle Q is decreased by 50%. What is the new circumference of Circle Q?

Name_____ Date_____

2.6 Enrichment and Extension

Getting an Art Project Covered

Alicia is starting an art project. Her first step is to cover the frames below with canvas and put ribbon around all the edges. All of the frames are similar figures. Help her decide how much material and ribbon to buy.

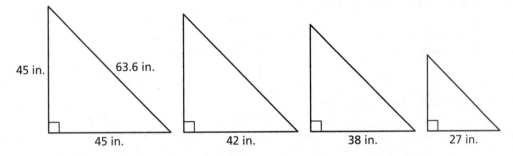

1. Ribbon costs $2.27 per yard and is sold to the nearest inch. What is the least that the ribbon will cost for all the frames?

2. Canvas is sold in rolls that are 45 inches wide. On the rectangle below, draw the best way for Alicia to arrange the 4 triangles in order to waste the least amount of material. Be sure to label each triangle. What is the least length of material (to the nearest inch) that she can buy and still have enough to cover all the triangles?

3. The canvas costs $3.99 per yard. What is the least that the material will cost?

4. How much material will she use?

5. How much material will she have left over?

6. What percent of the material will be left over? Round to the nearest whole percent.

7. Why do you think stores sell material this way?

8. What are some ways that Alicia could use the left over material?

2.6 Puzzle Time

Where Do Stinging Insects Go When They're Sick?

Write the letter of each answer in the box containing the exercise number.

In Exercises 1–7, use the following information.

An Olympic size swimming pool is 25 meters wide and 50 meters long. A similar pool that is smaller is 12 meters wide.

1. What is the ratio of the perimeters of the pools?

2. What is the ratio of the areas of the pools?

3. What is the perimeter of the Olympic size pool?

4. What is the perimeter of the smaller pool?

5. What is the area of the Olympic size pool?

6. What is the area of the smaller pool?

7. What is the length of the smaller pool?

In Exercises 8–13, use the following information.

Answers	
H. 24 m	**O.** 625 : 144
W. $10\frac{2}{3}$ in.^{2}	**T.** 3 : 4
T. 9 in.	**S.** 9 : 16
T. 1250 m^2	**I.** 150 m
A. 288 m^2	**L.** 72 m
E. 2 in.	**P.** 12 in.
A. 25 : 12	

A hexagon on a small soccer ball has a side length of $1\frac{1}{2}$ inches. The ratio of the side length of the hexagon to the side lengths of a hexagon from a larger soccer ball is 3 : 4.

8. What is the ratio of the perimeters of the hexagons?

9. What is the ratio of the areas of the hexagons?

10. What is the perimeter of the smaller hexagon?

11. What is the perimeter of the larger hexagon?

12. What is the side length of the larger hexagon?

13. The area of the smaller hexagon is about 6 square inches. What is the area of the larger hexagon?

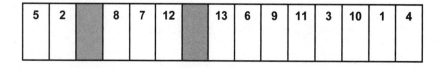

Activity 2.7 Start Thinking!

For use before Activity 2.7

Discuss with a partner real-life objects that can be enlarged or reduced.

Activity 2.7 Warm Up

For use before Activity 2.7

Multiply.

1. $2 \bullet 4$

2. $-5 \bullet 4$

3. $-6 \bullet 0.5$

4. $-3 \bullet 0.5$

5. $8 \bullet \frac{1}{4}$

6. $16 \bullet \frac{1}{4}$

Describe why it is important for a photographer to know how to enlarge and reduce photos.

Lesson 2.7 **Warm Up**
For use before Lesson 2.7

Draw the triangle with the given vertices. Multiply each coordinate of the vertices by 3 and then draw the new triangle. How are the two triangles related?

1. $(0, 3), (3, 3), (3, -1)$

2. $(0, -1), (0, 4), (3, 4)$

Name_____ Date _____

2.7 Practice A

Draw the triangle with the given vertices. Multiply each coordinate of the vertices by 3 and then draw the new triangle. How are the two triangles related?

1. $(0, 0), (1, 3), (2, 1)$

2. $(-3, -2), (-1, 4), (2, -2)$

Tell whether the dashed figure is a dilation of the solid figure.

3.

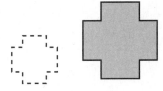

4.

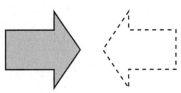

The vertices of a figure are given. Draw the figure and its image after a dilation with the given scale factor. Identify the type of dilation.

5. $A(-3, -2), B(2, 4), C(8, 1); k = \dfrac{1}{4}$

6. $D(1, 2), E(4, 1), F(1, -3), G(-3, -2); k = 5$

The dashed figure is a dilation of the solid figure. Identify the type of dilation and find the scale factor.

7.

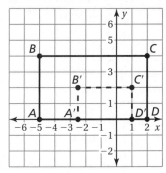

8.

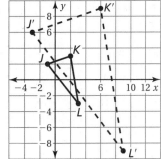

9. A triangle is dilated using a scale factor of 4. The image is then dilated using a scale factor of 3. What scale factor could you use to dilate the original triangle to get the final image?

10. The vertices of a figure are $P(1, 2), Q(3, 4),$ and $R(-1, 6)$. Dilate with respect to the origin using a scale factor of 2 and then translate 4 units right and 3 units down. Find the coordinates of the figure after the transformations given.

2.7 Practice B

Draw the triangle with the given vertices. Multiply each coordinate of the vertices by 3 and draw the new triangle. How are the two triangles related?

1. $(0, 4), (-1, -3), (5, 2)$

2. $(-40, -20), (-20, 30), (40, -10)$

Tell whether the dashed figure is a dilation of the solid figure.

3.

4.

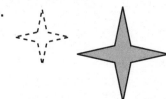

The vertices of a figure are given. Draw the figure and its image after dilation with the given scale factor. Identify the type of dilation.

5. $A(3, -1), B(-4, 4), C(-2, -3); k = 5$

6. $D(10, 20), E(-35, 10), F(25, -30), G(5, -20); k = \dfrac{1}{5}$

The dashed figure is a dilation of the solid figure. Identify the type of dilation and find the scale factor.

7.

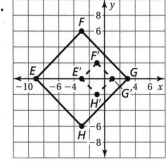

8.

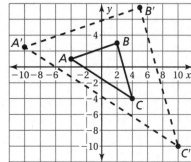

9. A scale factor of 2 is used to find the dilation of a quadrilateral. What is the sum of the angles in the original quadrilateral? What is the sum of the angles after the dilation? What is the difference between the perimeter of the original figure and the perimeter of the image?

10. A triangle is dilated using a scale factor of $\dfrac{1}{2}$. The image is then dilated using a scale factor of $\dfrac{1}{3}$. What scale factor could you use to dilate the original triangle to get the final image?

2.7 **Enrichment and Extension**

Surf Shop

Sven has selected a logo for his new surf shop. He has enlisted the help of a local print shop to assist him in creating merchandise to advertise his business by dilating the logo.

4.5 in.

2 in.

Use the logo to answer the questions.

1. Sven asks the owner of the print shop to dilate the logo so that the surf board leans to the left instead of to the right. Can the request be filled? Why or why not? Explain your reasoning.

2. Sven asks the owner of the print shop to dilate the logo so that it can be used in a magazine ad to advertise the shop. The logo needs to be increased using a scale factor of 2.5. What are the new dimensions of the logo?

3. The dimensions of Sven's logo need to be increased by 50% for a flyer. What are the new dimensions of the logo?

4. Sven asks the print shop to increase the size of the logo for posters. He wants the logo for the posters to measure 8 inches wide and 18 inches long.

   a. Which scale factor should the print shop use in order to create the logo?

   b. Find the percent increase of the dimensions used to produce the poster logo.

5. Sven asks the print shop to decrease the size of the logo for business cards. He wants the logo for the cards to measure 1 inch wide and 2.25 inches long.

   a. Which scale factor should the print shop use in order to create the logo?

   b. Find the percent decrease of the dimensions used to produce the business card logo.

6. The print shop increased the size of the logo so that it can be used on souvenir post cards that will be sold in Sven's Surf Shop. Explain why the new logo is not a dilation of the original.

8 in.

4 in.

2.7 Puzzle Time

What Do You Call A Surgeon With Eight Arms?

Write the letter of each answer in the box containing the exercise number.

The vertices of a triangle are $A(2, 2)$, $B(2, 5)$, and $C(4, 2)$. Find the coordinates of the image after a dilation with the given scale factor.

1. $k = 2$ **2.** $k = 5$ **3.** $k = 1\frac{1}{2}$

The vertices of a triangle are $A(-5, 5)$, $B(-2, -5)$, and $C(-2, 0)$. Find the coordinates of the image after a dilation with the given scale factor.

4. $k = \frac{1}{2}$ **5.** $k = 0.75$ **6.** $k = \frac{1}{5}$

The vertices of a triangle are $A(1, 3)$, $B(7, 3)$, and $C(7, 5)$. The vertices of its image after a dilation are given. Find the scale factor.

7. $A'(4, 12)$, $B'(28, 12)$, $C'(28, 20)$

8. $A'\left(\frac{1}{6}, \frac{1}{2}\right)$, $B'\left(1\frac{1}{6}, \frac{1}{2}\right)$, $C'\left(1\frac{1}{6}, \frac{5}{6}\right)$

9. $A'(0.5, 1.5)$, $B'(3.5, 1.5)$, $C'(3.5, 2.5)$

Answers

B. $k = \frac{1}{4}$

D. $A'(3, 3)$, $B'\left(3, 7\frac{1}{2}\right)$, $C'(6, 3)$

T. $A'(-3.75, 3.75)$, $B'(-1.5, -3.75)$, $C'(-1.5, 0)$

E. $k = 2$

C. $A'(4, 4)$, $B'(4, 10)$, $C'(8, 4)$

O. $k = 4$

A. $k = 0.5$

S. $A'\left(-2\frac{1}{2}, 2\frac{1}{2}\right)$, $B'\left(-1, -2\frac{1}{2}\right)$, $C'(-1, 0)$

F. $k = \frac{1}{7}$

P. $k = \frac{1}{6}$

U. $A'(10, 10)$, $B'(10, 25)$, $C'(20, 10)$

J. $k = 6$

O. $A'(-1, 1)$, $B'\left(-\frac{2}{5}, -1\right)$, $C'\left(-\frac{2}{5}, 0\right)$

T. $k = 7$

9		3	6	1		5	7	8	2	4
				-						

Name_____ Date_____

Transformations with Geometry Software

You can use geometry software to perform and explore various transformations.

EXAMPLE   How can you perform a reflection of △*ABC* in a line outside of the triangle?

SOLUTION

Step 1   Use the Segment tool $\boxed{/}$ to create a triangle. Use the $\boxed{A}$ tool to label the vertices *A*, *B*, and *C*.

Step 2   Draw another segment outside of the triangle. Double click on the segment. You should see two squares flash on the segment. This means that you have marked the segment as a line of reflection.

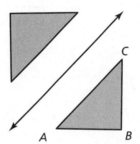

Step 3   Select the triangle. Then go to the TRANSFORM menu and select REFLECT.

Use geometry software to answer each question.

1. What happens to the reflection of △*ABC* when the line of reflection is moved?

2. Create a new triangle, △*DEF*. Draw a point outside of the triangle and double click on it. Go to the TRANSFORM menu and select DILATE to dilate the triangle. Describe the result.

3. Use the ROTATE command to perform a rotation on △*DEF*. How does moving the center of rotation affect the rotation?

Chapter 3

Name_____ Date _____

 Angles and Triangles

Dear Family,

Take a look at the structures in your neighborhood. What shapes do you see over and over again? Triangles can be seen everywhere. Peaked roofs are made with triangular sections; umbrellas use triangular wedges; bridges use triangular shapes to span great distances.

The triangle is used in many structures because it is a stable shape. There is only one way to form a polygon with three given segments and this makes the shape strong. A square can shift into a parallelogram. A circle can be deformed into an oval shape without changing the perimeter. But a triangle retains its shape.

You may want to use toothpicks and gum drops to create a triangle, square, and rectangle. Test the strength of each shape to reinforce that the triangle provides the most support.

Triangles can be used to form the sides of pyramids or the ends of prisms, making them popular for building roofs. More complicated patterns can be used to approximate nearly any shape. A geodesic dome uses triangles to create a sphere-like shape. Try this with your student. Choose a structure, such as your home or a nearby building or bridge.

- What types of triangles are used in the structure? Are they all similar, or are different triangles used?

- What types of angles are used? Are they acute (less than 90 degrees), right (equal to 90 degrees), or obtuse (greater than 90 degrees)? Why do you think those angles are chosen?

- Are there triangular parts inside of the structure? Try looking at the trusses in an attic or under a bridge. Why do you think the shapes you see were chosen?

You may want to build a model of your structure using toothpicks and gum drops or other similar materials.

Have fun looking at your structure from "every angle"!

Nombre _____ Fecha _____

Ángulos y triángulos

Estimada Familia:

Observe las estructuras en su barrio. ¿Qué formas observa una y otra vez? Los triángulos se pueden ver por todas partes. Los techos puntiagudos están compuestos de secciones triangulares; los paraguas utilizan pedazos triangulares, los puentes usan formas triangulares para cubrir grandes distancias.

El triángulo se utiliza en muchas estructuras porque es una forma estable. Sólo hay un modo para formar un polígono con tres segmentos dados y esto hace que la forma sea fuerte. Un cuadrado puede convertirse en un paralelogramo. Un círculo puede deformarse en una forma ovalada sin cambiar el perímetro. Pero un triángulo conserva su forma.

Puede querer usar palitos de dientes y gomitas dulces para crear un triángulo, un cuadrado y un rectángulo. Ponga a prueba la resistencia de cada forma para comprobar que el triángulo brinda el mayor soporte.

Los triángulos pueden ser usados para formar los lados de las pirámides o las terminaciones de un prisma, haciéndolos populares para construir techos. Los patrones más complicados pueden ser usados para aproximarse casi a cualquier forma. Un domo geodésico utiliza un triángulo para crear la forma de una esfera. Intente lo siguiente con su estudiante. Escojan una estructura, como su casa o un edificio o puente cercano.

- ¿Qué tipos de triángulos son usados en esta estructura? ¿Son todos similares o se utilizan distintos tipos de triángulos?

- ¿Qué clase de ángulos se utilizan? ¿Son agudos (menores de 90 grados), rectos (iguales a 90 grados) u obtusos (mayores de 90 grados)? ¿Por qué creen que se escogen estos ángulos?

- ¿Hay partes triangulares dentro de la estructura? Observen las estructuras en un ático o bajo un puente. ¿Por qué creen que las formas que observan fueron escogidas?

Querrán construir un modelo de sus estructuras usando palitos de dientes, gomitas dulces o materiales similares.

¡Diviértanse observando su estructura desde "todos los ángulos"!

Give some examples of parallel lines in your classroom.

Solve the proportion.

1. $\dfrac{16}{3} = \dfrac{x}{9}$

2. $\dfrac{2}{5} = \dfrac{5}{x}$

3. $\dfrac{15}{12} = \dfrac{x}{8}$

4. $\dfrac{x}{2} = \dfrac{11}{4}$

5. $\dfrac{100}{x} = \dfrac{25}{8}$

6. $\dfrac{x}{5} = \dfrac{3}{8}$

Start Thinking!
For use before Lesson 3.1

If you know the measure of one of the angles formed by two parallel lines and a transversal, can you find the measures of all the other angles without using a protractor? Why or why not?

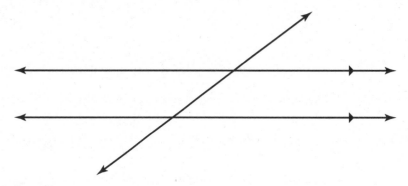

Lesson 3.1

Warm Up
For use before Lesson 3.1

Use the figure.

1. Identify the parallel lines.

2. Identify the transversal.

3. How many angles are formed by the transversal?

4. Which of the angles are congruent?

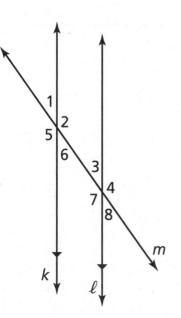

Name_____ Date_____

Use the figure to find the measures of the numbered angles.

1.
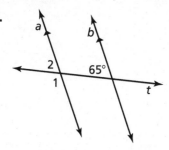

2.
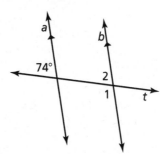

Use the figure to find the measures of the numbered angles. Explain your reasoning.

3.
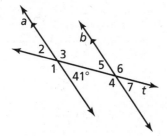

4.
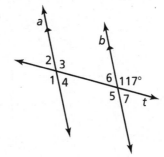

Complete the statement. Explain your reasoning.

5. If the measure of $\angle 1 = 160°$, then the measure of $\angle 5 = $ __?__ .

6. If the measure of $\angle 6 = 37°$, then the measure of $\angle 4 = $ __?__ .

7. If the measure of $\angle 8 = 82°$, then the measure of $\angle 3 = $ __?__ .

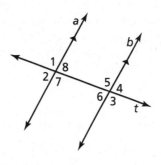

8. If the measure of $\angle 4 = 60°$, then the measure of $\angle 5 = $ __?__ .

Correct the following statements about the numbered angles by replacing the underlined words with the correct words.

9. $\angle 2$ is <u>congruent</u> to $\angle 4$. $\angle 4$ is <u>congruent</u> to $\angle 8$. So, $\angle 2$ is <u>supplementary</u> to $\angle 8$.

10. $\angle 6$ is <u>congruent</u> to $\angle 3$. $\angle 3$ is <u>congruent</u> to $\angle 1$. So, $\angle 6$ is <u>congruent</u> to $\angle 1$.

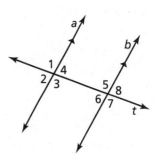

Name _____ Date _____

Use the figure to find the measures of the numbered angles. Explain your reasoning.

1.

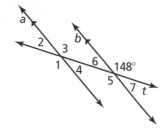

2.

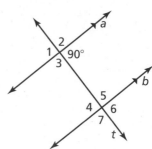

Complete the statement. Explain your reasoning.

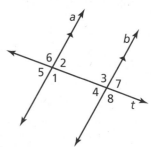

3. If the measure of $\angle 1 = 130°$, then the measure of $\angle 8 =$ __?__ .

4. If the measure of $\angle 5 = 53°$, then the measure of $\angle 3 =$ __?__ .

5. If the measure of $\angle 7 = 71°$, then the measure of $\angle 3 =$ __?__ .

6. If the measure of $\angle 4 = 65°$, then the measure of $\angle 6 =$ __?__ .

Using the diagram for angle placement only (the measurement of the angles may change), indicate if the following statements are *always*, *sometimes*, or *never* true. Explain.

7. $\angle 1$ is congruent to $\angle 3$.

8. $\angle 6$ is supplementary to $\angle 8$.

9. $\angle 2$ is complementary to $\angle 1$.

10. $\angle 8$ and $\angle 5$ are vertical angles.

11. $\angle 2$ is congruent to $\angle 8$.

12. If a transversal intersects two parallel lines, is it possible for all of the angles formed to be acute angles? Explain.

Name_____ Date_____

3.1 Enrichment and Extension

Telescopes

The most basic design for a telescope is a long tube with a lens at each end. The larger lens, called the objective lens, focuses a distant image to a point inside the tube, called the focal point. The smaller lens, called the eyepiece, has the same focal point and works like a magnifying glass. The result is that your eye sees an enlarged view of the image from the objective lens.

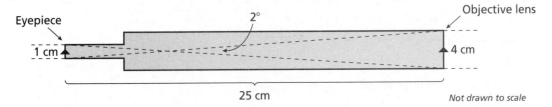

1. A lens and its focal point form an isosceles triangle. What are the angle measures of the triangle formed by the objective lens and the focal point?

2. Does the triangle formed by the eyepiece and the focal point have the same angle measures? Explain your reasoning.

3. What is the ratio of the diameters of the objective lens to the eyepiece?

4. The distance from a lens to its focal point is called the focal length. The ratio of the focal lengths is the same as the ratio of the diameters. Find the focal length (in centimeters) of each lens.

5. The focal length of the eyepiece determines the magnification of the telescope. The number of times m an image is magnified is represented by the equation $m = \dfrac{250}{f}$, where f is the focal length (in millimeters). How many times is the image magnified in the telescope above?

6. If the length of the telescope increased, would the magnification of the telescope increase or decrease? Explain.

Name _____ Date _____

3.1 Puzzle Time

Why Did The Rabbit Wear A Shower Cap?

A	B	C	D	E	F
G	H				

Complete each exercise. Find the answer in the answer column. Write the word under the answer in the box containing the exercise letter.

147 **HARE**
44 **WANT**
129 **ITS**
c **IT**

Use the figure to answer the questions.

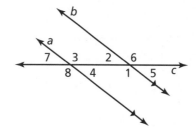

a, b **DIDN'T**
51 **GET**
112 **WET**
136 **TO**

A. Identify the transversal.

B. Identify the parallel lines.

C. If the measure of ∠1 = 136°, then the measure of
∠2 = _____°.

D. If the measure of ∠4 = 44°, then the measure of
∠8 = _____°.

E. If the measure of ∠8 = 129°, then the measure of
∠4 = _____°.

F. If the measure of ∠3 = 129°, then the measure of
∠1 = _____°.

Find the value of x.

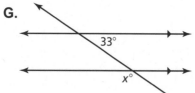

Start Thinking!

For use before Activity 3.2

Describe some real-life triangles. What kind of triangles are they?

Warm Up

For use before Activity 3.2

Classify the angle as *acute*, *right*, *obtuse*, **or** *straight*.

1.

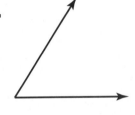

2.

3.

4.

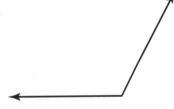

Give a real-life example of when it is important to know the angle measures of a triangle.

Find the measures of the interior angles.

1.

2.

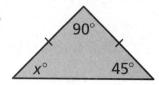

3.

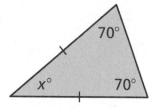

4.

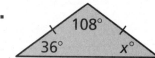

5.

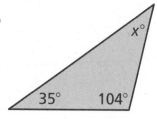

6.

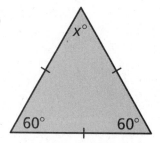

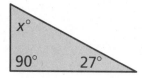

Name_____ Date _____

3.2 Practice A

Find the measures of the interior angles.

1.

2.
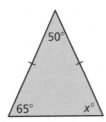

Find the measure of the exterior angle.

3.
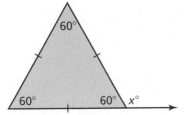

4.
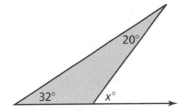

Tell whether a triangle can have the given angle measures. If not, change the first angle measure so that the angle measures form a triangle.

5. $36.9°, 110.4°, 33.7°$

6. $62°, 44\frac{3}{4}°, 73\frac{1}{4}°$

7. Consider the three isosceles right triangles.

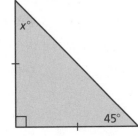
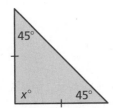

a. Find the value of x for each triangle.

b. What do you notice about the interior angle measures of each triangle?

c. Write a rule about the interior angle measures of an isosceles right triangle.

3.2 Practice B

Find the measures of the interior angles.

1.
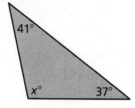

2.
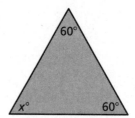

3.

4.

Find the measure of the exterior angle.

5.
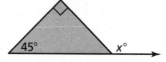

6.
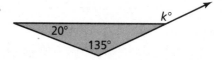

7.
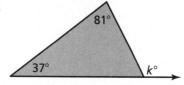

8.
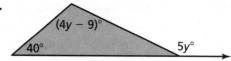

9. The ratio of the interior angle measures of a triangle is 1 : 4 : 5. What are the angle measures?

10. A right triangle has a exterior angles with a measure of 160°. Can you determine the measures of the interior angles? Explain.

Name_____ Date_____

3.2 Enrichment and Extension

Writing Ratios

The sides of a right triangle can be named by their location with respect to an angle of the triangle.

Trigonometry

It is possible to write ratios that compare the lengths of the sides in the triangle using special functions and a given angle. These ratios are called sine (sin), cosine (cos), and tangent (tan) and are studied in depth in a branch of mathematics called trigonometry.

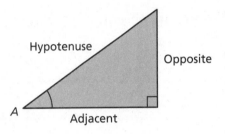

$$\sin A = \frac{\text{Opposite}}{\text{Hypotenuse}} \qquad \cos A = \frac{\text{Adjacent}}{\text{Hypotenuse}} \qquad \tan A = \frac{\text{Opposite}}{\text{Adjacent}}$$

Write the ratios. Use your answers and the color key to shade the mosaic.

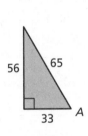
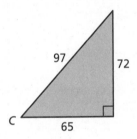

1. sin A

2. tan C

3. cos A

4. tan A

5. sin C

6. cos C

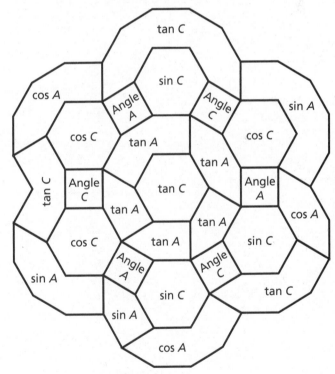

Key:
Angles = Blue
65 in the denominator = Red
97 in the denominator = Yellow
33 in the denominator = Purple

3.2 Puzzle Time

Did You Hear The Story About The Piece Of Butter?

A	B	C	D	E	F
G	H	I			

Complete each exercise. Find the answer in the answer column. Write the word under the answer in the box containing the exercise letter.

88° DON'T	
144° TOAST	
122° TO	
53° NEVER	
90° JELLY	
45° IT	

107° MIND	
124° SPREAD	
60° WHEAT	
87° AROUND	
41° I	
80° WANT	

Find the value of _x_.

A.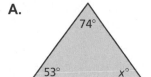

B.

C.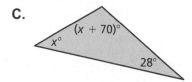

D.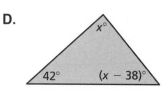

E. A triangle contains angles measuring 25° and 75°. What is the measure of the third angle?

Find the measure of the exterior angle.

F.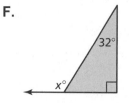

G.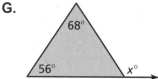

H.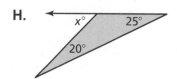

I.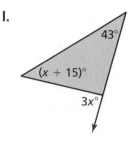

Many road signs are polygons. Try to come up with as many different road signs as you can. For each sign, classify the polygon by the number of sides.

Activity 3.3 | **Warm Up**
For use before Activity 3.3

Find the value of *y* for the given value of *x*.

1. $y = \dfrac{1}{2}x - 3;\ x = -2$

2. $y = -x + 2;\ x = 15$

3. $y = 10(x - 2);\ x = 10$

4. $y = 13(x - 3);\ x = 1$

5. $y = \dfrac{3}{2}x + \dfrac{5}{2};\ x = -2$

6. $y = 3(x + 4);\ x = -5$

Explain how you can draw an octagon on graph paper to make it easy to find the angle measures. Use this method to find each angle measure.

What is the sum of the angle measures?

Use triangles to find the sum of the interior angle measures of the polygon.

1.

2.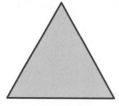

3.

4.

5.

6.

Name _____ Date _____

3.3 Practice A

Use triangles to find the sum of the interior angle measures of the polygon.

1.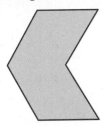

2.

Find the sum of the interior angle measures of the polygon.

3.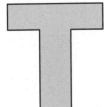

4.

5. Can an octagon have interior angles that measure 100°, 156°, 125°, 90°, 175°, 134°, 160°, and 140°? Explain.

Find the measures of the interior angles.

6.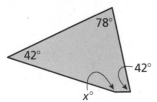

7.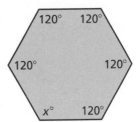

8. A stop sign is in the shape of a regular octagon. What is the measure of each interior angle?

Find the measures of the exterior angles of the polygon.

9.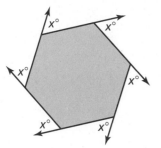

10.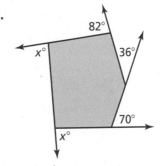

Name_____ Date _____

Use triangles to find the sum of the interior angle measures of the polygon.

1.

2.

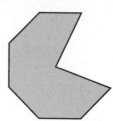

Find the sum of the interior angle measures of the polygon.

3.

4.

5. Four interior angles of a pentagon measure $50°$, $73°$, $146°$, and $161°$. Find the missing angle measure.

Find the measures of the interior angles.

6.

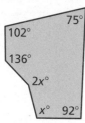

75°
102°
136°
2x°
x° 92°

7.

95°
x°
145°
(x + 1)° 101°

8. The interior angles of a regular polygon each measure $135°$. How many sides does the polygon have?

9. Use the polygon shown.

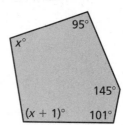

a. Is the polygon *convex* or *concave*?

b. Is the polygon *regular* or *not regular*?

c. What is the name of the polygon?

d. What is the sum of the interior angle measures in the polygon?

Name_____ Date _____

Area of Regular Polygons

To find the area of a regular polygon with more than four sides, you need to know the length of the *apothem*. The apothem is the distance from the center to any side of the polygon.

Once you know the length of the apothem, you can calculate the area of a regular polygon using the formula $A = \frac{1}{2}ans$, where a is the length of the apothem, n is the number of sides in the polygon, and s is the length of the sides.

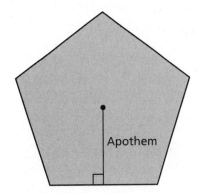

Apothem

Find the area of the regular polygon.

1.

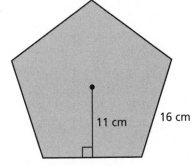

11 cm   16 cm

2.

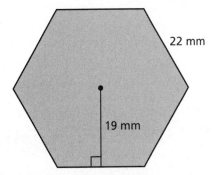

22 mm

19 mm

3.

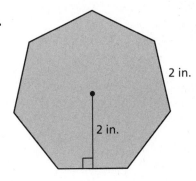

2 in.

2 in.

4.

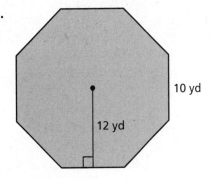

10 yd

12 yd

Name_____   Date _____

3.3 Puzzle Time

Why Did Old Mother Hubbard Scream When She Went To Fetch Her Poor Dog A Bone?

A	B	C	D	E	F
G	H				

Complete each exercise. Find the answer in the answer column. Write the word under the answer in the box containing the exercise letter.

720° GOT
135° WAS
124 THE
convex SHE

Tell whether the polygon is *convex* or *concave*.

A.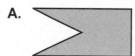

B.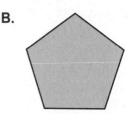

concave WHEN
15 CUPBOARD
1080° THERE
60° BEAR

Find the sum of the interior angle measures of the polygon.

C.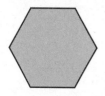

D.

Find the value of x.

E.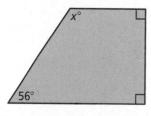

F.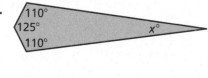

Find the measure of each interior angle of the regular polygon.

G.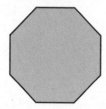

H.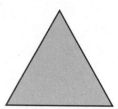

Which pairs of shapes appear to be *similar*?
How can you tell?

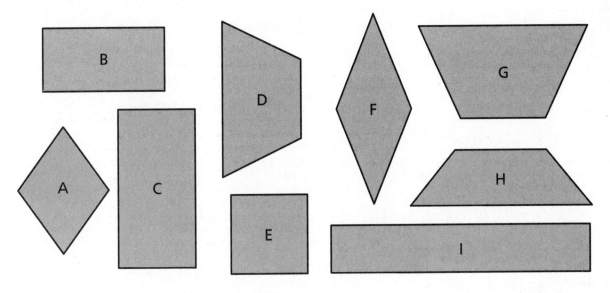

The triangles are similar. Find the value of *x*.

1.

10   4

5   *x*

2.

x   9

12   12

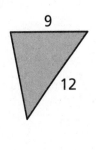

Lesson 3.4

Start Thinking!
For use before Lesson 3.4

Thales was a Greek philosopher and mathematician who lived around 600 B.C. There are several accounts of how he used indirect measurement to find the height of the Great Pyramid in Giza.

According to one account, when his shadow was the same length as his height, he measured the length of the Great Pyramid's shadow.

What does this have to do with similar triangles?

Lesson 3.4

Warm Up
For use before Lesson 3.4

Make a triangle that is larger or smaller than the one given and has the same angle measures. Find the ratios of the corresponding side lengths.

1.

2.

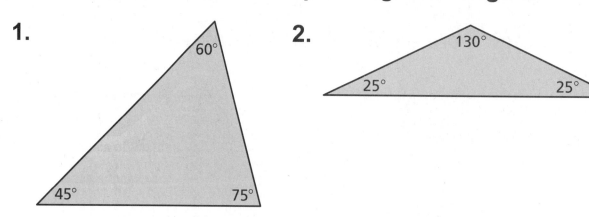

3.4 | Practice A

Tell whether the triangles are similar. Explain.

1.

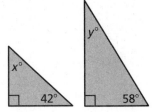

2.

3. The triangles are similar. Find the value of *x*.

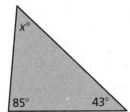 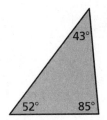

4. You can use indirect measurement to estimate the height of a building. First measure your distance from the base of the building and the distance from the ground to a point on the building that you are looking at. Maintaining the same angle of sight, move back until the top of the building is in your line of sight.

   a. Explain why △*ABC* and △*DBE* are similar.

   b. What is the height of the building?

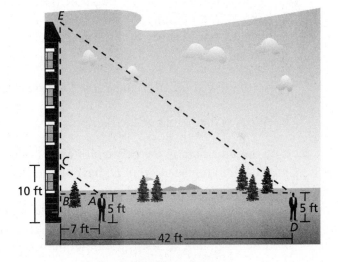

5. You and your friend are practicing for a rowing competition and want to know how far it is to an island in the Indian River Lagoon. You take measurements on your side of the lagoon and make the drawing shown.

   a. Explain why △*ABC* and △*DEC* are similar.

   b. What is the distance to the island?

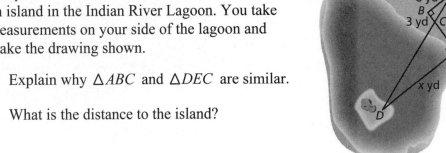
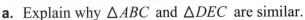

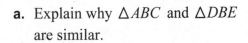

Name _____ Date _____

Tell whether the triangles are similar. Explain.

1.

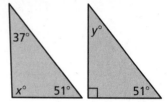

2.

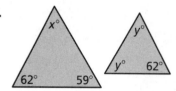

3. The triangles are similar. Find the value of x.

4. You can use indirect measurement to estimate the
height of a flag pole. First measure your distance
from the base of the flag pole and the distance from
the ground to a point on the flag pole that you are
looking at. Maintaining the same angle of sight,
move back until the top of the flag pole is in your
line of sight.

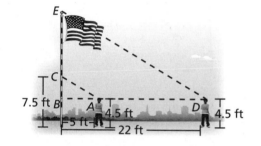

   a. Explain why $\triangle ABC$ and $\triangle DBE$ are similar.

   b. What is the height of the flag pole?

5. You are on a boat in the ocean, at Point A. You
locate a lighthouse at Point D, beyond the line
of sight of the marker at point C. You drive
0.2 mile west to Point B and then 0.1 mile south
to Point C. You drive 0.3 mile more to arrive at
Point E, which is due east of the lighthouse.

   a. Explain why $\triangle ABC$ and $\triangle DEC$ are
   similar.

   b. What is the distance from Point E to the
   lighthouse?

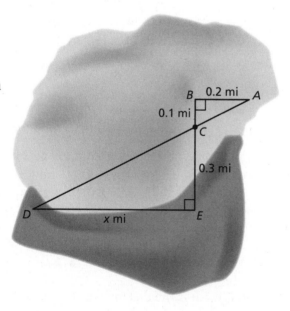

3.4 Enrichment and Extension

Tessellations

A *tessellation* is a collection of figures that covers a plane with no gaps or overlaps. A *semi-regular tessellation* is a pattern formed by using two or more regular polygons.

Use the tessellation to answer the questions.

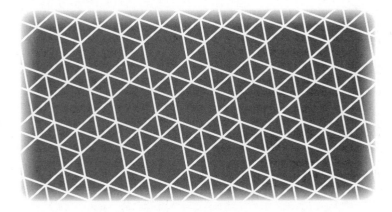

1. Is the tessellation semi-regular? How do you know?

2. Identify the two regular polygons used in the tessellation.

3. What is the measure of one angle of the triangle used in the tessellation?

4. What is the measure of one angle of the hexagon used in the tessellation?

5. A vertex is the point at which several polygons come together. Identify and mark one vertex in the tessellation.

6. Traveling clockwise, name the polygons that meet at your vertex.

7. What is the sum of the angles that meet at the vertex?

8. Give two examples where tessellations are used in real life.

9. Name the polygons that are found in your real-life examples from Exercise 8.

3.4 Puzzle Time

What Do You Call A Dandelion Floating In The Ocean?

Write the letter of each answer in the box containing the exercise number.

Choose the correct letter that describes the triangles.

1.

A. similar   **B.** not similar

2.

C. similar   **D.** not similar

3.

E. similar   **F.** not similar

4.

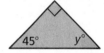

G. similar   **H.** not similar

Answers
R. B
A. D
T. H
E. 58
D. A
M. E
S. G
E. 18
W. 70
N. C
E. F

The triangles are similar. Find the value of x.

5.

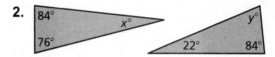

6.

7.

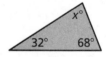
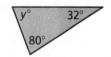
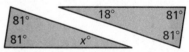
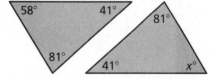

4	7	2		6	5	3	1

Name_____ Date _____

Exploring Tessellations

In Section 3.3, you learned that a *tessellation* is a covering (or tiling) of a surface with one or more geometric shapes so that there are no gaps or overlaps. Many computer software programs have the capability to produce tessellations; however, the process is much simpler if the program has the ability to draw regular polygons, maintain the polygon's shape when resizing, copy and paste, and color each shape in the drawing.

EXAMPLE Use a computer drawing program to create a tessellation of regular hexagons.

SOLUTION

Step 1 Use the Insert menu (or similar) to find and insert a graphic of a regular hexagon. When inserting or resizing the hexagon, usually holding the Shift key will keep the shape regular.

Step 2 After resizing your hexagon to your desired size, use the copy and paste commands to populate your screen with hexagons.

Step 3 Finish the tessellation by formatting the hexagons with a pattern of different colors.

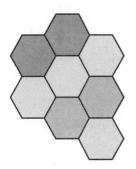

Use a computer program to produce tessellations of the following figures.

1. regular hexagons and equilateral triangles

2. squares and equilateral triangles

3. regular hexagons, squares, and equilateral triangles

Chapter 4

Name_____ Date _____

Dear Family,

Selling refreshments is a popular way to raise money at school events. You or your student may have volunteered to work at the refreshment table to help support a favorite activity or team.

Suppose you are working at a bake sale. The food is donated, so any sales are all profit. The cash box starts with $30 for making change. You can figure out how much money should be in the cash box with a linear equation.

Amount in cashbox = Initial amount + (Cookie price) × (Cookies sold)

$$y = 30 + 0.5x$$

In a graph of the equation, the line slopes upward because the amount of money in the cash box is increasing. The slope is positive and equal to the unit price: $0.50 per cookie or 0.5.

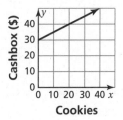

Suppose you give your student $5 to spend on snacks with a group of friends. The amount of money remaining depends on how many items they have already purchased.

Amount remaining = Initial amount − (Cookie price) × (Cookies bought)

$$y = 5 - 0.5x$$

In a graph of the equation, the line slopes downward because the money left to spend is decreasing. The slope is negative and equal to the cost of one cookie: −0.5. The intercepts (0, 5) and (10, 0) correspond to the starting point (no cookies and $5) and the possible ending point (10 cookies and no money remaining).

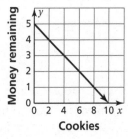

Enjoy your bake sale or snack bar work!

Capítulo 4 · Graficando y Escribiendo Ecuaciones Lineales

Estimada Familia:

Vender refrescos es una forma popular de obtener dinero en eventos escolares. Usted o su estudiante pueden haberse presentado como voluntarios para trabajar en la mesa de refrescos y ayudar a apoyar un equipo o actividad favorita.

Supongamos que están trabajando en una venta de pasteles. La comida es donada, así que cualquier venta que hagan se considera como ganancia completa. La caja con efectivo empieza con $30 para dar vuelto. Se puede averiguar cuánto dinero debe haber en la caja con una ecuación lineal.

Cantidad en caja con efectivo = Cantidad inicial + (Precio de la galleta)

× (Galletas vendidas)

$$y = 30 + 0.5x$$

En un gráfico de la ecuación, la línea va hacia arriba porque la cantidad de dinero en la caja está aumentando. La pendiente es positiva e igual al precio unitario: $0.50 por galleta ó 0.5.

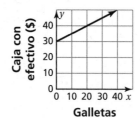

Supongamos que le entrega a su estudiante $5 para gastar en refrigerios con un grupo de amigos. La cantidad de dinero restante depende del número de objetos que ya han comprado.

Cantidad restante = Cantidad inicial − (Precio de la galleta) × (Galletas compradas)

$$y = 5 - 0.5x$$

En un gráfico de la ecuación, la línea va hacia abajo porque el dinero que queda para gastar está disminuyendo. La pendiente es negativa e igual al costo de una galleta: −0.5. Las intersecciones (0, 5) y (10, 0) corresponden al punto de inicio (sin galletas y $5) y el posible punto final (10 galletas y nada de dinero restante).

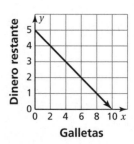

¡Disfruten su trabajo con la venta de pasteles o trabajo en la cafetería!

Start Thinking!

For use before Activity 4.1

Which of the following graphs do you think
show *linear* equations? Explain.

A.   **B.**   **C.**

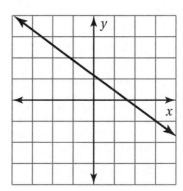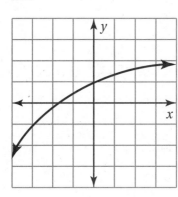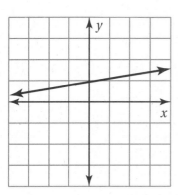

Activity 4.1

Warm Up

For use before Activity 4.1

Copy and complete the table using the given equation.

1. $y = 2x - 3$

x	−1	0	1	2
y				

2. $y = -x + 1$

x	−1	0	1	2
y				

3. $y = x + 5$

x	−1	0	1	2
y				

4. $y = \dfrac{1}{2}x + 2$

x	−1	0	1	2
y				

Think about how much energy you have on an average day.

Graph your energy level (on a scale of 0 to 10) throughout an average day.

Are any sections of your graph linear?

Copy and complete the table. Plot the two solution points and draw a line *exactly* through the two points. Find a different solution point on the line.

1.

x		
$y = 4x - 2$		

2.

x		
$y = -x + 5$		

Name_____ Date _____

4.1 Practice A

Copy and complete the table. Plot the two solution points and draw a line *exactly* through the two points. Find a different solution point on the line.

1.

x		
y = 4x + 3		

2.

x		
$y = \dfrac{3}{2}x - 1$		

Graph the linear equation. Use a graphing calculator to check your graph.

3. $y = -2x$

4. $y = \dfrac{2}{5}x$

5. $y = -4$

6. $y = x + 2$

7. $y = -5x + 3$

8. $y = \dfrac{x}{2} + 1$

9. The equation $y = \dfrac{2}{3}x$ represents the cost y (in dollars) for x pounds of bananas.

   a. Graph the equation.

   b. Use the graph to estimate the cost of 8 pounds of bananas.

   c. Use the equation to find the exact cost of 8 pounds of bananas.

Solve for *y*. Then graph the equation. Use a graphing calculator to check your graph.

10. $y - 2x = 5$

11. $6x + 5y = 15$

12. You have $110 in your lunch account and plan to spend $2.75 each school day.

   a. Write and graph a linear equation that represents the balance in your lunch account.

   b. How many school days will it take to spend all of the money in your lunch account?

4.1 Practice B

Graph the linear equation. Use a graphing calculator to check your graph, if possible.

1. $y = 3.5$

2. $y = \dfrac{4}{5}x$

3. $y = \dfrac{2}{3}x - 2$

4. $y = -\dfrac{1}{10}x + 4$

5. $y = \dfrac{10}{3}x$

6. $y = -\dfrac{x}{2} + \dfrac{3}{2}$

7. The equation $y = 1.5x + 35$ represents the cost y (in dollars) of the family meal when the food costs $35 and x beverages are purchased.

   a. Graph the equation.

   b. Use the graph to estimate the cost of the family meal when 5 beverages are purchased.

   c. Use the equation to find the exact cost of the family meal when 5 beverages are purchased.

Solve for y. Then graph the equation. Use a graphing calculator to check your graph.

8. $2y + 3x = -6$

9. $x + 0.25y = 1.5$

10. There are 10 coconuts at the base of your tree. The coconuts are falling off the tree at a rate of 6 coconuts per week. Assume that you do not pick up any coconuts.

   a. Write and graph a linear equation that represents the number of coconuts at the base of your tree after x weeks.

   b. The tree will have no coconuts on it when there are 52 coconuts at the base of the tree. After how many weeks will this occur?

11. The sum s of the first n positive integers is $s = \dfrac{1}{2}n(n + 1)$. Plot four points (n, s) that satisfy the equation. Is the graph of the equation a line?

4.1 Enrichment and Extension

Graphing Equations

You have studied the properties of linear equations. Now you will learn about two additional types of equations, the quadratic equation and the absolute value equation.

Copy and complete the table. Then plot the points and draw a graph of the equation.

1. $y = -2x + 3$

x	y
-2	7
-1	
0	
1	
2	

2. $y = 3x^2 - 1$

x	y
-2	11
-1	
0	
1	
2	

3. $y = -|x| + 2$

x	y
-2	0
-1	
0	
1	
2	

4. Linear equations have the form $y = mx + b$. Which of the given equations is linear?

5. An equation of the form $y = ax^2 + b$ is called a quadratic equation. Which of the given equations is quadratic? Describe the graph of the quadratic equation.

6. An equation of the form $y = a|x| + b$ is called an absolute value equation. Which of the given equations is an absolute value equation? Describe the graph of the absolute value equation.

7. Compare and contrast the three different types of graphs.

8. How would each graph change if a different b value was selected?

4.1 Puzzle Time

What Arctic Bird Can Be Found In A Bakery?

Write the letter of each answer in the box containing the exercise number.

Find the values of _y_ that correspond to the given values of _x_ for the linear equation.

1. $y = 4x + 3$ for $x = -1, 0, 1$

2. $y = -\dfrac{3}{2}x + 5$ for $x = 0, 2, 4$

3. $y = -9$ for $x = 0, 1, 2$

4. $y = -7x + 8$ for $x = -1, 0, 1$

5. $y = \dfrac{5}{3}x - 6$ for $x = -3, 0, 3$

6. $y = 1.4x - 9$ for $x = 0, 1, 2$

Solve for _y_. Then find the values of _y_ that correspond to the given values of _x_ for the linear equation.

7. $y + 8x = -2$ for $x = 0, 1, 2$

8. $12x + 3y = 15$ for $x = -1, 0, 1$

9. $\dfrac{1}{4}y - 3x = 9$ for $x = -2, 0, 2$

10. $0.4y + 2x = 1.2$ for $x = -3, 0, 3$

Answers
E. $y = -9, -7.6, -6.2$
F. $y = 12, 36, 60$
P. $y = 18, 3, -12$
I. $y = -2, -10, -18$
A. $y = 15, 8, 1$
F. $y = 6, 5, 4$
M. $y = 10, 9.5, 9$
U. $y = -11, -6, -1$
C. $y = 9, 5, 1$
N. $y = 5, 2, -1$
R. $y = -9, -9, -9$
A. $y = -1, 3, 7$

11. The equation $22 = 2y + x$ represents the perimeter of a flower garden with length _y_ (in feet) and width _x_ (in feet). Solve for _y_. Then find the length of the flower garden when the width is 2 feet, 3 feet, and 4 feet.

12. The equation $0.60 = 0.05x + 0.10y$ represents the number of nickels _x_ and dimes _y_ needed to add up to 60 cents. Solve for _y_. Then find the number of dimes that are needed to make 60 cents when the number of nickels is 0, 2, and 4.

1		8	3	6	4	11		10	5	9	12	7	2

Use the definition of ski slope to help you think of what the slope of a line is in mathematics.

Write the fraction in simplest form.

1. $\dfrac{6}{2}$ **2.** $\dfrac{8}{28}$ **3.** $\dfrac{10}{25}$

4. $\dfrac{10}{8}$ **5.** $\dfrac{6}{9}$ **6.** $\dfrac{16}{12}$

Choose a partner. Each student must choose an ordered pair and work together to find the slope of the line joining your two points. Use a graph to help you. Repeat the process several times with different ordered pairs.

Were any of the slopes positive? negative? zero?

Draw a line through each point using the given slope. What do you notice about the two lines?

1. Slope = 2

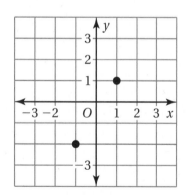

2. Slope = −2

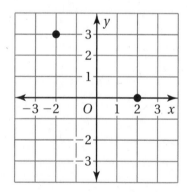

Name_____ Date_____

4.2 Practice A

1. Refer to the graph.

   a. Which lines have negative slopes?

   b. Which line has the steepest slope?

   c. Are any two of the lines parallel? Explain.

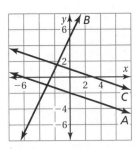

Draw a line through each point using the given slope. What do you notice about the two lines?

2. Slope $= -2$

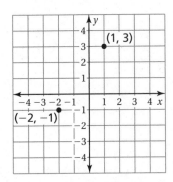

3. Slope $= \dfrac{1}{2}$

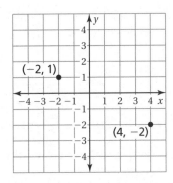

Find the slope of the line.

4.

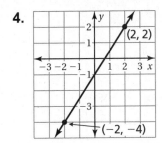

5.

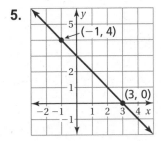

Find the slope of the line through the given points.

6. $(-1, -4), (1, 4)$

7. $(1, 2), (-3, 2)$

8. An awning covers a window that is 4 feet high. When the awning is opened, it extends 2 feet from the base of the window. Find the slope of the awning.

Name _____ Date _____

4.2 Practice B

Find the slope of the line.

1.

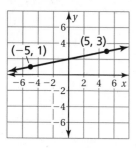

2.

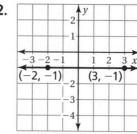

Find the slope of the line through the given points.

3. $(1, -6), (-1, 6)$

4. $(-3, -6), (6, 6)$

The points in the table lie on a line. Find the slope of the line.

5.

x	0	2	4	6
y	-4	-1	2	5

6.

x	-4	-1	0	3
y	7	4	3	0

7. A ramp used to remove furniture from a moving truck has a slope of $\frac{2}{5}$.

   The height of the ramp is 4 feet. How far does the base of the ramp extend from the end of the truck?

8. The graph shows the cost of a long distance phone call.

   a. Find the slope of the line.

   b. Explain the meaning of the slope as a rate of change.

   c. How much money is added to the phone bill if you talk for 5 extra minutes?

   d. How many minutes did you talk if the phone call costs $3?

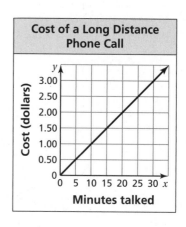

4.2 Enrichment and Extension

Slope of a Line

1. Draw an octagon in a coordinate plane with the vertices $(5, 2)$, $(2, 5)$, $(-2, 5)$, $(-5, 2)$, $(-5, -2)$, $(-2, -5)$, $(2, -5)$, and $(5, -2)$.

2. Without doing any calculations, do you think any of the line segments have the same slope? If so, which ones? Explain.

3. Calculate the slope of each side of the octagon. Were your predictions in Exercise 2 correct?

4. Two different lines are *parallel* if they do not intersect and have the same slope. Are any line segments in the graph parallel? Explain.

In Exercises 5–7, use the graph of the star.

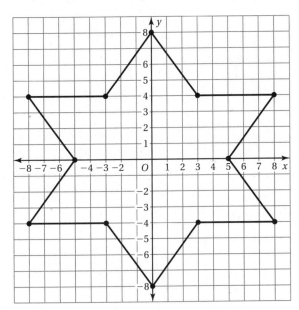

5. Without doing any calculations, do you think any of the line segments have the same slope? If so, which ones?

6. Calculate the slope of each line segment in the graph. Were your predictions in Exercise 5 correct?

7. Two lines in the same plane that intersect to form right angles are *perpendicular*. Two nonvertical lines are perpendicular if and only if the product of their slopes is -1. Are any line segments in the star perpendicular? Explain.

4.2 Puzzle Time

What Did One Poppy Seed Say To The Other?

Circle the letter of each correct answer in the boxes below. The circled letters will spell out the answer to the riddle.

Find the slope of the line through the given points.

1.
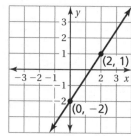

2.
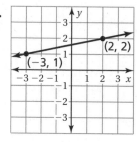

3.
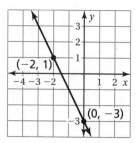

4.
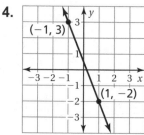

5.
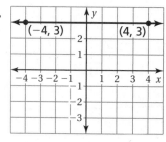

6.
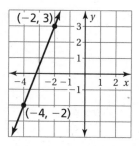

7. $(1, 4), (3, -2)$

8. $(1, 2), (1, -2)$

9.

x	−5	−3	3	5
y	15	7	−17	−25

I	T	M	S	A	O	N	H	A	P	L	R	O	M	E	L	S	L
−2	$\frac{2}{5}$	0	$\frac{1}{6}$	$\frac{4}{3}$	$\frac{1}{5}$	−3	$\frac{1}{4}$	$\frac{3}{2}$	$\frac{1}{50}$	1	−4	$\frac{5}{2}$	$-\frac{1}{3}$	2	$-\frac{5}{2}$	5	und.

Graph the linear equations $y = 3x + 2$ and $y = 3x - 4$ in a coordinate plane. What do you notice?

Graph the linear equations $y = -\dfrac{1}{2}x + 1$ and $y = 2x - 2$ in a coordinate plane. What do you notice?

Extension 4.2 **Warm Up**
For use before Extension 4.2

Find the slope of each line.

1.

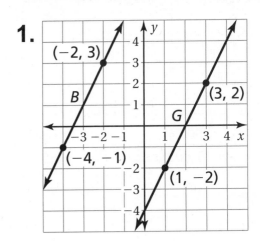

2.

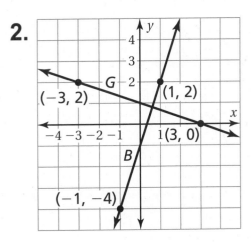

Name _____ Date _____

Which lines are parallel? How do you know?

1.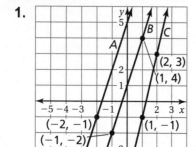

2.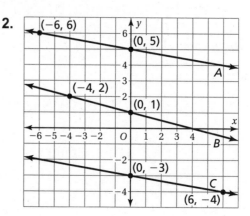

Are the given lines parallel? Explain your reasoning.

3. $x = -1, y = 2$

4. $x = 0, x = -3$

5. $y = 1, y = 5$

6. The vertices of a quadrilateral are $A(-4, -2)$, $B(-2, 1)$, $C(3, 2)$, and $D(1, -1)$. Is it a parallelogram? Justify your answer.

Which lines are perpendicular? How do you know?

7.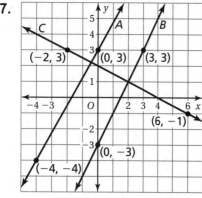

8.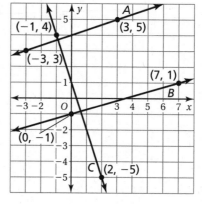

Are the given lines perpendicular? Explain your reasoning.

9. $x = 1, y = 0$

10. $y = -3, y = 2$

11. $x = -2, y = 2$

12. The vertices of a parallelogram are $J(2, 5)$, $K(5.5, 5)$, $L(0.5, -5)$, and $M(-3, -5)$. Is it a rectangle? Justify your answer.

Review with a partner how to graph the equation $y = 2x + 2$ using -1, 0, and 1 for the values of x.

Find the value of x.

1. $\dfrac{1}{2} = \dfrac{6}{x}$

2. $\dfrac{3}{4} = \dfrac{x}{24}$

3. $\dfrac{2}{x} = \dfrac{6}{18}$

4. $\dfrac{8}{12} = \dfrac{x}{3}$

5. $\dfrac{x}{21} = \dfrac{3}{9}$

6. $\dfrac{4}{x} = \dfrac{8}{20}$

Graph a line that passes through the origin. Next, graph a line that does not pass through the origin.

Which graph will have an equation in the form of $y = mx$?

Lesson 4.3 Warm Up
For use before Lesson 4.3

Tell whether x and y are in a proportional relationship. Explain your reasoning. If so, write an equation that represents the relationship.

1.

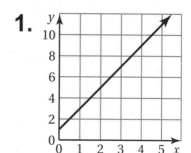

2.

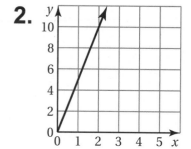

3.

x	4	8	12	16
y	2	4	6	8

4.

x	1	3	6	8
y	3	6	8	11

Name_____ Date_____

4.3 Practice A

Tell whether x and y are in a proportional relationship. Explain your reasoning. If so, write an equation that represents the relationship.

1.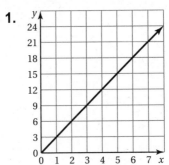

2.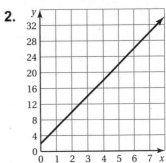

3.

x	5	10	15	20
y	1	3	5	7

4.

x	4	8	12	16
y	1	2	3	4

5. The distance your friend travels y (in miles) running x hours is represented by the equation $y = 7.5x$.

  a. Graph the equation and interpret the slope.

  b. How many minutes does it take for your friend to run one mile?

6. At a concession stand, hamburgers are selling at a rate of 160 hamburgers per hour. The table shows the rate at which wraps are selling.

Minutes	1	2	3	4
Wraps Sold	2.5	5	7.5	10

  a. Do hamburgers or wraps sell faster? Explain.

  b. Graph equations that represent the growth rates of hamburgers sold and wraps sold in the same coordinate plane. Compare the steepness of the graphs. What does this mean in the context of the problem?

4.3 Practice B

Tell whether *x* and *y* are in a proportional relationship. Explain your reasoning. If so, write an equation that represents the relationship.

1.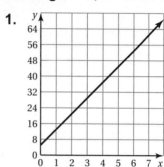

2.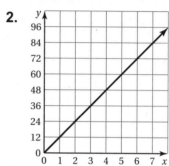

3.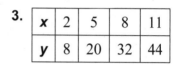

4.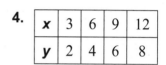

5. The cost *y* (in dollars) to rent a lane at the bowling alley is proportional to the number *x* of hours that you rent the lane. It costs $18 to rent the lane for 2 hours.

    a. Write an equation that represents the situation.

    b. Interpret the slope.

    c. How much does it cost to rent the lane for 3 hours?

6. The graph relates the height of the water in a tank *y* (in inches) to the volume of the water *x* (in gallons).

    a. Is the relationship proportional? Explain.

    b. Write an equation of the line. Interpret the slope.

    c. What is the height of the water in the tank when the volume is 250 gallons?

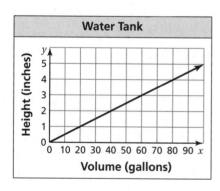

4.3 Enrichment and Extension

Inverse Variation

Two quantities x and y show *inverse variation* when $y = \dfrac{k}{x}$, where k is a nonzero constant.

1. Consider the inverse variation equation $y = \dfrac{1}{x}$.

    a. As x increases, does y increase or decrease?

    b. As x decreases, does y increase or decrease?

    c. What do you know about the product of x and y for any point (x, y) on the graph of the equation?

2. Is the graph of an inverse variation equation a line? Explain your reasoning.

Tell whether *x* and *y* show *direct variation*, *inverse variation*, or *neither*.

3. $y = \dfrac{x}{4}$ **4.** $y = \dfrac{10}{x}$ **5.** $y = 3x - 2$

6. $x = \dfrac{1}{y} + 5$ **7.** $y = 1.5x$ **8.** $8 - xy$

Tell whether the two quantities show *direct variation* or *inverse variation*. Write an equation that relates the variables.

9. You bring 200 cookies to a party. Let n represent the number of people at the party and c represent the number of cookies each person receives.

10. You work at a restaurant for 20 hours. Let r represent your hourly pay rate and p represent the total amount you earn.

4.3 Puzzle Time

What Do Ants Use For Hula Hoops?

Write the letter of each answer in the box containing the exercise number.

The cost *y* (in dollars) to spend an evening bowling is proportional to the number of games *x* that are bowled. It costs $16 to bowl 4 games.

1. Write an equation that represents the situation.

2. How much does it cost (in dollars) to bowl 6 games?

The gasoline *y* (in fluid ounces) is proportional to the number of fluid ounces of oil *x* used to run a 2-cycle motor. It takes 75 fluid ounces of gasoline for 3 fluid ounces of oil.

3. Write an equation that represents the situation.

4. How much gasoline (in fluid ounces) is needed for 8 fluid ounces of oil?

The number of pancakes *y* is proportional to the cups of pancake mix *x* that is used to make the pancake batter. The pancake batter will make 10 pancakes when 2 cups of pancake mix is used.

5. Write an equation that represents the situation.

6. How many pancakes are made when 5 cups of pancake mix are used in the pancake batter?

The toll charge *y* (in dollars) is proportional to the number of miles *x* traveled on the interstate. It cost $9 to travel 60 miles.

7. Write an equation that represents the situation.

8. How much does the toll charge cost (in dollars) when you travel 100 miles?

Answers
H. $y = 5x$
S. $y = 25x$
I. $y = 4x$
E. $y = 0.15x$
O. 25
C. 15
R. 200
E. 24

8	5	2	7	4	1	6	3

Start Thinking!
For use before Activity 4.4

The graph shows the attendance of a book fair over the last 7 days.

Explain what some points on the graph mean.

Is the graph linear?

What is the approximate slope? What does it represent?

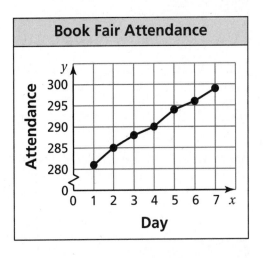

Book Fair Attendance

Activity 4.4

Warm Up
For use before Activity 4.4

Graph the linear equation using the input-output table.

1. $y = x - 1$

x	0	1	2	3
y				

2. $y = \dfrac{1}{2}x + 2$

x	-2	0	2	4
y				

Lesson 4.4

Start Thinking!

For use before Lesson 4.4

Describe a situation involving online shopping that can be modeled with a linear equation.

What is the slope?

What is the *y*-intercept?

Lesson 4.4

Warm Up

For use before Lesson 4.4

Match the equation with its graph. Identify the slope and *y*-intercept.

1. $y = 2x - 1$

2. $y = -x + 2$

3. $y = -2x - 1$

A.

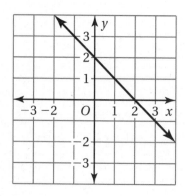

B.

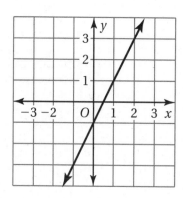

C.

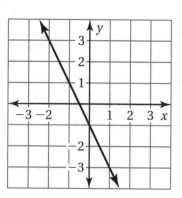

Name_____ Date_____

Match the equation with its graph. Identify the slope and *y*-intercept.

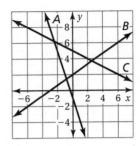

1. $y = -\dfrac{1}{2}x + 5$

2. $y = -3x - 1$

3. $y = \dfrac{2}{3}x + 2$

Find the slope and the *y*-intercept of the graph of the linear equation.

4. $y = x + 4$

5. $y = -8x + 3$

6. $y = -\dfrac{5}{7}x - 2$

7. $y = 1.75x - 1$

8. $y - 2 = 6x$

9. $y + 7 = \dfrac{1}{9}x$

10. The depreciated value *y* (in dollars) of a business car after *x* years is $y = -4200x + 21{,}000$.

   a. Graph the equation.

   b. Interpret the slope.

   c. Interpret the *y*-intercept.

   d. Interpret the *x*-intercept.

Graph the linear equation. Identify the *x*-intercept. Use a graphing calculator to check your answer.

11. $y = 3x - 6$

12. $y = -\dfrac{1}{4}x + 12$

13. $y = 3.2x + 9.6$

14. $y - 2 = 5x$

15. The amount of fertilizer *y* (in cups) that is needed for *x* square feet of grass is $y = \dfrac{1}{4}x$.

   a. Graph the equation.

   b. Interpret the slope.

4.4 Practice B

Find the slope and the *y*-intercept of the graph of the linear equation.

1. $y = -\dfrac{3}{8}x + 10$

2. $y = 4.5x + 7$

3. $y = -\dfrac{4}{5}x - \dfrac{1}{5}$

4. $y + 2.5 = 5.5x$

5. $y - \dfrac{2}{7} = 4x$

6. $y + 5 = \dfrac{2}{3}x$

Graph the linear equation. Identify the *x*-intercept. Use a graphing calculator to check your answer.

7. $y = \dfrac{5}{3}x - 2$

8. $y = -1.2x + 9$

9. $y - 6.6 = 1.1x$

10. $y + 3 = -\dfrac{6}{7}x$

11. There is a $10 monthly membership fee to download music. There is a $0.50 fee for each song downloaded.

  a. Write a linear equation that models the cost of downloading *x* songs per month.

  b. Graph the equation.

  c. What is the cost of downloading 15 songs?

12. An entrepreneur is opening a business to market pies and pie fillings based on her family's recipes. The price of every item in the store is $6.

  a. Write a linear equation that models the amount of revenue *y* (in dollars) taken in for selling *x* items.

  b. Graph the equation.

  c. The monthly cost of rent and utilities for the store space is $1100. What is the minimum number of items that must be sold each month in order to make a profit?

  d. Assuming 4 weeks in a month, what is the average number of items that need to be sold each week in order to turn a profit?

Name_____ Date_____

4.4 Enrichment and Extension

Matching Slopes and Intercepts

Each of the equations below is missing a *b*-value. Use each value in the B-hive only once to complete the seven linear equations below. The graph of each linear equation should pass through two of the given points on the graph. No two equations pass through the same given point.

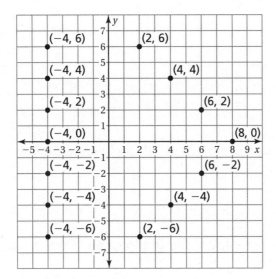

1. $y = -\dfrac{5}{4}x + \boxed{}$

2. $y = x + \boxed{}$

3. $y = \dfrac{3}{5}x + \boxed{}$

4. $y = \dfrac{1}{2}x + \boxed{}$

5. $y = \dfrac{1}{4}x + \boxed{}$

6. $y = \boxed{}$

7. $y = -\dfrac{5}{3}x + \boxed{}$

B-Hive

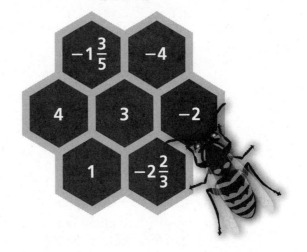

Name _____ Date _____

4.4 Puzzle Time

Did You Hear About...

A	B	C	D	E	F
G	H	I	J	K	L
M	N	O	P		

Complete each exercise. Find the answer in the answer column. Write the word under the answer in the box containing the exercise letter.

$\dfrac{3}{2}$ **MANY**	
$-\dfrac{1}{2}$ **WHO**	
-12 **THAT**	
-7 **SO**	
0.25 **SEASON**	
-5 **GAVE**	
-2 **FOR**	
16 **TICKETS**	
$\dfrac{2}{3}$ **THE**	
-8 **DRIVING**	

Find the slope of the graph of the linear equation.

A. $3y = 2x + 3$ **B.** $y = -x - 2$

C. $4y = -2x + 12$ **D.** $5y - 10 = x$

Find the y-intercept of the graph of the linear equation.

E. $y = 4x - 4$ **F.** $2y = x - 4$

G. $y - 12 = -9x$ **H.** $7 + y = 4.3x$

Find the x-intercept of the graph of the linear equation.

I. $y = 6x - 9$ **J.** $3y = 2x + 36$

K. $2y = -5x + 7$ **L.** $3y - 9 = 4x$

M. $y = 1.6x + 8$ **N.** $y + 15 = 12.5x$

O. Shannon's hair is 12 inches long and grows 0.25 inch per month. In an equation that represents the length y of her hair after x months, what number represents the slope?

P. You have a $20 gift card to a coffee shop. Each time you go there, you get chai tea for $1.25. The equation $y = -1.25x + 20$ represents how much you have left on the gift card after x visits. How many chai teas can you purchase before the balance on your card runs out?

-4 **STOPPED**	
5 **HAD**	
$-\dfrac{9}{4}$ **POLICE**	
-1 **LADY**	
22 **CAR**	
$\dfrac{7}{5}$ **THE**	
-18 **TIMES**	
$\dfrac{1}{5}$ **GOT**	
1.2 **HER**	
12 **SPEEDING**	

Consider the equation $y = -\dfrac{2}{5}x + 2$.

Which of the following is an equivalent equation?

$5x + 2y = 10$ or $2x + 5y = 10$

How do you know?

Solve the equation for *y*.

1. $x + y = 4$ **2.** $2x + y = 10$

3. $3x + 4y = 12$ **4.** $-5x + 10y = 8$

5. $-4x + 2y = 10$ **6.** $-x + 2y = 4$

You have $40 to spend on turkey and cheese for a party. At the deli, turkey is $10 per pound and cheese is $6 per pound.

Is it easier to write an equation to represent the situation in *slope-intercept form* or *standard form*? Why?

Define two variables for the verbal model. Write an equation in slope-intercept form that relates the variables. Graph the equation.

1. $\dfrac{25 \text{ miles}}{\text{hour}}$ · Non-highway hours + $\dfrac{60 \text{ miles}}{\text{hour}}$

    · Highway hours = $\dfrac{240}{\text{miles}}$

2. $\dfrac{\$5.00}{\text{hat}}$ · Number of hats + $\dfrac{\$10.00}{\text{T-shirt}}$

    · Number of T-shirts = $\$30$

Name_____ Date_____

Write the linear equation in slope-intercept form.

1. $4x + y = 10$

2. $3x - y = 7$

Graph the linear equation. Use a graphing calculator to check your graph.

3. $2x - 3y = 6$

4. $5x - 3y = 15$

Use the graph to find the *x*- and *y*-intercepts.

5.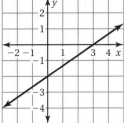

6.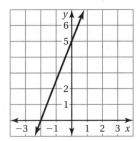

Graph the linear equation using intercepts. Use a graphing calculator to check your graph.

7. $4x + y = 8$

8. $3x - 2y = 12$

9. The total amount of fiber (in grams) in a package containing x apples and y oranges is given by the equation $5x + 10y = 110$.

   a. Find and interpret the y-intercept.

   b. Find and interpret the x-intercept.

   c. How many grams of fiber does an orange contain?

   d. How many grams of fiber does an apple contain?

   e. Is it possible for the package to contain 15 apples? Explain.

10. You have two jobs. You earn \$8 for each hour x that you work as a restaurant host and \$6 for each hour y that you work as a hair washer. Your earnings for the pay period are \$144.

   a. Write an equation in standard form that models your earnings.

   b. Find the x- and y-intercepts.

   c. Graph the equation.

   d. You worked 10 hours as a hair washer. How many hours did you work as a host?

Name _____ Date _____

Write the linear equation in slope-intercept form.

1. $\dfrac{2}{3}x + y = 4$

2. $4x - 2y = 10$

Graph the linear equation. Use a graphing calculator to check your graph.

3. $4.5x - 0.5y = 3$

4. $\dfrac{2}{3}x + \dfrac{1}{3}y = 2$

Use the graph to find the x- and y-intercepts.

5.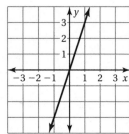

6.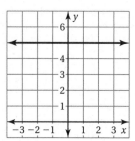

Graph the linear equation using intercepts. Use a graphing calculator to check your graph.

7. $\dfrac{1}{5}x + \dfrac{1}{10}y = \dfrac{2}{5}$

8. $2.5x - 1.25y = 5$

9. Your family is on a ski vacation. Lift tickets for the family cost $80 per day. Snowboard rentals cost $40 per day. You purchase lift tickets for x days and snowboard rentals for y days and spend $480.

    a. Write an equation in standard form that represents the situation.

    b. Find the x- and y-intercepts.

    c. Graph the equation.

    d. You rent snowboards for 2 days. How many days did you purchase lift tickets?

10. An electrician charges $80 plus $32 per hour.

    a. Write an equation that represents the total fee y (in dollars) charged by the electrician for a job lasting x hours.

    b. Find the x- and y-intercepts.

    c. Graph the equation.

    d. Is the value of the x-intercept applicable to the electrician? Explain.

4.5 Enrichment and Extension

Interpreting Intercepts

The graph shows the horizontal position y (in feet)
of a trapeze artist after x seconds during an act.

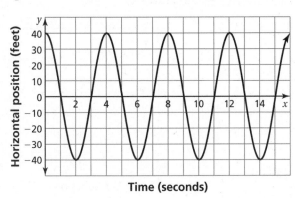

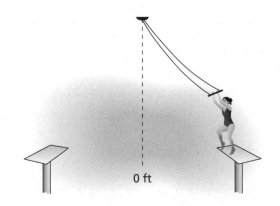

0 ft

1. Does the graph represent a linear equation? Explain.

2. What is the y-intercept of the graph?

3. Interpret the y-intercept.

4. How many x-intercepts does the graph have?

5. Why does the graph have more than one x-intercept?

6. How many seconds does the trapeze act last?

7. How many feet apart are the platforms?

8. Do you think the graph is a realistic representation of the situation?
   Why or why not?

9. Would it be a good idea to include Quadrants II and III in a realistic
   graph of the situation? Why or why not?

Name _____ Date _____

4.5 Puzzle Time

How Do Kangaroos Travel Across The Ocean?

Write the letter of each answer in the box containing the exercise number.

Write the linear equation in slope-intercept form.

1. $3x + y = 8$

2. $9x - y = \dfrac{1}{3}$

3. $-\dfrac{1}{4}x + y = 3$

4. $2x - 7y = 12$

Find the x- and y-intercepts of the linear equation.

5. $-3x + 5y = 15$

6. $2x - y = 4$

7. $4x - 9y = 36$

8. $x + \dfrac{1}{3}y = -3$

9. $\dfrac{2}{5}x - \dfrac{3}{4}y = 12$

10. $7.6x + 15.2y = 38$

11. The booster club sells popcorn at basketball games for $0.75 per bag. Their cost for supplies is $12. The equation $-0.75x + y = -12$ represents the booster club's income y after selling x bags of popcorn. Find the x- and y-intercepts of the linear equation.

12. You upload digital photos to an online photo processing website. You can print 4-inch-by-6-inch photos for $0.30 each and 5-inch-by-7-inch photos for $0.75 each. The linear equation $0.30x + 0.75y = 15$ represents the ways you can print x 4-inch-by-6-inch photos and y 5-inch-by-7-inch photos for $15. Find the x- and y-intercepts of the linear equation.

Answers

H. $y = \dfrac{2}{7}x - \dfrac{12}{7}$

S. x-intercept: 5; y-intercept: 2.5

H. x-intercept: -3; y-intercept: -9

J. x-intercept: 50; y-intercept: 20

M. x-intercept: 2; y-intercept: -4

Y. x-intercept: 30; y-intercept: -16

U. x-intercept: 9; y-intercept: -4

P. x-intercept: 16; y-intercept: -12

T. $y = -3x + 8$

E. x-intercept: -5; y-intercept: 3

P. $y = 9x - \dfrac{1}{3}$

I. $y = \dfrac{1}{4}x + 3$

1	4	5	9		12	7	6	2		10	8	3	11

Start Thinking!
For use before Activity 4.6

Use the graph to answer the questions.

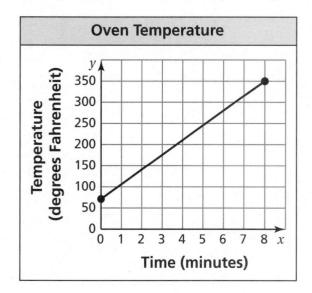

What does the graph show?

Estimate the *y*-intercept. What does it represent?

Estimate the slope. What does it represent?

Warm Up
For use before Activity 4.6

Find the slope of the line.

1.

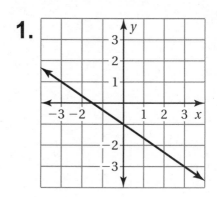

2.

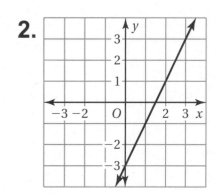

A gym membership has a $20 enrollment fee and costs $40 per month.

Write an equation in slope-intercept form that represents the cost *y* after *x* months of joining the gym.

What does the slope represent?

What does the *y*-intercept represent?

Lesson 4.6 **Warm Up**
For use before Lesson 4.6

Write an equation that represents each side of the figure.

1.

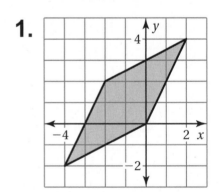

2.

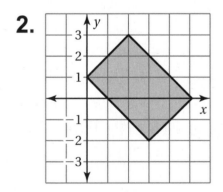

Name_____ Date _____

1. Write an equation that represents each side of the figure.

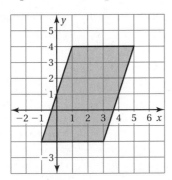

Write an equation of the line in slope-intercept form.

2.

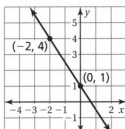

3.

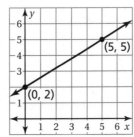

4. A plant is 3 inches tall when you purchase it and grows 2 inches per month. Write an equation that represents the height y (in inches) of a plant that you purchased x months ago.

Write an equation of the line that passes through the points.

5. $(0, 0), (4, -2)$

6. $(-2, 6), (0, 3)$

7. A bucket is empty. You are filling the bucket with water at a rate of 3 inches per second.

   a. Plot the points $(0, 0)$ and $(5, 15)$.

   b. What do the points in part (a) represent?

   c. Draw a line through the points.

   d. What does the line represent?

   e. Write an equation of the line.

4.6 Practice B

1. Write an equation that represents each side of the figure.

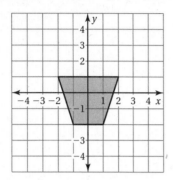

Write an equation of the line in slope-intercept form.

2.

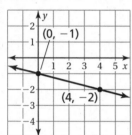

3.

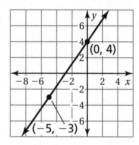

4. Your hair is 6 inches long and grows at a rate of 144 millimeters per year.

    a. Convert 144 millimeters per year to inches per year. Round your answer to the nearest tenth.

    b. Write an equation that represents the length y (in inches) of your hair after x years.

    c. How long is your hair after 4 years?

Write an equation of the line that passes through the points.

5. $(-4, -1), (0, 5)$ **6.** $(0, -3), (1, -5)$

7. Yesterday, you typed 8 pages in 48 minutes. Today, you typed 20 pages in 2 hours.

    a. Plot the two points (x, y), where x is the time (in minutes) and y is the number of pages.

    b. What is the rate of typing?

    c. Write an equation that represents the number of pages in terms of the number of minutes.

Name_____ Date _____

4.6 Enrichment and Extension

Matching Equations and Graphs

Copy the equations and graphs onto index cards. Mix the cards up and lay
them face down. With a friend, take turns turning over pairs of cards. If you
find a matching graph and equation, remove the pair and take another turn.
If the pair doesn't match, turn both cards face down again. Continue until
all pairs are removed. The player with the most pairs wins.

$y = \dfrac{1}{3}x + 2$	$y = 2x - 2$	$y = -x + 3$
$y = 4x$	$y = -\dfrac{2}{5}x + 1$	$y = \dfrac{3}{4}x - 3$
$y = -\dfrac{1}{2}x - 1$	$y = -3x$	$y = \dfrac{3}{5}x - 4$

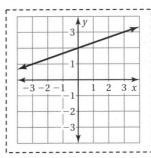
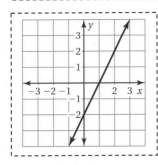
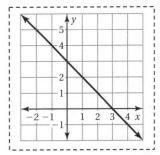

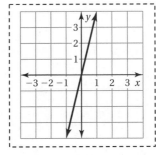
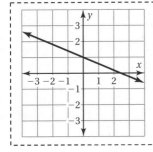
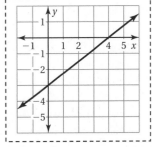

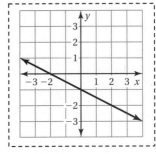
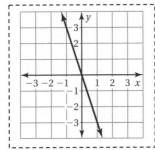
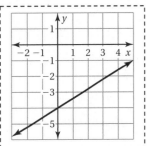

4.6 Puzzle Time

What Should You Know If You Want To Become A Lion Tamer?

Write the letter of each answer in the box containing the exercise number.

Write an equation of the line that passes through the points.

1. $(0, 3), (1, 4)$

2. $(0, 0), (5, -2)$

3. $(-2, 0), (0, 4)$

4. $(-3, 2), (0, -3)$

5. $(-7, 4), (0, 4)$

6. $(0, -8), (4, 8)$

7. $(0, -2), (-5, -2)$

8. $(-12, -9), (0, -3)$

9. $(0, 10), (5, 0)$

10. $(-14, 12), (0, 6)$

11. $(0, -6), (6, -24)$

12. $(0, -15), (5, 0)$

13. You are planning to make a scrapbook. The album costs $20 and each of the scrapbook papers costs an additional $1. Write an equation that represents the cost of the completed scrapbook where x represents the number of scrapbook papers you purchase.

14. A hot tub that holds 300 gallons of water drains at a rate of 8 gallons per minute. Write an equation that represents how many gallons of water are left in the tub after it has drained for x minutes.

15. An elevator in a tall building is at a point 180 feet above the ground. The elevator descends at a rate of 12 feet per second. Write an equation that represents how far above the ground the elevator is after descending for x seconds.

Answers

T. $y = -2x + 10$

N. $y = \dfrac{1}{2}x - 3$

H. $y = x + 3$

R. $y = -12x + 180$

E. $y = 2x + 4$

A. $y = -\dfrac{2}{5}x$

H. $y = -\dfrac{3}{7}x + 6$

N. $y = x + 20$

E. $y = 4$

T. $y = 4x - 8$

I. $y = 3x - 15$

L. $y = -3x - 6$

M. $y = -8x + 300$

O. $y = -2$

O. $y = -\dfrac{5}{3}x - 3$

14	7	15	3		6	10	2	13		9	1	5		11	12	4	8

Activity 4.7

Start Thinking!

For use before Activity 4.7

Choose an ordered pair that is not on the y-axis. Choose a slope.

Can you write an equation of a line with the slope you chose that goes through the point you chose? If so, explain the method you used. If not, explain why not.

Activity 4.7

Warm Up

For use before Activity 4.7

Graph the linear equation.

1. $y = 2x + 3$

2. $y = -x + 2$

3. $y = \frac{2}{3}x - 1$

4. $y = -\frac{1}{2}x + 4$

5. $y = 5x - 10$

6. $y = -\frac{5}{7}x + 14$

How is writing the equation of a line given the slope and a point on the line similar to writing the equation of a line given the slope and y-intercept? How is it different?

Use the point-slope form to write an equation of the line with the given slope that passes through the given point.

1. $m = 2$

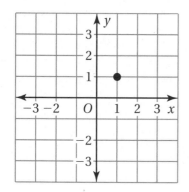

2. $m = -1$

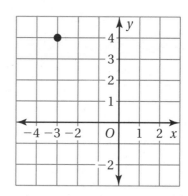

3. $m = -\dfrac{1}{2}$

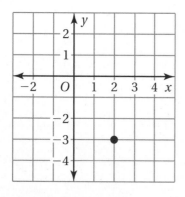

4. $m = \dfrac{2}{3}$

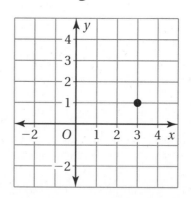

Name_____ Date_____

4.7 Practice A

Use the point-slope form to write an equation of the line with the given slope that passes through the given point.

1. $m = 3$

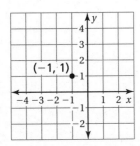

2. $m = -\dfrac{2}{3}$

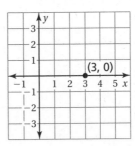

Write in point-slope form an equation of the line that passes through the given point and has the given slope.

3. $(4, -2); \; m = \dfrac{1}{4}$

4. $(-3, 5); \; m = -\dfrac{4}{3}$

5. $(2, 2); \; m = -1$

6. $(-1, -5); \; m = 4$

Write in slope-intercept form an equation of the line that passes through the given points.

7. $(-3, -4), (6, -1)$

8. $(-4, 12), (2, -3)$

9. $(-1, -2), (1, -6)$

10. $(-2, -9), (1, 6)$

11. After a laptop is purchased, its value decreases by $150 each year. After 2 years, the laptop is worth $600.

    a. Write an equation that represents the value V (in dollars) of the laptop x years after it is purchased.

    b. What was the original value of the laptop?

    c. What is the value of the laptop 5 years after it is purchased?

Name _____ Date _____

Write an equation of the line with the given slope that passes through the given point.

1. $m = \dfrac{5}{4}$

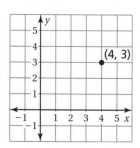

2. $m = -4$

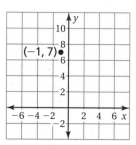

Write in point-slope form an equation of the line that passes through the given point and has the given slope.

3. $(-6, 3);\ m = \dfrac{1}{3}$

4. $(8, -7);\ m = -\dfrac{3}{4}$

5. $(-1, -5);\ m = 2$

6. $(-2, 8);\ m = -3$

Write in slope-intercept form an equation of the line that passes through the given points.

7. $(2, 3), (3, 7)$

8. $(-5, -8), (10, 4)$

9. $(-6, 4), (6, 0)$

10. $(2, 4), (4, 9)$

11. You are pulling a kite back to the ground at a rate of 2 feet per second. After 4 seconds, the kite is 16 feet above the ground.

   a. Write an equation that represents the height y (in feet) above the ground after x seconds.

   b. At what height was the kite when you started pulling it in?

   c. When does the kite touch the ground?

4.7 Enrichment and Extension

Ski Slopes

The grade of a ski trail describes the steepness of the ski slope. A skier can calculate the grade by dividing the vertical decrease (in meters) of the slope by the horizontal distance (in meters) it covers.

Frosty's Ski Center	
Trail	**Grade of Trail**
Bunny Slope	4%
Medium Trail	15%
Expert Route	30%

1. How does the grade of a trail relate to the slope of a line?

2. What is the slope of each of the ski trails?

3. There is a first aid station located at the point $(750, 28)$ on the Bunny Slope. Write an equation that describes the Bunny Slope.

4. What is the y-intercept of your equation? What does the y-intercept mean in terms of the Bunny Slope?

5. What is the x-intercept of your equation? What does the x-intercept mean in terms of the Bunny Slope?

6. The halfway point on the Medium Trail is located at $(5100, 765)$. Write an equation that describes the Medium Trail.

7. The Expert Route passes by the ski lodge located at the point $(15,000, 1500)$. Write an equation that describes the Expert Route.

8. Beginner slopes for new skiers have a maximum grade of 5%. Two skiers on a trail are located at the points $(700, 30)$ and $(450, 50)$. Is the trail a beginner slope? Explain.

4.7 Puzzle Time

What Do You Call A Ghost Cheerleader?

Write the letter of each answer in the box containing the exercise number.

Write in point-slope form an equation of the line that passes through the given point and has the given slope.

1. $(1, 5)$; $m = 2$ **2.** $(-2, 4)$; $m = -3$

3. $(4, 2)$; $m = 3$ **4.** $(-1, 5)$; $m = -2$

5. $(2, -4)$; $m = -3$ **6.** $(-5, 1)$; $m = 2$

Write in slope-intercept form an equation of the line that passes through the given points.

7. $(-5\ -5)$, $(5, -7)$ **8.** $(-3, -4)$, $(3, 0)$

9. $(-2, -7)$, $(2, -1)$ **10.** $(-6, -4)$, $(6, 4)$

11. You go to an arcade and purchase a card with game credits. After playing 5 games, you have 33 credits left. You play 4 more games and have 21 credits left. Write an equation that represents the number of credits y on the card after x games.

12. You go to a school dance. There is an entrance fee, and there are slices of pizza for sale. After having 1 slice of pizza, you have spent a total of $6. After having 2 more slices of pizza, you have spent a total of $10. Write an equation that represents the total cost y after buying x slices of pizza at the dance.

13. You make 2 headbands and have 6 feet of ribbon left. You make 1 more headband and have 4 feet of ribbon left. Write an equation that represents the amount of ribbon y you have left after making x headbands.

Answers

R. $y - 4 = -3(x + 2)$

M. $y = \dfrac{2}{3}x$

E. $y = 2x + 4$

I. $y + 4 = -3(x - 2)$

P. $y = -2x + 10$

I. $y = -3x + 48$

A. $y - 2 = 3(x - 4)$

T. $y = \dfrac{2}{3}x - 2$

E. $y - 5 = 2(x - 1)$

T. $y - 1 = 2(x + 5)$

S. $y = \dfrac{3}{2}x - 4$

T. $y - 5 = -2(x + 1)$

H. $y = -\dfrac{1}{5}x - 6$

4	7	1		6	12	3	10		9	13	5	2	11	8

Name_____ Date _____

Finding Slope

Use a calculator to find the slope of a line, given two points on the line.

EXAMPLE Find the slope of the line that passes through the points (8, 3) and (2, 5).

SOLUTION

Press $\boxed{(}\,5\,\boxed{-}\,3\,\boxed{)}\,\boxed{\div}\,\boxed{(}\,2\,\boxed{-}\,8\,\boxed{)}\,\boxed{=}$.

ANSWER −0.33...

You need to keep track of where you use each value. Either point can be used as (x_1, y_1). But the y-values or x-values cannot be switched.

In this set of exercises, you will explore what happens when the values are switched.

1. Find the slope of the line that passes through the points (3, 1) and (5, 4).

2. What happens when you change the order of the points in mid-calculation?

   a. Press $\boxed{(}\,4\,\boxed{-}\,1\,\boxed{)}\,\boxed{\div}\,\boxed{(}\,3\,\boxed{-}\,5\,\boxed{)}\,\boxed{=}$.

   b. Compare your answer in part (a) to your answer to Exercise 1. How are the slopes related?

   c. Describe a quick check you can use to ensure that you do not accidentally make this mistake when entering the problem.

3. What happens when you find the run over the rise?

   a. Press $\boxed{(}\,5\,\boxed{-}\,3\,\boxed{)}\,\boxed{\div}\,\boxed{(}\,4\,\boxed{-}\,1\,\boxed{)}\,\boxed{=}$.

   b. Compare your answer in part (a) to your answer to Exercise 1. How are the slopes related?

   c. Describe a quick check you can use to ensure that you do not accidentally make this mistake when entering the problem.

Use a calculator to find the slope. Round to the nearest hundredth.

4. (7, −3) and (0, 1)   5. (−1, −1) and (2, 9)

6. (3, 9) and (5, 9)   7. (6, 3) and (5, −2)

Chapter 5

Name_____ Date _____

Dear Family,

Some people have a side business to supplement their income: delivering papers, selling crafts, or running a website, to name a few. The goal is to make a *profit*—to have more income than expenses.

The *break-even point* is where the income equals the expenses. Making a graph is a good way to keep track of income and expenses and will show at a glance when the business will break even. On a graph, the break-even point is where the income line crosses the expense line.

My Woodworking Business

Selling Stools at Craft Fair		Units	Expense	Income
		0	$370.00	$0.00
		10	$475.00	$149.50
Craft Fair Booth:	$160.00	20	$580.00	$299.00
Business Cards:	$85.00	30	$685.00	$448.50
New Tools:	$125.00	40	$790.00	$598.00
Initial Investment:	$370.00	50	$895.00	$747.50
		60	$1,000.00	$897.00
Electricity:	$0.50	70	$1,105.00	$1,046.50
Rough Lumber:	$3.00	80	$1,210.00	$1,196.00
Fasteners & Glue:	$0.75	90	$1,315.00	$1,345.50
Stain & Sandpaper:	$1.25	100	$1,420.00	$1,495.00
My Time:	$5.00	110	$1,525.00	$1,644.50
Unit Cost:	$10.50	120	$1,630.00	$1,794.00
Unit Price:	$14.95	130	$1,735.00	$1,943.50

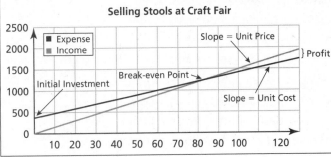

Selling Stools at Craft Fair

Have your student help you make a plan for a small business. A few basic steps will get your business plan started.

- How much money will you need for supplies to get started? This represents your *initial investment*. Plot this point on your graph.

- How much does it cost you to produce each item? This is the *unit cost*. Use this to plot more points on the graph to make an expense line.

- What price will you charge for each item? Starting at the origin of the graph, use this unit price to make an income line.

- Do the two lines cross? This is your break-even point—the number of items you must sell to pay for your expenses.

If the two lines do not cross, you will have to make some changes. Can you increase your unit price? You may not be able to charge more than your competitors. In that case, you will have to find a way to cut expenses.

What effect do changes to your initial investment have on the break-even point? What effect do changes to the unit cost have on the break-even point? Ask your student which one has a greater impact over time.

May your collaboration be a profitable one!

Nombre _____ Fecha _____

Estimada Familia:

Algunas personas tienen un negocio para complementar sus ingresos: repartir el diario, vender artesanías, administrar un sitio web, por nombrar algunos ejemplos. El objetivo es generar utilidades—tener más ingresos que gastos.

El punto de equilibrio se da cuando los ingresos son iguales a los egresos. Hacer un gráfico es una buena manera de monitorear los ingresos y gastos y muestra a simple vista cuando un negocio alcanza este punto. En un gráfico el punto de equilibrio se da cuando la línea de ingresos cruza la línea de gastos.

Mi negocio de carpintería

Vender bancos en feria artesanal		Unidades	Gastos	Ingresos
		0	$370.00	$0.00
Stand en la feria:	$160.00	10	$475.00	$149.50
Tarjetas de presentación:	$85.00	20	$580.00	$299.00
Herramientas nuevas:	$125.00	30	$685.00	$448.50
Inversión inicial:	**$370.00**	40	$790.00	$598.00
		50	$895.00	$747.50
Electricidad:	$0.50	60	$1,000.00	$897.00
Madera:	$3.00	70	$1,105.00	$1,046.50
Grapas y adhesivos:	$0.75	80	$1,210.00	$1,196.00
Barniz y lijas:	$1.25	90	$1,315.00	$1,345.50
Tiempo:	$5.00	100	$1,420.00	$1,495.00
Costo unitario:	**$10.50**	110	$1,525.00	$1,644.50
		120	$1,630.00	$1,794.00
Precio unitario:	**$14.95**	130	$1,735.00	$1,943.50

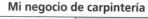

Vender bancos en feria artesanal

Gráfico con leyenda: ■ Gasto, Ingreso. Ejes: vertical de 0 a 2500, horizontal de 10 a 120. Etiquetas: Pendiente = Costo unitario, Pendiente = Precio unitario, Punto de equilibrio, Inversión inicial, Rentabilidad.

Haga que su estudiante lo ayude a preparar un plan para un pequeño negocio. Con unos cuantos pasos básicos empezarán su plan de negocios.

- ¿Cuánto dinero necesitarán para comenzar? Esto representa su inversión inicial. Ubiquen este punto en su gráfico.

- ¿Cuánto les costará producir cada artículo? Este es el costo unitario. Con este dato, coloquen más puntos con el fin de trazar una línea de gastos.

- ¿Qué precio cobrarán por cada artículo? Comenzando en el origen del gráfico, utilicen este precio unitario para dibujar la línea de ingresos.

- ¿Se cruzan estas dos líneas? Este es su punto de equilibrio—el número de artículos que deben vender para cubrir sus gastos.

Si las dos líneas no se cruzan deberán hacer ciertos cambios. ¿Pueden aumentar su precio unitario? Tal vez no puedan cobrar más que la competencia. En ese caso, tendrán que hallar un modo de recortar los gastos.

¿Cómo afectan al punto de equilibrio las modificaciones en su inversión inicial? ¿Cómo afectan al punto de equilibrio las modificaciones del costo unitario? Pregunte a su estudiante cuál tiene mayor impacto a largo plazo.

Activity 5.1

Start Thinking!

For use before Activity 5.1

Can you find an ordered pair (x, y) that is a solution to both of the equations below?

$$x + y = 5$$

$$x = y + 1$$

Can you find more than one solution to both equations? What method did you use to find a solution? Can you think of any other methods for finding the solution of a set of two equations?

Activity 5.1

Warm Up

For use before Activity 5.1

Graph the linear equation.

1. $y = \frac{1}{2}x - 2$

2. $y = -\frac{3}{4}x + 3$

3. $y = -2x + 1$

4. $y = 3x - 7$

5. $y = \frac{2}{3}x - 4$

6. $y = -\frac{1}{5}x + 5$

The table and graph below relate to the system of equations at the right.

$$y = -x - 5$$
$$y = -2x - 6$$

x	−3	−2	−1	0	1	2	3
−x − 5	−2	−3	−4	−5	−6	−7	−8
−2x − 6	0	−2	−4	−6	−8	−10	−12

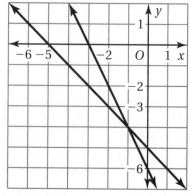

What is the solution of the system? Is it easier to see the solution of the system using the table or the graph? In general, is using a table or graph a better method? Explain.

Use a table to find the break-even point. Check your solution.

1. $C = 15x + 100$

$R = 65x$

2. $C = 10x + 30$

$R = 16x$

3. $C = 25x + 80$

$R = 45x$

4. $C = 8x + 21$

$R = 15x$

5. $C = 8x + 24$

$R = 12x$

6. $C = 11x + 6$

$R = 12.5x$

5.1 Practice A

Match the system of linear equations with the corresponding graph. Use the graph to estimate the solution. Check your solution.

1. $y = 2.5x + 1$

$y = x$

2. $y = 2x - 3$

$y = -\dfrac{1}{2}x + 1$

3. $y = \dfrac{1}{4}x - 2$

$y = -\dfrac{2}{5}x + 4$

A.

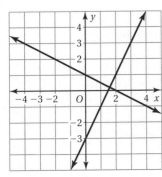

B.

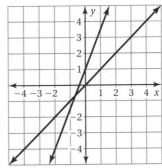

C.

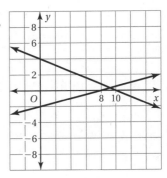

Solve the system of linear equations by graphing.

4. $y = x + 4$

$y = -x$

5. $y = x - 7$

$y = -4x + 3$

6. $y = -x - 1$

$y = -3x + 9$

7. The cost C (in dollars) for beads to make bracelets is $C = 4x + 180$, where x is the number of bracelets. Each bracelet sells for $34.

   a. Write an equation for the revenue R in terms of the number of bracelets.

   b. How many bracelets need to be sold for the business to break even?

8. You have a total of 21 pens and pencils on your desk. You have 3 more pens than pencils.

   a. Write a system of linear equations that represents this situation.

   b. How many of each do you have?

Name _____ Date _____

5.1 Practice B

Solve the system of linear equations by graphing.

1. $x + y = 18$
   $y = x + 12$

2. $y = 6x - 1$
   $x - y = 11$

3. $y + x = 6$
   $y = -1.5x + 10$

4. The cost C (in dollars) to rent the convention hall is $C = 10x + 1500$, where x is the number of admission tickets. Admission tickets to the convention are $16 each.

   a. Write an equation for the revenue R in terms of the number of admission tickets.

   b. How many admission tickets need to be sold in order for the convention to break even?

Use a graphing calculator to solve the system of linear equations.

5. $x + 1.2y = 12.4$
   $-1.5x + 2y = 8$

6. $3.4x + 1.5y = 0.4$
   $3x - 2.4y = 7.8$

7. $-1.2x + 3.3y = 3.6$
   $2.5x - 4y = -7.5$

8. A building has a total of 60 one-bedroom and two-bedroom apartments. There are twice as many one-bedroom apartments as two-bedroom apartments. How many apartments of each type are in the building? Use a system of linear equations to justify your answer.

9. Is it possible for a system of two linear equations to have no solution? Explain your reasoning.

10. The hare challenged the tortoise to a race from the water fountain to the park bench. In order to ensure a fair race, the tortoise will start 100 feet in front of the hare. The tortoise is walking at a rate of 2 feet per minute. The hare is walking at a rate of 6 feet per minute.

    a. How long will it take for the hare to catch up to the tortoise?

    b. How long did the hare wait before walking (in order for the tortoise to walk 100 feet)?

    c. The distance from the water fountain to the park bench is 130 feet. Who won the race?

Name_____ Date_____

5.1 Enrichment and Extension

Solving Systems Game

Set Up

With a partner, create game cards with each system of equations below on a separate card. Make or find game pieces for each player.

$y = x$
$y = \dfrac{1}{2}x$

$y = -x + 7$
$y = 2x - 2$

$y = -2x - 1$
$x + y = 6$

$y = 2x + 3$
$y = \dfrac{1}{2}x + 4$

$y = -x$
$y = x + 4$

$y = \dfrac{3}{2}x$
$y = \dfrac{1}{2}x + 4$

$y = \dfrac{3}{5}x - 5$
$y = -\dfrac{1}{5}x - 1$

$y = x$
$y = 3x - 4$

$y = -x + 1$
$-y = 8x$

$y = 3x + 7$
$y = 3x - 1$

$y = 2x + 1$
$y = -2x + 5$

$y = -x + 3$
$y = \dfrac{2}{3}x - 2$

How to Play

1. The first player chooses a card, graphs the two equations, and finds the solution of the system.

2. The player calculates the sum of the x- and y-coordinates of the solution, and moves ahead that number of spaces.

   Bonus: If there is no solution, the player can move ahead 5 spaces.

3. The players take turns. The first player to reach or pass the finish space wins.

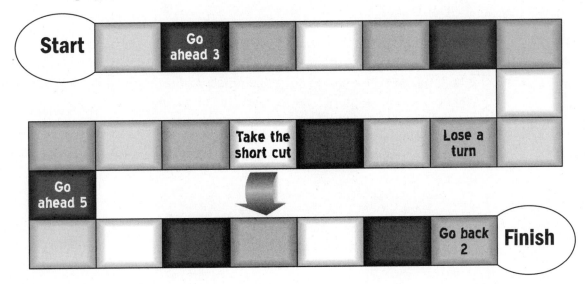

5.1 Puzzle Time

Why Did The Student Eat His Homework?

A	B	C	D	E	F
G	H	I	J		

Complete each exercise. Find the answer in the answer column. Write the word
under the answer in the box containing the exercise letter.

(−4, 4) STUDENT	
(0, 0) THE	
(1, 8) PIECE	
(−2, 1) DOG	
(3, 0) IT	
(5, −3) HER	
(3, 3) CAKE	
(−3, 5) ICING	
(0, 2) HIM	

Solve the system of linear equations by graphing.

A. $y = x$
$y = -x$

B. $y = x + 1$
$y = -x - 3$

C. $y = 2x$
$y = 4x + 2$

D. $y = -4x + 2$
$y = 2x + 2$

E. $y = -\dfrac{1}{4}x + \dfrac{3}{4}$
$y = \dfrac{1}{4}x - \dfrac{3}{4}$

F. $y = \dfrac{1}{2}x - 1$
$y = -x + 2$

G. $x + y = 3$
$y = x - 1$

H. $4x + y = 12$
$y = 4x + 4$

I. $-x + y = -3$
$4x + y = 2$

J. At a grocery store, Candy buys 2 cantaloupes at
x dollars each and 1 watermelon at y dollars. Her
total bill is $9. Chip goes to the same grocery store
and buys 1 cantaloupe at x dollars and 1 watermelon
at y dollars. His total bill is $6. Write and solve a
system of linear equations by graphing to find the
cost x of a cantaloupe and the cost y of a watermelon.

(−1, −2) TOLD	
(1, −2) OF	
(5, 0) HERSELF	
(2, 0) WAS	
(8, 1) ATE	
(2, 1) A	
(0, −6) HOMEWORK	
(−2, −1) TEACHER	
(7, 7) SAID	

Amelia is 3 years older than Caleb, and Caleb is 2 years more than half of Amelia's age. The system of equations represents this situation.

$A = 3 + C$

$C = 2 + 0.5A$

Solve the system of equations to find the ages of the children. Instead of graphing the equations to solve, try substituting $2 + 0.5A$ for C into the first equation.

How old is Amelia? How old is Caleb?

Complete the following exercises.

1. Solve $2x + y = 5$ for y.

2. Solve $a - b = 3$ for b.

3. Solve $5y - x = 12$ for x.

4. Solve $3c - 7d = 12$ for c.

5. Solve $4x + 3y = 24$ for y.

6. Solve $2x + 3y = 4$ for x.

Solve each system first by graphing and then by substitution. Which system is easier to solve by graphing? Which system is easier to solve by substitution? Explain.

$$2x + y = 5$$
$$3x + 5y = 18$$

$$y = \frac{1}{2}x + 3$$
$$y = -\frac{3}{4}x - 2$$

Write a system of linear equations that has the ordered pair as its solution.

1. $(1, 1)$ **2.** $(4, 5)$

3. $(6, 2)$ **4.** $(2, 4)$

5. $(5, 6)$ **6.** $(3, 1)$

5.2 Practice A

Tell which equation you would choose to solve for one of the variables when solving the system by substitution. Explain your reasoning.

1. $y = 5x - 2$
$2x + 9y = 10$

2. $3x - 7y = 12$
$3x - 12y = 6$

3. $\frac{1}{5}x + y = 8$
$4x - 3y = 1$

Solve the system of linear equations by substitution. Check your solution.

4. $y = x + 3$
$y = 5x - 5$

5. $y = 3x - 1$
$y = x - 7$

6. $x = 5y + 2$
$x - 4y = 5$

7. The gym has a total of 25 treadmills and stationary bikes. There are 7 more stationary bikes than treadmills.

    a. Write a system of linear equations that represents this situation.

    b. How many treadmills are in the gym?

    c. How many stationary bikes are in the gym?

Solve the system of linear equations by substitution. Check your solution.

8. $x - y = 9$
$2x + 5y = 4$

9. $2x + 3y = 25$
$4x - y = 15$

10. $3x - 6y = 2$
$4x + 3y = -1$

11. A drawer contains 24 spoons and forks. There are three times as many spoons as forks.

    a. Write a system of linear equations that represents this situation.

    b. How many spoons are in the drawer?

    c. How many forks are in the drawer?

12. The perimeter of a rectangle is 34 centimeters. The length is two more than twice the width. Write and solve a system of linear equations to find the length and the width of the rectangle.

13. A parking lot has a total of 60 cars and trucks. The ratio of cars to trucks is 7 : 3. How many cars are in the parking lot? How many trucks are in the parking lot? Justify your answers.

5.2 Practice B

Solve the system of linear equations by substitution. Check your solution.

1. $x + 4y = -1$
$-3x - 14 = y$

2. $3y = -2x$
$y = x - 5$

3. $\frac{1}{2}x + 2y = 3$
$6y + 1 = x$

4. The revenue for a vehicle rental store is $5460. There were 208 cars and 52 vans rented. A van rents for $10 more than a car.

   a. Write a system of equations that represents this situation.

   b. What is the cost of the car rental?

   c. What is the cost of the van rental?

Solve the system of linear equations by substitution. Check your solution.

5. $2x - y = 6$
$x = y - 1$

6. $2x + 4y = -4$
$x - 3y = -12$

7. $4x + 2y = 8$
$6x - 4y = 5$

8. The sum of the digits of a two-digit number is 11. The tens digit is one less than three times the ones digit. Find the original number.

9. The farmers' market has a total of 98 tents. The ratio of food tents to retail tents is 9 : 5.

   a. Write a system of linear equations that represents this situation.

   b. How many food tents are at the farmers' market?

   c. How many retail tents are at the farmers' market?

10. Forty-five children attend a preschool. The number of two-year-olds is one half the number of three-year-olds. The number of four-year-olds is the same as the number of three-year-olds.

   a. How many two-year-olds attend the preschool?

   b. How many three-year-olds attend the preschool?

   c. How many four-year-olds attend the preschool?

5.2 Enrichment and Extension

Solving Systems of Linear Equations

In Exercises 1–12, choose a pair of equations from the list of equations below that has the given solution.

$$y = x \qquad\qquad y = 2x \qquad\qquad y = 3x + 4$$
$$y = x + 2 \qquad\quad x = -2 \qquad\qquad y = 4x + 1$$
$$y = 6 \qquad\qquad y = -x + 6 \qquad\quad y = 2x - 2$$
$$y = -x + 12 \qquad x = 1 \qquad\qquad y = -x$$

1. $(0, 0)$ **2.** $(-2, -4)$ **3.** $(6, 6)$

4. $(-2, 14)$ **5.** $(2, 4)$ **6.** $(3, 3)$

7. $(-2, 0)$ **8.** $(5, 7)$ **9.** $(1, 3)$

10. $(4, 8)$ **11.** $(3, 13)$ **12.** $(1, 5)$

13. Write a system of equations whose solution is $(-120, 52)$.

Name _____ Date _____

5.2 Puzzle Time

Where Do High Jumpers Store Their Valuables?

Write the letter of each answer in the box containing the exercise number.

Solve the system of linear equations by substitution.

1. $y = x$
$y = 2x - 1$

2. $y = -x$
$y = 3x - 4$

3. $y = 5x - 6$
$y = 4x - 2$

4. $x + y = 7$
$7x + y = 1$

5. $-8x + y = 9$
$5x - y = 3$

6. $x - y = 0$
$9x + y = 0$

7. $x + y = 5$
$3x - y = 7$

8. $3x - 2y = 12$
$4x + 2y = 16$

9. $\dfrac{1}{2}x + y = 2$
$-x + y = 2$

10. $\dfrac{1}{2}x + \dfrac{1}{4}y = 2$
$x + y = 1$

11. $6x - y = 24$
$6x + y = -12$

12. There are a total of 52 students on the soccer team and the field hockey team. The field hockey team has 12 more students than the soccer team. Write a system of linear equations that fits this situation. How many students are on the soccer team x and the field hockey team y?

Answers
P. $(20, 32)$
V. $(0, 0)$
L. $(7, -6)$
I. $(-1, 8)$
T. $(4, 0)$
U. $(4, 14)$
A. $(1, -18)$
N. $(1, -1)$
E. $(-4, -23)$
O. $(0, 2)$
A. $(3, 2)$
L. $(1, 1)$

4	2		11		12	9	1	5		6	7	3	10	8

Consider the following equations: $3 + 7 = 10$

$$2 + 4 = 6$$

Add the equations.
$$
\begin{array}{r}
3 + 7 = 10 \\
2 + 4 = 6 \\
\hline
5 + 11 = 16
\end{array}
$$

Perform the operation on the given equations.

1. Subtract the second equation from the first.

2. Multiply both sides of the first equation by 2 and add it to the second equation.

Are the resulting equations true?

How can you use this method to solve the following system?

$$x + y = 10$$
$$x - y = 4$$

Warm Up
For use before Activity 5.3

Solve the equation.

1. $6y = 90$

2. $-17x = 102$

3. $9x = -144$

4. $-11y = -209$

5. $4x + 20 = 4$

6. $-2y + 4 = -10$

Students were asked to solve the system by using elimination.

$$2x + 3y = 10$$
$$x + y = 4$$

Compare and contrast the students' work.

Maddie

$2x + 3y = 10$
$-2(x + y = 4)$

$2x + 3y = 10$
$-2x - 2y = -8$
$\overline{ y = 2}$

$2x + 3(2) = 10$
$2x = 4$
$x = 2$

The solution is $(2, 2)$.

Sophie

$2x + 3y = 10$
$-3(x + y = 4)$

$2x + 3y = 10$
$-3x - 3y = -12$
$\overline{ -x = -2}$
$x = 2$

$2(2) + 3y = 10$
$3y = 6$
$y = 2$

The solution is $(2, 2)$.

Solve the system by adding or subtracting the equations.

1. $x + y = 10$

$x - y = 7$

2. $x + 2y = 8$

$-x + 2y = 20$

3. $2x - 3y = 14$

$2x + 4y = 21$

4. $3x + y = -5$

$2x - y = 10$

Name_____ Date_____

5.3　Practice A

Solve the system of linear equations by elimination. Check your solution.

1. $x - y = 4$
　　$x + y = 2$

2. $x + 3y = 5$
　　$2x - 3y = 1$

3. $4x - y = 7$
　　$4x - 2y = 2$

4. You purchase 5 pounds of apples and 2 pounds of oranges for $9. Your friend purchases 5 pounds of apples and 6 pounds of oranges for $17.

   a. Write a system of linear equations that represents this situation.

   b. What is the price per pound for apples?

   c. What is the price per pound for oranges?

Solve the system of linear equations by elimination. Check your solution.

5. $2x + 3y = -2$
　　$3x - y = -14$

6. $x - 3y = 1$
　　$4x + 5y = 4$

7. $3x - 5y = 9$
　　$6x - 6y = 6$

8. A 100-point test contains a total of 20 questions. The multiple choice questions are worth 3 points each and the short response questions are worth 8 points each.

   a. Write a system of linear equations that represents this situation.

   b. How many multiple choice questions are on the test?

   c. How many short response questions are on the test?

   d. If the teacher changed the test to 15 questions, then how many of each type of question would be on the test?

9. One customer purchases 8 bags of cat food and 2 bags of dog food. The total weight of the purchase is 44 pounds. Another customer purchases 5 bags of cat food and 2 bags of dog food. The total weight of the purchase is 35 pounds.

   a. You write the following system of linear equations to represent this situation. Is your answer correct?

$$8x + 2y = 44$$
$$5x + 2y = 35$$

   b. Your answer for the next step is $13x = 79$, which is incorrect. Explain the error.

Name _____ Date _____

Solve the system of linear equations by elimination. Check your solution.

1. $3x - y = 0$
   $-3x + 5y = 0$

2. $2x - 4y = -2$
   $2x + 3y = -16$

3. $x + 3y = 17$
   $-2x + 3y = -7$

4. You and your friend are selling magazine subscriptions. You sell 8 fewer magazine subscriptions than your friend. Together you sell 42 magazine subscriptions.

   a. Write a system of linear equations that represents this situation.

   b. How many magazine subscriptions did you sell?

   c. How many magazine subscriptions did your friend sell?

Solve the system of linear equations by elimination. Check your solution.

5. $2x + 5y = -3$
   $3x - y = 21$

6. $2y = -5x - 3$
   $4x - 2 = -6y$

7. $3y = x - 6$
   $2x = 3y + 3$

8. For what values of a and b should you solve the system by elimination?

   a. $3x + 5y = 10$
      $2x + ay = 4$

   b. $-4x - 3y = 9$
      $bx + 7y = 2$

9. Your friend rents 10 chairs and 2 tables for $300. Another friend rents 8 chairs and 4 tables for $360. You want to rent 12 chairs and 3 tables. How much do you expect to pay?

10. One equation in a system of linear equations is $x - 3y = 1$. The solution of the system of linear equations is (4, 1).

    a. Find the value of a such that the equation $2x + ay = 5$ is the second equation in the system.

    b. Find the value of b such that the equation $bx + 5y = 1$ is the second equation in the system.

    c. Find the value of c such that the equation $2x - 7y = c$ is the second equation in the system.

5.3 Enrichment and Extension

Which Method is Best?

You have learned about three different methods to solve systems of linear equations: graphing, substitution, and elimination. Complete the following exercises.

1. Explain when it is best to use each method.

2. Discuss the advantages and disadvantages of each method.

3. Which method is your favorite? Explain your answer.

Tell which method—*graphing*, *substitution*, or *elimination*—is best to solve the system. Then find the solution using that method.

4. $y = 2x + 5$
   $y = -x + 2$

5. $3x + 4y = 36$
   $-2x + 2y = 4$

6. $-6x - y = -6$
   $-2x + 14 = y$

7. $y = x$
   $y = 2x - 3$

8. $2x - 3y = -18$
   $-2x + 5y = 26$

9. $2x - 3y = 15$
   $-4x + 3y = -9$

10. $x + 2y = -15$
    $3x - y = -17$

11. $y = x + 1$
    $2x - 3y = -3$

Name_____ Date _____

5.3 Puzzle Time

Does It Take Longer To Run From First Base To Second Base Or From Second Base To Third Base?

A	B	C	D	E	F
G	H	I	J		

Complete each exercise. Find the answer in the answer column. Write the word under the answer in the box containing the exercise letter.

$(2, 9)$ BECAUSE	**Solve the system of linear equations by elimination.**	$(-1, 2)$ TO
$\left(\dfrac{9}{2}, -1\right)$ A	**A.** $x + y = 6$ $x - y = 2$ **B.** $x + 5y = 15$ $-x - 2y = 0$	$(0, 0)$ BAT
$(-2, 1)$ REFEREE	**C.** $3x + 4y = 5$ $3x - 4y = -11$ **D.** $-x - 2y = 9$ $x + 4y = 9$	$(6, 0)$ HOMERUN
$(4, 2)$ SECOND	**E.** $x - 6y = -11$ $8x + 6y = 20$ **F.** $3x + 2y = 24$ $-x + 2y = 16$	$(1, 2)$ BASE
$(5, 5)$ CATCHER	**G.** $4x + 9y = -12$ $4x - 7y = 20$ **H.** $3x + 7y = 9$ $4x - 7y = 12$	$(20, 40)$ SHORTSTOP
$(-27, 9)$ THIRD	**I.** $2x + 5y = 4$ $4x + 7y = 11$	$(2, 4)$ MITT
$(0, 3)$ FIRST	**J.** The local theater is showing a matinee and offering a special deal for the community. A ticket for an adult costs \$11 and a ticket for a child costs \$6. The theater sells a total of 60 tickets and collects \$460. How many adult tickets x and children tickets y are sold?	$\left(\dfrac{3}{2}, -2\right)$ THERE
$(-9, 8)$ BALL		$(5, -6)$ FOUL
$(3, 0)$ IS		$(-10, 5)$ BASE

Consider the system:

$x + y = 2$

$x + y = 5$

Are there any two numbers x and y that add up to 2 *and* add up to 5? Is there a solution to the system?

Can you write a different system of equations that has no solution?

Tell whether the lines are *parallel*, *coincide*, or *intersect at one point*.

1. $y = x - 3$

$y = x + 1$

2. $x + 3y = 9$

$2x + 6y = 18$

3. $y = 2x + 5$

$2x + y = 5$

4. $-8x = 4y + 12$

$3y = -6x - 9$

5. $-4x + 2y = 4$

$2x + 4y = -4$

6. $6x = -9y + 18$

$10x + 15y = 15$

How is solving a linear equation with no solution similar to solving a system of linear equations with no solution? How is it different?

How is solving a linear equation whose solution is all real numbers similar to solving a system of linear equations with infinitely many solutions? How it is different?

Lesson 5.4 **Warm Up**
For use before Lesson 5.4

Let *x* and *y* be two numbers. Find the solution of the puzzle.

1. y is 10 more than twice x.
The difference of $16x$ and $8y$ is 12.

2. x is 3 less than y.
The sum of $2x$ and $2y$ is 4.

3. The sum of x and y is 10.
The difference of $2x$ and 20 is equal to twice y.

4. 5 less than $2y$ is $6x$.
y is 2 more than $3x$.

5.4 Practice A

Without graphing, determine whether the system of linear equations has *one solution, infinitely many solutions,* or *no solution*. Explain your reasoning.

1. $y - 3x = 5$

$y = 3x + 5$

2. $y = 6x + 2$

$y = 6x - 2$

3. $y = 5x + 9$

$y = 3x - 2$

Solve the system of linear equations. Check your solution.

4. $y = 4x - 5$

$y + 2 = 4x$

5. $y = 2 - 3x$

$2x - y = 13$

6. $y = \dfrac{2}{3}x - 3$

$2x - 3y = 9$

7. A gift basket has 2 soaps and 5 lotions and costs \$20. A second gift basket has 6 soaps and 15 lotions and costs \$50. Is it possible to determine the price of the soap?

8. Both equations in a system of linear equations have y-intercepts at $(0, 2)$.

  a. Is it possible for this system to have only *one solution*? Explain your reasoning.

  b. Is it possible for this system to have *no solution*? Explain your reasoning.

  c. Is it possible for this system to have *infinitely many solutions*? Explain your reasoning.

9. For a given two-digit number, the second digit is 2 more than 5 times the first digit. Also, 5 times the first digit is 3 more than the second digit. Find the two-digit number.

10. Find the values of a and b so the system shown has infinitely many solutions.

$2x + 9y = 3$

$4x + ay = b$

Name _____ Date _____

Solve the system of linear equations. Check your solution.

1. $y = \dfrac{1}{4}x - 1$

   $y = \dfrac{1}{4}x + 5$

2. $y = -2x - 1$

   $5x + 2y = -5$

3. $3\left(x - \dfrac{2}{3}y\right) = 4$

   $3x + 5 = 2y$

4. $\pi x - 2y = 2\pi$

   $y = \dfrac{\pi}{2}x - \pi$

5. $x = 2y$

   $6y + 3x = 0$

6. $4x + 3y = 10$

   $2x + \dfrac{3}{2}y = 5$

7. y is 6 less than 3 times x. x is 2 more than one-third of y. Find the solution of the puzzle.

8. Both equations in a system of linear equations have a slope of $\dfrac{1}{2}$. Does this system have infinitely many solutions? Explain.

9. You and a friend go to a farmers' market. You spend $13 on fruit. Then you and your friend each buy the same number of tomato plants for $4 each.

   a. Write a system of linear equations that represents this situation.

   b. Will you and your friend spend the same amount of money? Explain.

10. Write a system of linear equations that has infinitely many solutions.

11. Write a system of linear equations that has the solution (2, 1).

12. Write a system of linear equations that has no solution.

13. Find the values of a and b so the system shown has no solution.

    $5x = 2y + 1$
    $ax = 6y + b$

5.4 Enrichment and Extension

Solving Special Systems of Linear Equations

Find the values of *a* and *b* so that the system shown has the given solution.

1. $y = ax - 5$

$y = -2x - b$

The solution is $(2, -3)$.

2. $y = \dfrac{1}{2}x + b$

$y = ax - 2$

The system has infinitely many solutions.

3. $y = 2x + b$

$y = ax + 3$

The solution is $(-1, 4)$.

4. $y = -2x + b$

$y = ax - 1$

The solution is $(1, 0)$.

5. $y = 3x + 1$

$y = ax + b$

There is no solution.

6. $y = ax + 4$

$y = \dfrac{1}{2}x + b$

The solution is $(6, 6)$.

7. $x + y = b$

$ax + 3y = 13$

The solution is $(4, 7)$.

8. $y = 12x - b$

$-ax + y = 4$

The system has infinitely many solutions.

9. Write a system of linear equations in *x* and *y* that contains unknown values *a* and *b* and that has infinitely many solutions. Exchange problems with a partner and see if your partner can find the values of *a* and *b*.

Name _____ Date _____

5.4 Puzzle Time

What Should You Do When a Bull Charges You?

Write the letter of each answer in the box containing the exercise number.

Solve the system of linear equations.

1. $x - y = 5$
$-x + y = 5$

   H. infinitely many   **I.** no solution   **J.** $(0, 5)$ **K.** $(5, 0)$

2. $4x - 3y = 5$
$-8x + 6y = -10$

   A. infinitely many   **B.** no solution   **C.** $(4, -3)$ **D.** $(-3, 4)$

3. $-7x - 7y = -14$
$x + y = -2$

   L. infinitely many   **M.** no solution   **N.** $(2, 0)$ **O.** $(0, 2)$

4. $2x + y = 5$
$x - y = 1$

   W. infinitely many   **X.** no solution   **Y.** $(2, 1)$ **Z.** $(1, 2)$

5. $3x + 9y = 12$
$-x - 3y = -4$

   H. infinitely many   **I.** no solution   **J.** $(3, 9)$ **K.** $(9, 3)$

6. $2x - 3y = 8$
$4x - 6y = 16$

   P. infinitely many   **Q.** no solution   **R.** $\left(4, \dfrac{8}{3}\right)$ **S.** $\left(\dfrac{8}{3}, 4\right)$

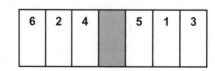

6	2	4		5	1	3

Start Thinking!

For use before Extension 5.4

How does the graph below relate to the equation
$-2x + 4 = x - 5$?

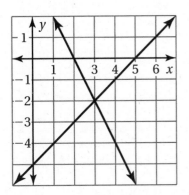

Warm Up

For use before Extension 5.4

Solve the equation. Check your solution.

1. $m - 8 = 2m$

2. $3x - 5 = 2x + 1$

3. $12 - 4p = p - 3$

4. $2(x - 8) = -x + 5$

5. $-2r - 9 = -3(r + 2)$

6. $4(x + 8) = -2(x - 1)$

Name _____ Date _____

Solve the equation algebraically and graphically.

1. $\frac{1}{2}x - 2 = -\frac{1}{4}x + 1$

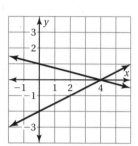

2. $\frac{2}{3}x + 4 = \frac{1}{6}x + \frac{5}{2}$

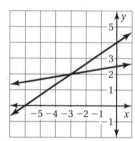

Use a graph to solve the equation. Check your solution.

3. $x + 4 = -2x + 7$

4. $\frac{1}{2}x + \frac{9}{2} = -5x - 1$

5. You have $4x + 10$ CDs and your friend has $5x + 22$ CDs. Is it possible that you both have the same number of CDs? Explain your reasoning.

Use a graph to solve the equation. Check your solution.

6. $0.75x = 2x - 10$

7. $1.2x + 4.8 = -0.8x - 0.2$

8. One tank contains 50 gallons of water and another tank contains 75 gallons of water. Water is draining out of both tanks at a rate of 6 gallons per minute. Do the tanks ever have the same amount of water before either is empty? Explain.

9. You and your friend sell lemonade. You get $\frac{1}{3}$ of the total money collected. Your friend gets $20 less than the total money collected.

    a. Write an equation to represent that you both earn the same amount of money.

    b. What is the total amount of money collected?

    c. How much does each of you earn?

    d. Describe a situation to explain the unclaimed money.

Chapter 5 **Technology Connection**
For use after Section 5.1

Solving a Linear System

You can use the *intersect* feature of a graphing calculator to solve a system of two linear equations.

EXAMPLE Solve the system: $2x + 5y = 10$

$x - 3y = 16$

SOLUTION

Step 1 Rewrite each equation in slope-intercept form.

$$y = -\frac{2}{5}x + 2$$

$$y = \frac{x}{3} - \frac{16}{3}$$

Step 2 Press $\boxed{Y=}$ and enter the equations in Y1 and Y2.

Step 3 Press $\boxed{\text{GRAPH}}$ to graph the system. Adjust the viewing window until the point of intersection is visible.

Step 4 Press $\boxed{\text{2nd}}$ [CALC] 5 to use the *intersect* feature.

The solution is $(10, -2)$.

Solve the system using a graphing calculator.

1. $y = 5x - 8$

$y = \frac{x}{3} + 6$

2. $y = -3$

$2x + 4y = -7$

3. $-2x + 6y = 2$

$9x - 7y = -9$

4. $y - \frac{2}{3}x = 4$

$5x + \frac{y}{2} = -62$

Chapter 6

Name_____ Date _____

Dear Family,

Many people enjoy putting their photos on their computers and sharing them online with friends and family. Sometimes, when sharing a photo online, you can see jagged edges that don't appear in the actual photo. These jagged edges happen because digital photos are actually created by a grid of colored dots.

The colors in the world we see are an example of a continuous range—any number of colors can exist. However, the colors in our camera are an example of a discrete range—a limited number of colors can exist.

When an edge passes through a dot, the camera has to decide whether to choose the color on one side of the edge or the other. Over a long edge, this can lead to a jagged look as the camera chooses one color or the other.

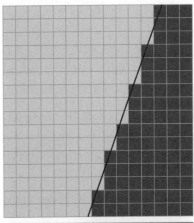

You and your student can model this using graph paper. Draw a slanted line on the graph paper. Color the blocks on one side of the line with red and the other side with blue. Choose one color or the other for blocks that the line passes through.

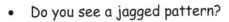

- Do you see a jagged pattern?

- What if you change the angle of the line—is the line *more jagged* or *less jagged*?

- What happens if you draw the line using blocks? Does the line look straight or jagged?

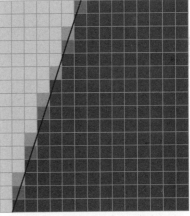

To see this, it might help to stand some distance away from the paper so the blocks appear smaller.

Modern computer applications try to eliminate the jagged edges by blending the colors on each side of the line. Try this with your student on a piece of graph paper. Does it improve the appearance of the line—especially from a distance?

Take a picture of your project and share it!

Funciones

Estimada Familia:

Muchas personas disfrutan colocando sus fotografías en la computadora y compartiéndolas en línea con familiares y amigos. A veces, cuando se comparten fotografías en línea, se pueden ver líneas que no están definidas, las cuales no aparecen en la foto real. Estos bordes irregulares ocurren porque las fotos digitales son creadas mediante una cuadrícula de puntos de colores.

Los colores que vemos en el mundo son un ejemplo de un rango continuo—puede existir un sinfín de colores. Sin embargo, los colores en nuestras cámaras son un ejemplo de un rango definido—existe un número limitado de colores.

Cuando un borde pasa por un punto, la cámara tiene que decidir si escoge entre un color u otro. En un borde largo, esto puede producir una apariencia irregular al elegir la cámara un color u otro.

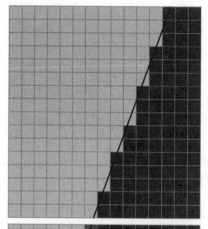

Usted y su estudiante pueden replicar este modelo usando papel cuadriculado. Dibujen una línea oblicua en el papel. Coloreen los cuadrados de un lado con rojo y los del otro lado con azul. Escojan un color u otro para los cuadrados por donde pasa la línea.

- ¿Observan el patrón irregular?

- Y si cambiara el ángulo de inclinación de la línea—¿la línea *es más o menos irregular*?

- ¿Qué pasaría si dibujaran la línea usando cuadrados? La línea aparece recta o irregular?

Para ver esto, ayudaría apreciar el papel a cierta distancia para que los cuadrados aparezcan más pequeños.

Los programas modernos de computadora tratan de eliminar los bordes irregulares mezclando los colores en cada lado de la línea.

Intente hacerlo con su estudiante en un pedazo de papel cuadriculado. ¿Esto mejora la apariencia de la línea—particularmente desde una distancia?

¡Tomen una foto de su proyecto y compártanlo!

Start Thinking!
For use before Activity 6.1

Use the cost of a container of milk at your school cafeteria to complete the diagram.

Containers of Milk   **Cost**

This type of diagram is called a *mapping diagram*. Why do you think it is called that?

Warm Up
For use before Activity 6.1

Solve the equation. Check your solution.

1. $-2.3 + x = 9.1$

2. $6\frac{1}{2} + x = -4\frac{3}{4}$

3. $x - 7.74 = -0.4$

4. $x - \left(-2\frac{1}{4}\right) = -5$

5. $-\frac{4}{7}x = 15$

6. $-8x = 4\frac{4}{5}$

Start Thinking!
For use before Lesson 6.1

The function machine shown is for the rule "Add 3." Using this function machine, what is the output for an input of 12?

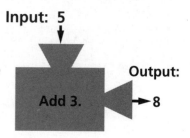

Input: 5

Add 3.

Output: 8

Guess the Function Game (2 players)

1. Decide who will be Player A and Player B.
2. Player A makes up a function rule. Do NOT tell Player B!
3. Player B gives an input number.
4. Player A uses the rule and mental math to calculate the output. Tell Player B the output.
5. Repeat Steps 3 and 4 until Player B can correctly guess the function rule.
6. Switch roles and play again.

Warm Up
For use before Lesson 6.1

Describe the pattern in the mapping diagram.
Copy and complete the diagram.

1. Input   Output

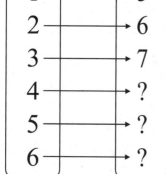

Input	Output
1	5
2	6
3	7
4	?
5	?
6	?

2. Input   Output

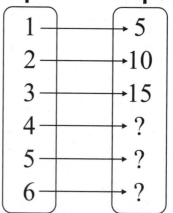

Input	Output
1	5
2	10
3	15
4	?
5	?
6	?

Name_____ Date_____

6.1 Practice A

Describe the pattern in the mapping diagram. Copy and complete the diagram.

1.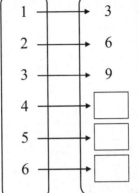

2.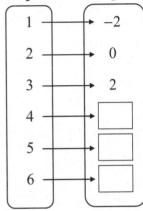

List the ordered pairs shown in the mapping diagram.

3.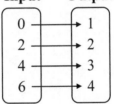

4.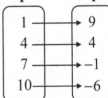

Draw a mapping diagram of the set of ordered pairs.

5. $(1, 2), (3, 5), (6, 9), (10, 12)$

6. $(-2, 7), (0, 5), (5, 8), (4, 9)$

7. The table shows the number of tickets purchased and the total cost.

   a. Use the table to draw a mapping diagram.

   b. Is the relation a function? Explain.

   c. Describe the pattern. How does the cost per ticket change as you buy more tickets?

   d. Based on this pattern, how much would you expect to pay for 5 tickets?

   e. Compare the costs for 3 tickets and 5 tickets. What can you suggest?

   f. Explain why this pattern could not continue for up to 8 tickets.

Tickets	Total Cost
1	$14
2	$24
3	$30
4	$32

6.1 Practice B

List the ordered pairs shown in the mapping diagram.

1. Input   Output

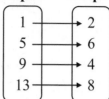

2. Input   Output

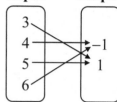

Draw a mapping diagram of the set of ordered pairs.

3. $(0, -3), (4, 12), (6, 13), (7, 0)$

4. $(1, 0), (3, 0), (5, 4), (7, 4), (9, 4)$

Draw a mapping diagram for the graph. Then describe the pattern of inputs and outputs.

5.

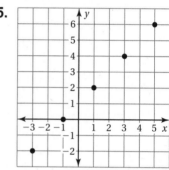

6.

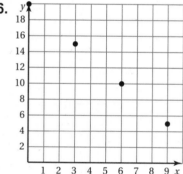

7. The table shows the cost of a collect call.

Minutes	1	2	3	4	5	6	7
Cost	$3	$3.25	$3.50	?	?	?	?

   a. Complete the table.

   b. Draw a mapping diagram for the table.

   c. Is the relation a function? Explain.

   d. List the ordered pairs.

   e. Graph the ordered pairs in a coordinate plane.

   f. Describe the pattern. How does the cost change as the number of minutes increases?

Name_____   Date_____

Identifying Functions

You learned that a *function* pairs each input with exactly one output. Tell whether the mapping diagram represents a function. Explain.

1. Input   Output

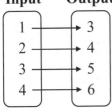

2. Input   Output

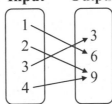

3. Input   Output

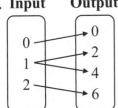

4. Input   Output

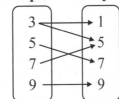

(a) Draw arrows to complete a mapping diagram of a function. (b) Draw one more arrow so that the mapping diagram does not represent a function.

5. Input   Output

3	2
4	3
5	4
6	5

6. Input   Output

0	
1	4
2	5
3	6

(a) Find another point (x, y) so that the set of points represents a function.

(b) Find a point so that the set of points does not represent a function.

7. $(0, 0), (1, 1), (2, 2), (x, y)$

8. $(0, 9), (2, 8), (4, 7), (6, 6), (8, 5), (x, y)$

9. $(1, 3), (2, 3), (3, 4), (4, 4), (5, 5), (6, 5) (x, y)$

Name _____ Date _____

6.1 Puzzle Time

What Flowers Grow Between Your Nose and Your Chin?

Write the letter of each answer in the box containing the exercise number.

List the ordered pairs shown in the mapping diagram.

1.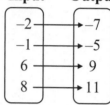

2.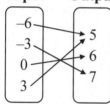

Draw a mapping diagram of the ordered pairs.

3. $(-15, -17), (-9, -11), (-6, 4), (-2, 8)$

4. $(-5, 3), (-3, 1), (2, 1), (6, 3)$

Describe the pattern of inputs and outputs.

5.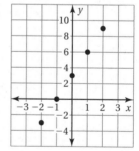

6.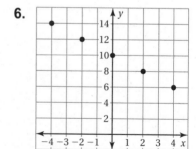

Answers

S. As each input increases by 2, the output decreases by 2.

L. $(-2, -7), (-1, -5), (6, 9), (8, 11)$

P.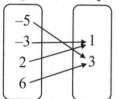

M. As each input decreases by 2, the output decreases by 2.

R. $(2, 11), (4, 9), (6, 7), (8, 5)$

I.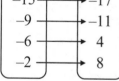

U. $(-6, 5), (-3, 7), (0, 6), (3, 5)$

T. As each input increases by 1, the output increases by 3.

A. $(1, 5), (2, 6), (3, 7), (4, 5)$

D. As each input increases by 1, the output decreases by 3.

5	2	1	3	4	6

Think about the function rule "Multiply by 7."

How can you write an equation for this function?

Explain how this equation can be used to describe the area of a rectangle with a length of 7 meters.

Activity 6.2 **Warm Up**
For use before Activity 6.2

Name the ordered pair.

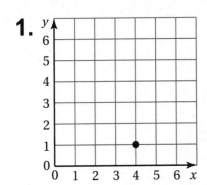

1.

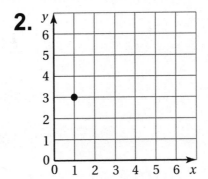

2.

Big Ideas Math Blue **189**
Resources by Chapter

Using two variables, write an equation for a function that describes a real-life situation. Explain the situation and what each of the variables represents. Which variable represents input values? Which variable represents output values? Then make a mapping diagram that includes four different input values.

Write an equation that describes the function.

1. Input, *x* Output, *y*

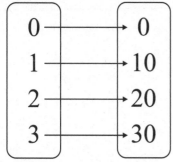

2. Input, *x* Output, *y*

3. Input, *x* Output, *y*

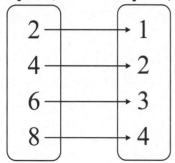

4. Input, *x* Output, *y*

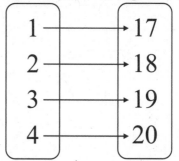
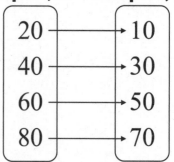

Name_____ Date _____

6.2 Practice A

Write an equation that describes the function.

1. Input, x Output, y

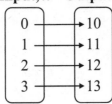

2. Input, x Output, y

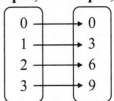

Write a function rule for the statement.

3. The output is eight less than the input.

4. The output is double the input.

Find the value of *y* for the given value of *x*.

5. $y = x - 8$; $x = 5$

6. $y = 8x$; $x = 3$

7. $y = 4x - 1$; $x = 10$

8. $y = \dfrac{x}{2} + 5$; $x = -4$

Graph the function.

9. $y = x + 5$

10. $y = 9x$

11. $y = 2x + 3$

12. $y = \dfrac{x}{2} - 4$

13. You are running at a rate of 6 miles per hour.

   a. Write a function that represents the distance d traveled in h hours.

   b. How many miles do you run in 2 hours?

14. The cost of admission for a student is $4 less than the cost of admission for an adult.

   a. Write a function that relates the cost of admission for a student s with the cost of admission for an adult a.

   b. What is the cost of admission for a student when the cost of admission for an adult is $7.50?

   c. What is the cost of admission for an adult when the cost of admission for a student is $2?

6.2 Practice B

Write an equation that describes the function.

1. **Input, x   Output, y**

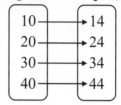

2. **Input, x   Output, y**

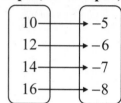

Write a function rule for the statement.

3. The output is five times the input.

4. The output is two less than the input.

Find the value of *y* for the given value of *x*.

5. $y = 3x - 4; \; x = 2$

6. $y = \dfrac{x}{3} - 1; \; x = -6$

Graph the function.

7. $y = \dfrac{x}{3} - 4$

8. $y = 2x + 7$

9. You are traveling on a turnpike at a rate of 70 miles per hour.

   a. Write a function that represents the distance *d* traveled in *h* hours.

   b. How many miles do you travel in 3.5 hours?

Find the value of *x* for the given value of *y*.

10. $y = 6x - 4; \; y = 20$

11. $y = \dfrac{x}{2} + 3; \; y = 1$

12. Your school club is selling popcorn at the football game. The cost of making the popcorn is $90. You charge $1.50 for each bag of popcorn.

    a. Write a function you can use to find the profit *P* for selling *b* bags of popcorn.

    b. You will *break even* if the cost of making the popcorn equals your income. How many bags of popcorn must you sell to break even?

13. Write a function for the area *A* of a square given the perimeter *P* of the square.

Name_____ Date_____

6.2 Enrichment and Extension

Function Notation

In Lesson 6.2, you wrote functions as equations in two variables, x and y, with x as the input and y as the output. Another way to write a function is to use *function notation*.

Function in x and y		Function notation
$y = 4x$	$\longrightarrow$	$f(x) = 4x$
$y = 3x + 5$	$\longrightarrow$	$f(x) = 3x + 5$

$f(x)$ is the output. The symbol $f(x)$ is read as "*f* of *x*."

Example: Find $f(4)$ for $f(x) = x + 3$.

$$f(x) = x + 3 \qquad \text{Write function.}$$

$$f(4) = 4 + 3 \qquad \text{Substitute 4 for } x.$$

$$f(4) = 7 \qquad \text{Add.}$$

So, f of 4 is equal to 7.

Rewrite the function using function notation.

1. $y = 2x$ 2. $y = x - 1$ 3. $y = 4x + 7$ 4. $\dfrac{3}{4}x + 5 = y$

Find $f(0)$, $f(2)$, and $f(4)$ for the function.

5. $f(x) = 8x$ 6. $f(x) = 7 + x$ 7. $f(x) = 5 - x$

8. $f(x) = 3x + 8$ 9. $f(x) = 9 - 2x$ 10. $f(x) = \dfrac{1}{2}x$

11. $f(x) = \dfrac{1}{4}x + 6$ 12. $f(x) = 3 + 1.6x$ 13. $f(x) = x^2 + 1$

14. **Critical Thinking** Find a function where $f(0) = 2$ and $f(1) = 2$.

Name _____ Date _____

6.2 Puzzle Time

Did You Hear The Story About The Smog?

A	B	C	D	E	F
G	H	I	J	K	

Complete each exercise. Find the answer in the answer column. Write the word under the answer in the box containing the exercise letter.

44 IS
y = x − 5 HAVE
y = 3x YOU
y = 10x TOWN
y = 8x TO
−1 ALL

Write an equation that describes the function.

A. Input, x   Output, y
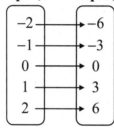

B. Input, x   Output, y
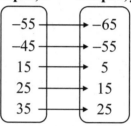

Write a function rule for the statement.

C. The output is five less than the input.

D. The output is eight times the input.

E. The output is one-third the input.

F. The output is thirteen more than four times the input.

Find the value of y for the given value of x.

G. $y = x + 7$; $x = -5$ **H.** $y = 6x - 4$; $x = 8$

I. $y = 2x + 4$; $x = -2.5$ **J.** $y = 9x - 3$; $x = 3$

K. The number of multiple-choice questions on a test y is 10 times the number of open-ended questions x. Write a function that describes the relationship.

21 AIR
y = $\frac{1}{3}$x TELL
24 OVER
2 IT
y = x − 10 DON'T
y = 4x + 13 ME

In the block pattern below, two blocks are added in each step to form a pattern.

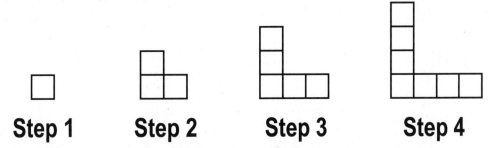

Step 1   **Step 2**   **Step 3**   **Step 4**

Use blocks to come up with a different pattern in which the same number of blocks is added in each step. Sketch the first 4 steps in your pattern.

Complete the table. Then graph the function.

Step number, x				
Number of blocks, y				

Write an equation of the line in slope-intercept form.

1.
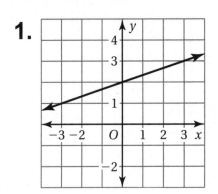

2.
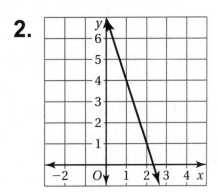

Think about the term *linear function*.

What do you think it means?

Give an example.

The table shows a familiar pattern from geometry.

x	1	2	3	4	5
y	4	8	12	16	20

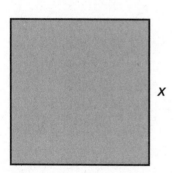

1. Write a function that relates y to x.

2. What do the variables x and y represent?

3. Graph the function.

6.3 Practice A

Use the graph or table to write a linear function that relates y to x.

1.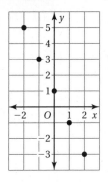

2.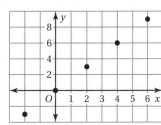

3.

x	−1	0	1	2
y	3	0	−3	−6

4.

x	−10	−5	0	5
y	−2	−1	0	1

5. The table shows the cost y (in dollars) of x fluid ounces of brewed coffee.

    a. Which variable is independent? dependent?

Fluid Ounces, x	0	8	16	24
Cost, y		0	0.5	1	1.5

    b. Write a linear function that relates y to x. Interpret the slope.

    c. Graph the linear function.

    d. How much does it cost to purchase 32 fluid ounces of brewed coffee?

6. The table shows the area y (in square feet) of a triangle with a height of x feet.

    a. Which variable is independent? dependent?

Height, x	0	1	2	3
Area, y	0	3	6	9

    b. Write a linear function that relates the area of the triangle to the height of the triangle.

    c. Graph the linear function.

    d. The formula for the area of a triangle is $A = \dfrac{1}{2}bh$. What is the length (in feet) of the base of the triangle?

6.3 Practice B

Use the graph or table to write a linear function that relates _y_ to _x_.

1.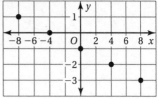

2.

3.

x	-4	-2	0	2
y	8	4	0	-4

4.

x	-5	0	5	10
y	1	3	5	7

5. The table shows the time _y_ (in minutes) it takes to make _x_ burritos.

   a. Which variable is independent? dependent?

   b. Write a linear function that relates _y_ to _x_. Interpret the slope.

   c. Graph the linear function.

   d. How long does it take to make 7 burritos?

Burritos, x	1	2	3	4
Minutes, y	0.75	1.5	2.25	3

6. The table shows the distance traveled _y_ (in miles) in a car in _x_ hours.

   a. Which variable is independent? dependent?

   b. Write a linear function that relates distance traveled to hours.

   c. Graph the linear function.

   d. What was the distance traveled in 5 hours?

   e. The formula $d = rt$ relates distance with time for a given rate. Use the formula to determine the rate at which the car was traveling.

   f. How long will it take to travel 400 miles?

Hours, x	0	2	4	6
Miles, y	0	128	256	384

Name_____ Date _____

6.3 Enrichment and Extension

Describing a Pattern

A *fractal* is a geometric object that is self-similar. In other words, if you enlarge any part of the fractal, it will be similar to the whole fractal.

Fractals can be produced by repeating the same set of steps multiple times. The number of times you have performed the procedure is call the *iteration number*.

This example is called the *Box Fractal*.

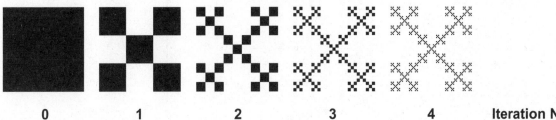

| 0 | 1 | 2 | 3 | 4 | Iteration Number |

1. Describe the procedure used to transform the box at iteration 0 into the box at iteration 1.

2. What is the relationship between the original box and each of the five boxes in iteration 1?

3. Copy and complete the table using the fractal pattern.

Iteration	Number of Squares
0	1
1	5
2	
3	
4	

4. What pattern do you notice in the table? Can you generalize the pattern?

5. Is the pattern in the table linear? Explain your reasoning.

6. How many iterations do you expect to perform in this pattern? Explain your reasoning.

6.3 Puzzle Time

What Would You Get If You Crossed A Vampire With A Snowman?

Write the letter of each answer in the box containing the exercise number.

Use the graph or table to write a linear function that relates y to x.

1.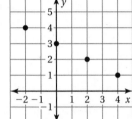

2.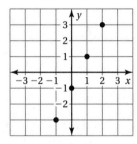

Answers

S. $y = 2x - 1$

R. $y = \dfrac{1}{2}x + 5$

E. $y = -\dfrac{1}{2}x + 3$

3.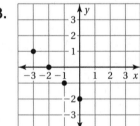

4.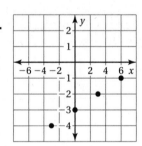

O. $y = \dfrac{1}{3}x - 3$

T. $y = \dfrac{3}{2}x - 5$

I. $y = -x - 2$

B. $y = 6x$

5.

x	−2	0	2	4
y	4	5	6	7

6.

x	−4	−2	0	2
y	0	−2	−4	−6

F. $y = -x + 2$

T. $y = -x - 4$

7.

x	−2	0	2	4
y	−8	−5	−2	1

8.

x	0	2	4	6
y	2	0	−2	−4

9. The table shows how many cups of pancake mix x are needed to make y pancakes. Find the linear function that relates the number of pancakes to the number of cups of pancake mix.

Cups of Mix, x	1	2	3	4
Pancakes, y	6	12	18	24

8	5	4	2	7	9	3	6	1

Start Thinking!
For use before Activity 6.4

Consider the following:

- the height of a bouncing ball

- the height of a plane during takeoff

- the height of a baseball hit over an outfield fence

- the height of a roller coaster car

Draw a graph to represent each situation and then tell whether it is *linear* or *nonlinear*.

Warm Up
For use before Activity 6.4

Find the perimeter and area of the rectangle.

1.
4 cm

6 cm

2.
2 cm

10 cm

3.
16 ft

12 ft

4.
7 in.

13 in.

Describe two real-life situations at an amusement park: one that can be represented by a linear function and one that can be represented by a nonlinear function.

Graph the data in the table. Decide whether the graph is *linear* or *nonlinear*.

1.

x	0	1	2	3
y	6	4	2	0

2.

x	0	1	2	3
y	3	5	8	12

3.

x	0	1	2	3
y	15	25	20	30

4.

x	0	1	2	3
y	−7	−2	3	8

Name_____ Date _____

6.4 Practice A

Graph the data in the table. Decide whether the graph is *linear* or *nonlinear*.

1.

x	0	1	2	3
y	5	10	15	20

2.

x	1	2	3	4
y	4	6	9	13

Does the table or graph represent a *linear* or *nonlinear* function? Explain.

3.
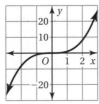

4.
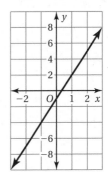

5.

x	3	5	7	9
y	5	3	0	3

6.

x	4	7	10	13
y	-2	0	2	4

7. The table shows the area A (in square centimeters) of a circle with radius r centimeters. Does the table represent a *linear* or *nonlinear* function? Explain.

Radius, r	1	2	3	4	5	6	7	8
Area, A	π	4π	9π	16π	25π	36π	49π	64π

8. The table shows the cost y (in dollars) of x ounces of cereal.

a. What is a missing y-value that makes the table represent a nonlinear function?

b. What is the missing y-value that makes the table represent a linear function?

Ounces, x	8	12	16
Cost, y	?	2.5	3.5

c. Write a linear function that represents the cost y of x ounces of cereal. Interpret the slope.

Name _____ Date _____

6.4 Practice B

Graph the data in the table. Decide whether the graph is *linear* or *nonlinear*.

1.

x	4	3	2	1
y	1	3	7	11

2.

x	2	5	8	11
y	3	6	9	12

Does the graph or equation represent a *linear* or *nonlinear* function? Explain.

3.
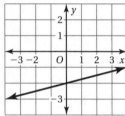

4.

5. $y = \dfrac{3}{x} - 1$

6. $5x - y = 8$

7. The table shows the profit P (in dollars) of selling x pairs of flip flops. Does the table represent a *linear* or *nonlinear* function? Explain.

Flip Flops, x	1	2	3	4	5
Profit, P	4	8	12	16	20

8. The table shows the commission y (in dollars) of selling x cell phone plans.

Cell Phone Plans, x	1	2	3	4
Commission, y	100	150	250	400

   a. Does the table represent a *linear* or *nonlinear* function? Explain.

   b. Based on the pattern in the table, what is the commission of selling 5 cell phone plans?

9. The formula for the volume V of a sphere with radius r is $V = \dfrac{4}{3}\pi r^3$.

   Does this formula represent a *linear* or *nonlinear* function? Explain.

6.4 Enrichment and Extension

Linear and Nonlinear Functions

In Exercises 1–6, describe two real-life patterns for each topic—one that is linear and one that is nonlinear.

1. monthly allowance   **2.** music   **3.** television

4. airplane flight   **5.** geometric shape   **6.** shopping mall

A family is baking sugar cookies using the recipe at the right. The graph below shows the oven temperature (in degrees Fahrenheit) over time.

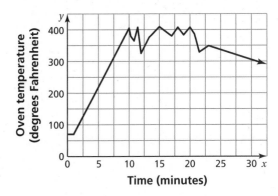

7. Is the graph *linear* or *nonlinear*?

8. Describe the graph as it relates to baking cookies. Be sure to include the following in your description:

- starting temperature
- time it took to preheat the oven
- times when the oven door was opened
- time that the oven was turned off

9. Why do you think the oven temperature fluctuates once the oven reaches the desired temperature?

10. Use the graph to complete Step 6 of the recipe.

Super Easy Sugar Cookies

Ingredients

1 cup butter

1 cup sugar

1 large egg

1 teaspoon vanilla extract

2 teaspoons baking powder

2 ¾ cups flour

Directions

1. Cream butter and sugar.

2. Add egg and vanilla.

3. Mix all dry ingredients and add slowly to butter cream mixture until incorporated

4. Roll out on lightly floured board to ¼-inch thickness.

5. Cut out 2½-inch hearts.

6. Bake at _____ degrees for _____ minutes.

6.4 Puzzle Time

What Belongs To You, But Is Used More By Other People?

Write the letter of each answer in the box containing the exercise number.

Choose the equation that represents a *nonlinear* function.

1.   **N.** $y + x = 2x - 1$ **O.** $xy = 2x - 1$ **P.** $2y + 1 = 2x$

2.   **P.** $3y = 4x + 3$ **Q.** $x - y = 4$ **R.** $y = 3x^2 + 4$

3.   **A.** $5y = \dfrac{7}{x}$ **B.** $7y = 5x$ **C.** $5y + x = 7x$

4.   **C.** $y = 6\pi$ **D.** $y = 6\pi x$ **E.** $y = 6\pi x^2$

Choose the missing *y*-value that makes the points represent a linear function.

5. $(1, 15), (2, 19), (3, ?)$

   U. 23   **V.** 24   **W.** 25

6. $(-3, 9), (-2, ?), (-1, 7)$

   K. 12   **L.** 6   **M.** 8

7. $(4, ?), (7, -3), (10, -3)$

   X. -2 **Y.** -3 **Z.** -4

8. $(25, 360), (40, 320), (55, ?)$

   L. 300   **M.** 380   **N.** 280

7	1	5	2		8	3	6	4

Start Thinking!

For use before Activity 6.5

Review with a partner what the difference is between a *linear function* and a *nonlinear function*. Give an example of each.

Warm Up

For use before Activity 6.5

Graph the data.

1.

Input, x	1	2	3	4
Output, y	2	4	6	8

2.

Input, x	0	2	4	6
Output, y	1	2	3	4

3.

Input, x	1	2	3	4
Output, y	3	5	7	9

Start Thinking!
For use before Lesson 6.5

Draw a graph that represents the following situation.

You go shopping. You buy a shirt and spend half of your money. You meet a friend who owes you a quarter of the amount of money you have left and pays you back. You buy lunch with the rest of your money.

Warm Up
For use before Lesson 6.5

Describe the relationship between the two quantities.

1.

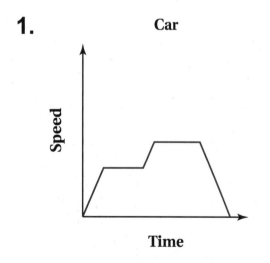

2.

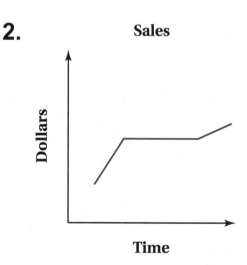

Name_____ Date_____

6.5 Practice A

Describe the relationship between the two quantities.

1.

Wind

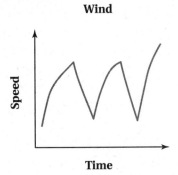

2.

Grass

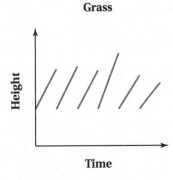

3.

Airplane

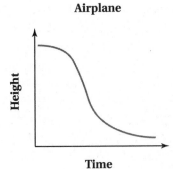

4.

Gas Tank

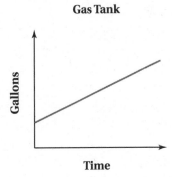

5. The graph shows the number of cars in the parking lot over a 24 hour period.

   a. Describe the change in the number of cars from 7:00 A.M. to 9:00 A.M.

   b. Describe the change in the number of cars from 5:00 P.M. to 7:00 P.M.

Parking Lot

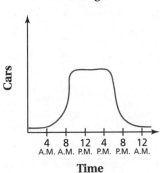

Sketch a graph that represents a situation.

6. The flu virus spreads quickly at first and then more slowly.

7. The sales of a new cell phone increase at an increasing rate, then the sales remain the same, and then the sales decrease at a constant rate.

8. The outside temperature decreased at a decreasing rate and then decreased at a constant rate.

Name_____ Date _____

Describe the relationship between the two quantities.

1. Customers

2. Hiker

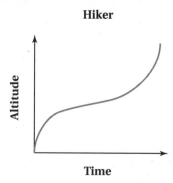

3. Postage

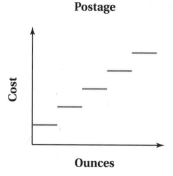

4. Water Level

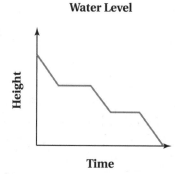

5. The supply and demand model shows how the price of the shares of a new stock changes in a market.

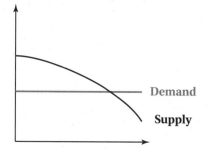

   a. Describe and interpret each curve.

   b. Which part of the graph represents a surplus? a shortage? Explain your reasoning.

   c. The curve intersects at the *equilibrium point*, which is where the number of shares equals the quantity demanded. Suppose that demand for the shares suddenly increases, causing the entire demand curve to shift up. What happens to the equilibrium point?

6.5 Enrichment and Extension

Discrete and Continuous Data

In some situations, only certain numbers in an interval make sense in a graph. Data that fit this description are called **discrete data**. Data that are not discrete are continuous. **Continuous data** use any number in an interval in a graph.

Example: Keenan performs an experiment in which he measures the temperature of tap water when he turns on the hot water nozzle to his kitchen sink. He records the temperatures in 5-second intervals. Determine whether the data are discrete or continuous.

The data are discrete, because Keenan only records the temperature every five seconds.

Determine if the situation describes *discrete data* or *continuous data*. Explain your reasoning.

1. Keenan's next experiment is to record the temperature for each day in October. He will record the temperature at 1:00 P.M. each day.

2. Keenan's father works at a large corporation. His job requires him to make a graph showing a employee's salary each year.

3. Keenan works at a photo booth in the local mall. Keenan keeps track of how many people buy photos.

4. One of Keenan's classmates is making a chart showing people's weights on the moon.

5. On the wall in Keenan's science room is a graph of his teacher's hike into the Grand Canyon. The graph shows how far beneath the edge of the canyon she hiked.

6.5 **Puzzle Time**

What Has Many Keys That Fit No Locks?

Write the letter of each answer in the box containing the exercise number.

Describe the relationship between the two quantities.

1. Test
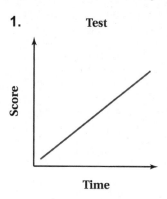

2. Shopping
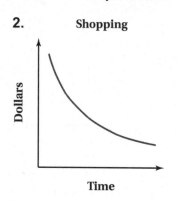

3. Electricity
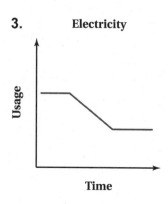

4. Cell Phone
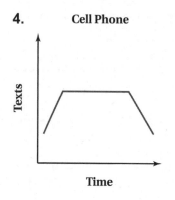

5. Sales of Radios
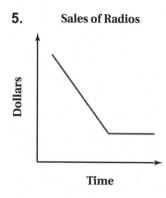

Answers

P. The amount of money in sales of radios decreased at a constant rate then remained constant.

K. Test scores decreased at a constant rate.

L. The amount of usage of electricity was constant, increased at a constant rate, then remained constant.

N. The number of texts increased at a constant rate, then was constant, and finally decreased at a constant rate.

A. During the shopping trip, the amount of money increased at an increasing rate.

I. The amount of usage of electricity was constant, decreased at a constant rate, then remained constant.

E. The number of texts decreased at a constant rate, then was constant, and finally increased at a constant rate.

A. Test scores increased at a constant rate.

B. The amount of money in sales of radios increased at a constant rate then remained constant.

O. During the shopping trip, the amount of money decreased at a decreasing rate.

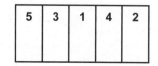

Name_____ Date_____

Making Graphs from Spreadsheets

A spreadsheet is a computer application used to organize and work with data.
Each cell in a spreadsheet can be empty, or it can contain letters, numbers, or
a formula. Spreadsheets can perform calculations with numeric data. They
can also generate graphs from the data.

**Open a spreadsheet. Column A should be headed *x* with the values
of 1, 2, 3, 4, 5, 6 listed below. Column B should be headed *y*. Use the
formula $y = 2x - 1$ to fill in the values for *y*. (You may calculate the
values yourself, or use the formula function of the spreadsheet.)**

1. Find the *chart or graph* function on the spreadsheet. One of the choices
   should be a scatter plot. Make a scatter plot of the data.

2. Change the *y*-value in cell B5 from 7 to 8. This new value is within the
   range of *y*-values already included in the graph. Does the graph change
   automatically? Describe what happens.

3. Change the *y*-value in cell B5 to 12. This new value is outside the range
   of the original graph. Does this change the graph automatically? Describe
   what happens.

4. Return the value in cell B5 to 7. Add the value $x = 10$ and the
   corresponding *y*-value to your spreadsheet in row 8. Does this change the
   graph automatically? Describe what happens.

5. Add a new column of data, *y*2 in column C. Use the formula $y = 2x + 1$ to
   generate the values for the column. Does the graph change automatically?

6. If the graph did not change in Exercise 5, make a new graph that includes
   all the new data. You may need to highlight all the data. Describe your
   new graph.

7. What other chart options would be a good choice to display the data?
   Explain your reasoning.

Chapter 7

Name_____ Date _____

Chapter 7 Real Numbers and the Pythagorean Theorem

Dear Family,

When adding or multiplying small numbers, you rely on tables you memorized long ago. For larger numbers, you follow the rules you've learned. For example, when adding large numbers, you line up the place values and start adding from the right, carrying digits to the left.

The "add and carry" method is an example of a rule that follows a strict, predictable procedure. Perhaps surprisingly, not all problems in mathematics have rules that are this straightforward. One of the oldest ways of solving problems is to use the "guess and check" method.

This method requires us to make a reasonable guess about the answer and check how close it is. You then refine your guess and check the new estimate. Each time you do this, you try to get closer to the answer.

Try this with your student to find the square root of a number. For example, to find the square root of 19, you might do the following steps.

- The square root of 16 is 4 $\left(\text{because } 4^2 = 16\right)$ and the square root of 25 is 5 $\left(\text{because } 5^2 = 25\right)$. Because 19 is between 16 and 25, the square root of 19 is greater than 4 and less than 5, so guess 4.5.

- Check: $(4.5)^2 = 20.25$, which is too big, so refine your guess. Try 4.2.

- Check: $(4.2)^2 = 17.64$, which is too small, so refine your guess. Try 4.4.

- Check: $(4.4)^2 = 19.36$, which is getting closer, but still a little too big.

If you continue this method, you will soon find out that $19 \approx (4.36)^2$. You could keep going to get the precision you need.

It may appear that computers and calculators have functions like these memorized, because the answers are shown immediately. However, many types of calculations are done using a process very similar to "guess and check." Because computers and calculators can make millions of guesses per second, the answer simply appears to be memorized.

So don't be afraid to guess the answer—just remember to check it!

Nombre _____ Fecha _____

Números reales y el Teorema Pitagórico

Capítulo 7

Estimada Familia:

Al sumar o multiplicar números pequeños, dependemos de tablas que memorizamos hace muchos años. Para números más grandes, seguimos reglas que hemos aprendido. Por ejemplo, al sumar números grandes, alineamos las posiciones de valores y empezamos a sumar desde el lado derecho, llevando dígitos hacia el lado izquierdo.

El método de "sumar y llevar" es un ejemplo de una regla que sigue un procedimiento estricto y predecible. Quizás, y sorprendentemente, no todos los problemas en matemáticas tienen reglas tan simples como ésta. Una de las formas más antiguas de resolver problemas es usando el método de "predecir y verificar".

Este método requiere que hagamos una predicción razonable sobre la respuesta y que verifiquemos qué tan cerca estamos. Luego refinamos la predicción y verificamos la nueva aproximación. Cada vez que hacemos esto, estamos más cerca de la respuesta.

Intente esto con su estudiante para hallar la raíz cuadrada de un número. Por ejemplo, para encontrar la raíz cuadrada de 19, pueden hacer los siguientes pasos:

- La raíz cuadrada de 16 es 4 $\left(\text{porque } 4^2 = 16\right)$ y la raíz cuadrada de 25 es 5 $\left(\text{porque } 5^2 = 25\right)$. Ya que 19 se encuentra entre 16 y 25, la raíz cuadrada de 19 es mayor que 4 y menor que 5, entonces predecimos 4.5.

- Verifique: $(4.5)^2 = 20.25$, que es demasiado grande, así que refine su predicción. Intente con 4.2.

- Verificar: $(4.2)^2 = 17.64$, que es demasiado pequeño, así que refine su predicción. Intente con 4.4.

- Verificar: $(4.4)^2 = 19.36$, lo cual está más cerca, pero todavía es un poco más grande.

Si continúa con este método, pronto averiguará que $19 \approx (4.36)^2$. Puede continuar para obtener la precisión deseada.

Puede parecer que las computadoras y calculadoras tengan funciones como éstas memorizadas, ya que las respuestas se muestran inmediatamente. Sin embargo, muchos tipos de cálculos se realizan con un proceso muy similar al de "predecir y verificar." Ya que las computadoras y calculadoras pueden hacer millones de predicciones por segundo, la respuesta simplemente aparece como memorizada.

Así que no tema predecir la respuesta—¡sólo recuerde verificarla!

Activity 7.1 Start Thinking!
For use before Activity 7.1

When you know the area of a rectangle, can you determine the lengths of its sides? Why or why not?

When you know the area of a square, can you determine the lengths of its sides? Why or why not?

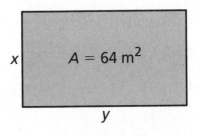

Activity 7.1 Warm Up
For use before Activity 7.1

Find the product.

1. 12×12 **2.** 9×9 **3.** 18×18

4. 1.6×1.6 **5.** 2.5×2.5 **6.** $\dfrac{2}{3} \times \dfrac{2}{3}$

Start Thinking!

For use before Lesson 7.1

Shelley says that there are two solutions of the equation $x^2 = 400$. Gina says that there is only one solution. Who is correct? Explain.

Warm Up

For use before Lesson 7.1

Find the dimensions of the square or circle. Check your answer.

1.

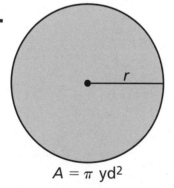

$A = 81$ in.^{2} s

s

2.

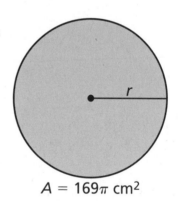

r

$A = 169\pi$ cm^2

3.

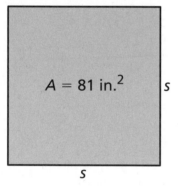

r

$A = \pi$ yd^2

4.

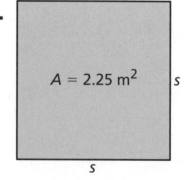

$A = 2.25$ m^2 s

s

Name_____ Date_____

7.1 Practice A

Find the dimensions of the square or circle. Check your answer.

1. Area $= 196$ in.^{2}

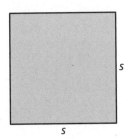

s

s

2. Area $= 36\pi$ m^2

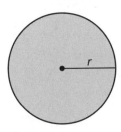

r

Find the two square roots of the number.

3. 16

4. 0

Find the square root(s).

5. $\sqrt{121}$

6. $-\sqrt{\dfrac{1}{36}}$

7. $\pm\sqrt{\dfrac{289}{49}}$

8. $-\sqrt{0.64}$

Evaluate the expression.

9. $2\sqrt{25} + 3$

10. $7 - 12\sqrt{\dfrac{1}{9}}$

Copy and complete the statement with <, >, or =.

11. $\sqrt{64}$ __?__ 5

12. 0.6 __?__ $\sqrt{0.49}$

13. The volume of a right circular cylinder is represented by $V = \pi r^2 h$, where r is the radius of the base (in feet). What is the radius of a right circular cylinder when the volume is 144π cubic feet and the height is 9 feet?

14. The cost C (in dollars) of producing x widgets is represented by $C = 4.5x^2$. How many widgets are produced if the cost is $544.50?

15. Two squares are drawn. The larger square has area of 400 square inches. The areas of the two squares have a ratio of 1 : 4. What is the side length s of the smaller square?

Name_____ Date _____

Find the dimensions of the square or circle. Check your answer.

1. Area $= \dfrac{169}{225}$ cm^2

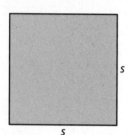

2. Area $= 121\pi$ yd^2

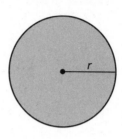

Find the two square roots of the number.

3. 225

4. 400

Find the square root(s).

5. $-\sqrt{484}$

6. $\pm\sqrt{\dfrac{25}{64}}$

7. $\sqrt{6.25}$

8. $\pm\sqrt{1.69}$

Evaluate the expression.

9. $6\sqrt{2.25} - 4.2$

10. $3\left(\sqrt{\dfrac{48}{3}} - 2\right)$

Copy and complete the statement with <, >, or =.

11. $\sqrt{\dfrac{49}{9}}$ ___?___ 2

12. $\dfrac{2}{5}$ ___?___ $\sqrt{\dfrac{12}{75}}$

13. The area of a sector of a circle is represented by $A = \dfrac{5}{18}\pi r^2$, where r is the radius of the circle (in meters). What is the radius when the area is 40π square meters?

14. Two squares are drawn. The smaller square has an area of 256 square meters. The areas of the two squares have a ratio of 4 : 9. What is the side length s of the larger square?

Name_____ Date_____

7.1 Enrichment and Extension

Solving Equations with Square Roots

A variable is used to represent an unknown number. Variables also have square roots and can be used to solve equations. Use inverse operations prior to taking the square root to solve the equation.

Example: Solve $2x^2 - 4 = 4$.

$$2x^2 - 4 = 4 \qquad \text{Write the equation.}$$
$$2x^2 = 8 \qquad \text{Add 4 to each side.}$$
$$x^2 = 4 \qquad \text{Divide each side by 2.}$$
$$x = \pm 2 \qquad \text{Find both square roots of 4.}$$

Solve the equation using square roots.

1. $p^2 - 49 = 0$

2. $a^2 - 100 = 0$

3. $r^2 - 16 = 0$

4. $8 = j^2 + 4$

5. $d^2 - 12 = 4$

6. $y^2 + 2 = 6$

7. $4x^2 - 81 = 19$

8. $s^2 - 2 = -1$

9. $5t^2 + 2 = 127$

10. $-p^2 - 15 = -24$

11. An oil tank holds about 785 cubic feet of oil and has a height of 10 feet. The formula for the volume of a cylinder is $V = \pi r^2 h$. Find the radius of the tank. Use 3.14 for π.

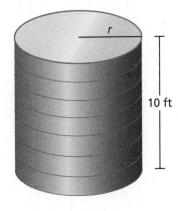

7.1 Puzzle Time

How Did The Man At The Seafood Restaurant Cut His Mouth?

Circle the letter of each correct answer in the boxes below. The circled letters will spell out the answer to the riddle.

Find the two square roots of the number.

1. 169

2. 576

3. $\dfrac{49}{64}$

4. 2.56

Find the square root(s).

5. $\sqrt{400}$

6. $-\sqrt{225}$

7. $\pm\sqrt{\dfrac{9}{16}}$

8. $\sqrt{\dfrac{36}{25}}$

9. $\pm\sqrt{7.84}$

10. $-\sqrt{56.25}$

Evaluate the expression.

11. $6 - 2\sqrt{81}$

12. $\sqrt{53.29} + \sqrt{2.89}$

13. $\sqrt{21.16} - \sqrt{1.69}$

14. $7\sqrt{\dfrac{25}{49}} + \sqrt{\dfrac{36}{64}}$

15. The bottom of a circular swimming pool has an area of 200.96 square feet. What is the radius (in feet) of the swimming pool? Use 3.14 for π.

R	E	L	C	A	F	T	M	I	H	N	U	S	B	G	R	D
25	±2.8	−10	7.5	±1.6	2.3	$\pm\dfrac{3}{4}$	$4\dfrac{3}{4}$	±13	28	$\pm\dfrac{7}{8}$	±3.4	$4\dfrac{1}{3}$	−5.5	−12	30	±5.2

S	I	T	W	N	O	P	R	G	D	V	F	I	Y	S	L	H
−15	$3\dfrac{1}{4}$	−6.5	$5\dfrac{3}{4}$	3.4	20	±1.8	$\dfrac{6}{5}$	12	8	−1.6	3.3	±24	−6.1	−7.5	14	9

Start Thinking!
For use before Activity 7.2

Your friend says that $\sqrt{169}$ is 13. Another friend says that $\sqrt{169}$ is −13. Who is correct? Explain.

Warm Up
For use before Activity 7.2

Find the square root(s).

1. $\sqrt{36}$

2. $-\sqrt{64}$

3. $\sqrt{\dfrac{49}{81}}$

4. $-\sqrt{225}$

5. $\sqrt{121}$

6. $\sqrt{\dfrac{144}{169}}$

Explain to a partner what the difference is between finding the square root of a number and finding the cube root of a number. Use an example to support your reasoning.

Find the edge length of the cube.

1. Volume $= 64{,}000$ ft^3

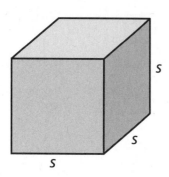

2. Volume $= \dfrac{1}{216}$ ft^3

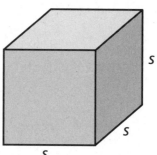

Name_____ Date_____

Find the edge length of the cube.

1. Volume = 27,000 cm³

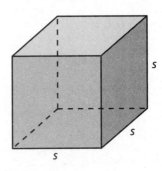

2. Volume = $\frac{1}{8}$ in.³

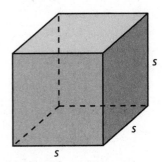

Find the cube root.

3. $\sqrt[3]{125}$

4. $\sqrt[3]{-1}$

5. $\sqrt[3]{-8}$

6. $\sqrt[3]{-1000}$

7. $\sqrt[3]{8000}$

8. $\sqrt[3]{512}$

9. $\sqrt[3]{-\frac{1}{64}}$

10. $\sqrt[3]{0.001}$

Copy and complete the statement with <, >, or =.

11. $-\sqrt[3]{27}$ __?__ -4

12. $\sqrt[3]{64}$ __?__ $\sqrt{16}$

Find the circumference of the circle.

13.

Area = $\sqrt[3]{729}\pi$ in.²

14.

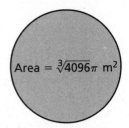

Area = $\sqrt[3]{4096}\pi$ m²

15. Which cube has a greater edge length? How much greater is it?

Volume = 343 ft³   Surface Area = 384 ft²

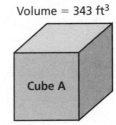

Cube A   Cube B

7.2 Practice B

Find the cube root.

1. $\sqrt[3]{343}$

2. $\sqrt[3]{-1331}$

3. $\sqrt[3]{-8000}$

4. $\sqrt[3]{3375}$

5. $\sqrt[3]{\dfrac{1}{64}}$

6. $\sqrt[3]{-\dfrac{125}{27}}$

Evaluate the expression.

7. $13 + \left(\sqrt[3]{125}\right)^3$

8. $2\dfrac{2}{3} - \left(\sqrt[3]{\dfrac{1}{27}}\right)^3$

9. $24 + \left(\sqrt[3]{-1000}\right)^3$

Evaluate the expression for the given value of the variable.

10. $\sqrt[3]{4t} + 3t,\ t = 54$

11. $\sqrt[3]{\dfrac{n}{24}} - \dfrac{n}{25},\ n = 375$

12. The volume of storage pod that is shaped like a cube is 1728 cubic feet.

   a. What is the edge length of the storage pod?

   b. What is the surface area of the storage pod?

   c. What is the area of the floor space of the storage pod?

Copy and complete the statement with <, >, or =.

13. $0.25 \underline{\quad ? \quad} \sqrt[3]{0.008}$

14. $\sqrt{729} \underline{\quad ? \quad} \sqrt[3]{729}$

15. There are infinitely many pairs of numbers of which the sum of their cube roots is zero. Give two of these pairs.

16. The radius of a sphere can be represented by $r = \sqrt[3]{\dfrac{3V}{4\pi}}$, where V is the volume of the sphere. What is the radius of a sphere with a volume of 36π cubic meters?

Solve the equation.

17. $(4x - 1)^3 = 343$

18. $(15x^3 - 2)^3 = 2197$

7.2 Enrichment and Extension

Finding *n*th Roots

A square root of a number is a number that, when multiplied by itself, equals the given number. A cube root of a number is a number that, when used as a factor in a product three times, equals the given number. The *n*th root of a number x is a number r that, when used as a factor in a product n times, equals the given number x. The notation for the nth root of x is $\sqrt[n]{x}$.

$$r \bullet r \bullet r \bullet \ldots \bullet r = r^n = x \qquad\qquad \sqrt[n]{x} = r$$

1. Complete the table.

r	n	$x = r^n$	$\sqrt[n]{x}$	Check
1	7	1	1	$1 \bullet 1 \bullet 1 \bullet 1 \bullet 1 \bullet 1 \bullet 1$
2	6			
3	5			
4	4			

Simplify the expression.

2. $\sqrt[5]{32}$ **3.** $\sqrt[4]{81}$ **4.** $\sqrt[4]{625}$ **5.** $\sqrt[6]{729}$

6. Find the least whole number by which 9000 can be multiplied so that the product is a perfect cube. Explain your method.

7. Find the least whole number by which 3072 can be divided so that the quotient is a perfect cube. Explain your method.

Name _____ Date _____

7.2 Puzzle Time

What Kind of Coat Is Made Without Buttons?

Write the letter of each answer in the box containing the exercise number.

Find the cube root.

1. $\sqrt[3]{216}$

2. $\sqrt[3]{-343}$

3. $\sqrt[3]{\dfrac{27}{64}}$

4. $\sqrt[3]{-\dfrac{1000}{1331}}$

Evaluate the expression.

5. $21 - \sqrt[3]{729}$

6. $\sqrt[3]{-\dfrac{1}{125}} + 6\dfrac{1}{2}$

7. $6\sqrt[3]{-512} + 13$

8. $\left(\sqrt[3]{-2744}\right)^3 + 2800$

Evaluate the expression for the given value of the variable.

9. $3a - \sqrt[3]{5a}, \ a = 25$

10. $\sqrt[3]{-\dfrac{x}{5}} + \dfrac{x}{10}, \ x = 320$

Answers
A. $-\dfrac{10}{11}$
I. 6
T. 56
A. $\dfrac{3}{4}$
T. -35
C. 20
F. 12
N. 70
O. -7
P. 28
O. $6\dfrac{3}{10}$

11. The volume of a box is 8000 cubic millimeters. What is the edge length of the box?

11	6	3	8	■	2	5	■	10	4	1	9	7

Activity 7.3 Start Thinking!

For use before Activity 7.3

Cut three narrow strips of paper that are 3 inches, 4 inches, and 5 inches long.

Form a triangle using the three strips. What kind of a triangle is formed?

Notice that $3^2 + 4^2 = 5^2$.

Do you know any other triangles whose side lengths would satisfy a similar equation?

Activity 7.3 Warm Up

For use before Activity 7.3

Find the square root(s).

1. $\sqrt{1.44}$

2. $\pm\sqrt{900}$

3. $\sqrt{\frac{4}{9}}$

4. $-\sqrt{441}$

5. $\pm\sqrt{484}$

6. $-\sqrt{2500}$

Start Thinking!
For use before Lesson 7.3

How can you use the Pythagorean Theorem in sports?

Lesson 7.3

Warm Up
For use before Lesson 7.3

Find the missing length of the triangle.

1.

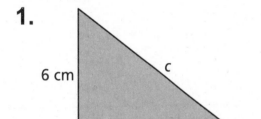

6 cm

c

8 cm

2.

c

5 in.

12 in.

3.

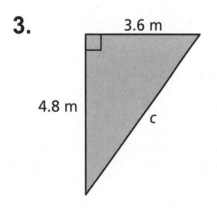

3.6 m

4.8 m

c

4.

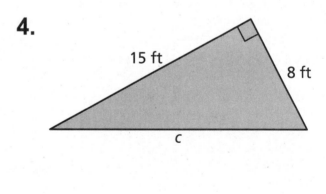

15 ft

8 ft

c

Name_____ Date_____

7.3 Practice A

Find the missing length of the triangle.

1.

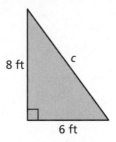

8 ft   c

6 ft

2.

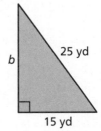

13 cm   5 cm

b

3.

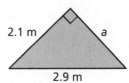

2.1 m   a

2.9 m

4.

25 yd

b

15 yd

5. A small shelf sits on two braces that are in the shape of a right triangle. The leg (brace) attached to the wall is 4.5 inches and the hypotenuse is 7.5 inches. The leg holding the shelf is the same length as the width of the shelf. What is the width of the shelf?

Find the missing length of the figure.

6.

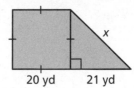

x

20 yd   21 yd

7.

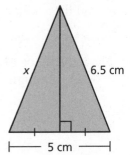

x   6.5 cm

5 cm

8. Can a right triangle have a leg that is 10 meters long and a hypotenuse that is 10 meters long? Explain.

9. One leg of a right triangular piece of land has a length of 24 yards. The hypotenuse has a length of 74 yards. The other leg has a length of $10x$ yards. What is the value of x?

7.3 Practice B

Find the missing length of the triangle.

1.

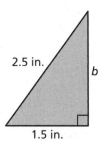

35 mm

c

12 mm

2.

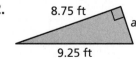

8.75 ft

a

9.25 ft

3.

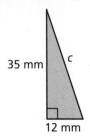

2.5 in.

b

1.5 in.

4.

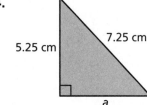

7.25 cm

5.25 cm

a

5. You built braces in the shape of a right triangle to hold your surfboard. The leg (brace) attached to the wall is 10 inches and your surfboard sits on a leg that is 24 inches. What is the length of the hypotenuse that completes the right triangle?

6. Laptops are advertised by the lengths of the diagonals of the screen. You purchase a 15-inch laptop and the width of the screen is 12 inches. What is the height of its screen?

7. In a right isosceles triangle, the lengths of both legs are equal. For the given isosceles triangle, what is the value of *x*?

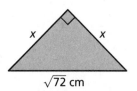

x   *x*

$\sqrt{72}$ cm

8. To get from your house to your school, you ride your bicycle 6 blocks west and 8 blocks north. A new road is being built that will go directly from your house to your school, creating a right triangle. When you take the new road to school, how many fewer blocks will you be riding to school and back?

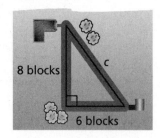

8 blocks

c

6 blocks

7.3   Enrichment and Extension

The Bermuda Triangle

The Bermuda Triangle is in the Atlantic Ocean between Bermuda, Miami, Florida, and San Juan, Puerto Rico. There are many stories about strange events that occur within the Bermuda Triangle.

The Bermuda Triangle is not a right triangle. In order to find the area, you need to use a different method.

1. Find the perimeter of the triangle.

2. The semi-perimeter of a triangle is equal to half the perimeter. Find the semi-perimeter s of the triangle.

3. Find the differences between the semi-perimeter and each side of the triangle, $s - a$, $s - b$, and $s - c$.

4. Use the values you found to evaluate the product $R = s(s - a)(s - b)(s - c)$.

5. The area of the triangle is equal to $\sqrt{R}$. What is the area (in square miles) of the Bermuda Triangle?

6. This method of finding the area of a triangle is called Heron's Formula. Use this method to find the area of the triangle below.

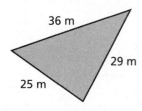

Name _____ Date _____

7.3 Puzzle Time

What Did One Dog Say To The Other Dog?

Write the letter of each answer in the box containing the exercise number.

Find the hypotenuse c of the right triangle with the given side lengths a and b.

1. $a = 15, b = 20$

2. $a = 5, b = 12$

3. $a = 13, b = 84$

4. $a = 65, b = 72$

5. $a = 6, b = 17.5$

6. $a = 6\frac{2}{3}, b = 7$

Find the side length b of the right triangle with the given hypotenuse c and side length a.

7. $c = 61, a = 11$

8. $c = 82, a = 80$

9. $c = 34, a = 16$

10. $c = 65, a = 63$

11. $c = 13, a = 6.6$

12. $c = 10\frac{3}{5}, a = 5\frac{3}{5}$

13. The flap of an envelope has two side lengths that are each 10 centimeters long and meet at a right angle. How long is the envelope? Round your answer to the nearest tenth.

14. A middle school gym is 60 feet wide and 100 feet long. If you stand in one corner of the gym, how many feet away is the corner diagonally across from you? Round your answer to the nearest tenth.

Answers
T. $9\frac{2}{3}$
P. 14.1
E. 18.5
D. 18
N. 25
U. 9
O. 97
H. 116.6
N. 60
G. 30
O. 13
M. 11.2
I. 85
S. 16

10	6	2	13		14	4	12	1	8	3	7	9		11	5

Start Thinking!
For use before Activity 7.4

An irrational number is a number that cannot be written as a ratio of integers. Decimals that do not repeat and do not terminate are irrational.

Do you know any examples of irrational numbers?

Warm Up
For use before Activity 7.4

Use the Pythagorean Theorem to find the hypotenuse of a right triangle with the given leg lengths.

1. 30, 40

2. 10, 24

3. 16, 30

4. 9, 40

5. 54, 72

6. 2.5, 6

How can you find the side length of a square that has the same area as an 8.5-inch-by-11-inch piece of paper?

Tell whether the rational number is a reasonable approximation of the square root.

1. $\dfrac{577}{408}$, $\sqrt{2}$

2. $\dfrac{401}{110}$, $\sqrt{8}$

3. $\dfrac{271}{330}$, $\sqrt{21}$

4. $\dfrac{521}{233}$, $\sqrt{5}$

5. $\dfrac{795}{153}$, $\sqrt{27}$

6. $\dfrac{441}{150}$, $\sqrt{12}$

Name_____ Date _____

7.4 Practice A

Tell whether the rational number is a reasonable approximation of the square root.

1. $\dfrac{277}{160}, \sqrt{3}$

2. $\dfrac{590}{160}, \sqrt{17}$

Classify the real number.

3. $-\sqrt{14}$

4. $1.\overline{3}$

5. 2.375

6. $\sqrt{100}$

7. You are finding the area of a circle with a radius of 2 feet. Is the area a *rational* or *irrational* number? Explain.

Estimate the square root to the nearest (a) integer and (b) tenth.

8. $\sqrt{33}$

9. $\sqrt{630}$

10. $-\sqrt{8}$

11. $\sqrt{\dfrac{7}{2}}$

12. A swimming pool is in the shape of a right triangle. One leg has a length of 10 feet and one leg has a length of 15 feet. Estimate the length of the hypotenuse to the nearest integer.

Which number is greater? Explain.

13. $\sqrt{70}, 8$

14. $-\sqrt{16}, 3$

15. $\sqrt{210}, 16\dfrac{1}{4}$

16. $\sqrt{\dfrac{4}{25}}, \dfrac{3}{10}$

17. Find a number a such that $2 < \sqrt{a} < 3$.

18. Is $\sqrt{\dfrac{1}{9}}$ a rational number? Explain.

19. Is $\sqrt{\dfrac{5}{9}}$ a rational number? Explain.

20. Is $\sqrt{\dfrac{2}{18}}$ a rational number? Explain.

7.4 Practice B

Tell whether the rational number is a reasonable approximation of the square root.

1. $\dfrac{2999}{490}$, $\sqrt{41}$

2. $\dfrac{2298}{490}$, $\sqrt{22}$

Classify the real number.

3. $2\dfrac{2}{9}$

4. $-\sqrt{576}$

5. $2.\overline{41}$

6. $\sqrt{130}$

7. You are finding the circumference of a circle with a diameter of 10 meters. Is the circumference a *rational* or *irrational* number? Explain.

Estimate the square root to the nearest (a) integer and (b) tenth.

8. $-\sqrt{\dfrac{250}{9}}$

9. $\sqrt{395}$

10. $\sqrt{0.79}$

11. $\sqrt{1.48}$

12. A patio is in the shape of a square, with a side length of 35 feet. You wish to draw a black line down one diagonal.

   a. Use the Pythagorean Theorem to find the length of the diagonal. Write your answer as a square root.

   b. Find the two perfect squares that the length of the diagonal falls between.

   c. Estimate the length of the diagonal to the nearest tenth.

Which number is greater? Explain.

13. $\sqrt{220}$, $14\dfrac{3}{4}$

14. $-\sqrt{135}$, $-\sqrt{145}$

15. $\sqrt{\dfrac{7}{64}}$, $\dfrac{3}{8}$

16. -0.25, $-\sqrt{\dfrac{1}{4}}$

17. Find two numbers a and b such that $7 < \sqrt{a} < \sqrt{b} < 8$.

7.4 Enrichment and Extension

Approximating Square Roots

Before there were calculators and computers, mathematicians developed several methods of approximating square roots by hand. One popular method is sometimes called the divide-and-average method. It uses the following steps.

Use the divide-and-average method to calculate $\sqrt{47}$.

1. What two perfect squares is 47 between?

2. Let $g = \sqrt{47}$. Estimate g to the nearest whole number.

3. Find the quotient $q = 47 \div g$. Round your answer to two decimal places.

4. Find the average of g and q. This gives the approximate value of $\sqrt{47}$. To get a closer approximation, you can repeat this process multiple times by using the average as g.

5. Check the accuracy by squaring the average and comparing it to 47. How close are the numbers?

6. Use this method to estimate $\sqrt{30}$ by repeating the process three times. How close is the square of the estimate to 30?

7.4 Puzzle Time

Did You Hear About...

A	B	C	D	E	F
G	H	I	J	K	L
M					

Complete each exercise. Find the answer in the answer column. Write the word under the answer in the box containing the exercise letter.

18.5 **BECAUSE**
$\sqrt{\dfrac{4}{9}}$ **AND**
7 **BECAME**
−34 **SEASHELL**
6.8 **POLICEMAN**
$\sqrt{55}$ **OCEAN**
11.7 **A**
14 **THE**
$-\sqrt{83}$ **COURT**
12 **BELIEVED**

Estimate to the nearest integer.

A. $\sqrt{195}$

B. $-\sqrt{1220}$

C. $-\sqrt{306}$

D. $\sqrt{\dfrac{315}{6}}$

Estimate to the nearest tenth.

E. $\sqrt{137}$

F. $\sqrt{45.9}$

G. $\sqrt{342.5}$

H. $\sqrt{\dfrac{38}{7}}$

Which number is greater?

I. $\sqrt{55}, 12$

J. $-\sqrt{83}, -9$

K. $-\sqrt{0.75}, -\sqrt{0.85}$

L. $\sqrt{\dfrac{4}{9}}, \dfrac{1}{2}$

M. You are standing 15 feet from a 25-foot-tall tree. Estimate the distance from where you are standing to the top of the tree? Round your answer to the nearest tenth.

−9 **IN**
13 **DUTY**
−18 **SAND**
−35 **LOBSTER**
$-\sqrt{0.85}$ **CLAM**
2.3 **HE**
29.2 **ORDER**
$-\sqrt{0.75}$ **CLAW**
$\dfrac{1}{2}$ **LAWYER**
−17 **THAT**

Extension 7.4 **Start Thinking!**
For use before Extension 7.4

Given a number written in decimal form, how do you determine if it is a repeating decimal?

Extension 7.4 **Warm Up**
For use before Extension 7.4

Determine if the decimal is *repeating* or *terminating*.

1. 1.222

2. $0.1\overline{22}$

3. $23.\overline{546576}$

4. 43.76676

5. $2.\overline{4439}$

6. $0.3\overline{4}$

Extension 7.4 Practice

Write the decimal as a fraction or mixed number.

1. $0.\overline{2}$

2. $-0.\overline{7}$

3. $-2.\overline{3}$

4. $8.\overline{7}$

5. $-10.\overline{5}$

6. $24.\overline{8}$

7. $0.5\overline{7}$

8. $-1.4\overline{5}$

9. $-3.8\overline{6}$

10. $-0.\overline{32}$

11. $6.\overline{13}$

12. $7.\overline{90}$

Complete the statement:

The Pythagorean Theorem states that if a triangle with legs *a* and *b* and hypotenuse *c* is a right triangle, then _____.

Give an example of three side lengths of a right triangle.

Can those three side lengths form a triangle that is not a right triangle?

Find the missing side length.

1.

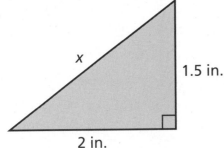

x   1.5 in.

2 in.

2.

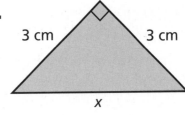

3 cm   3 cm

x

3.

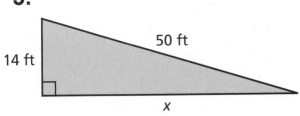

14 ft   50 ft

x

4.

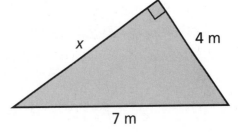

x   4 m

7 m

Lesson 7.5

Start Thinking!
For use before Lesson 7.5

Write a word problem that can be solved using the Pythagorean Theorem. Be sure to include a sketch of the situation.

Lesson 7.5

Warm Up
For use before Lesson 7.5

Write the converse of the true statement. Determine whether the converse is true or false. If it is true, justify your reasoning. If it is false, give a counterexample.

1. If a is a negative number, then $|a| = -a$.

2. If one line is vertical and another line is horizontal, then the two lines are perpendicular.

3. If a is a negative number, then a^2 is a positive number.

4. If a is an odd number, then $a - 1$ is an even number.

5. If the side lengths of a triangle are 3, 4, and 5, then the triangle is a right triangle.

6. If a line is given by the equation $y = 2x - 3$, then the y-intercept of the graph is -3.

7.5 Practice A

Write the converse of the true statement. Determine whether the converse is true or false. If it is true, justify your reasoning. If it is false, give a counterexample.

1. If a is an odd number, then $2a$ is an even number.

2. If a is negative, then $\dfrac{1}{a}$ is negative.

Tell whether the triangle with the given side lengths is a right triangle.

3.

4.

Find the distance between the two points.

5. $(2, -4), (3, -1)$

6. $(3, 2), (7, 5)$

7. $(-9, -2), (-7, 5)$

8. The side of the clip on a clip board appears to be a right triangle. The leg lengths are 2 millimeters and 2.1 millimeters and the hypotenuse is 2.9 millimeters. Is the side of the clip a right triangle?

Tell whether a triangle with the given side lengths is a right triangle.

9. $18, 80, 82$

10. $\sqrt{28}, 63, 65$

11. $2, \sqrt{96}, 10$

12. You are standing 6 feet away from the stage and your friend is standing 7 feet away from the stage.

   a. You are standing on a platform, which places your eyes at 6.5 feet. What is the distance from your eyes to the stage?

   b. Your friend's eyes are at 5 feet. What is the distance from your friend's eyes to the stage?

   c. Do you or your friend have a closer visual?

13. On the Junior League baseball field, you run 60 feet to first base and then 60 feet to second base. You are out at second base and then run directly along the diagonal to home plate. Find the total distance that you ran. Round your answer to the nearest tenth.

7.5 Practice B

Tell whether the triangle with the given side lengths is a right triangle.

1. 11 in., 60 in., 61 in.

2. 45 cm, 26 cm, 51 cm

Find the distance between the two points.

3. $(5, 5), (8, 7)$

4. $(-6, 2), (3, -2)$

5. $(10, -3), (-1, -8)$

6. Describe and correct the error in finding the distance between the points $(-5, -2)$ and $(-1, 4)$.

$$\times \quad d = \sqrt{(-5 - 1)^2 + (-2 - 4)^2}$$
$$= \sqrt{36 + 36}$$
$$= \sqrt{72}$$

Tell whether a triangle with the given side lengths is a right triangle.

7. $9, \sqrt{54}, 8$

8. $\sqrt{704}, 27, 5$

9. $88, 103, 137$

10. Your teacher gives you and your friend two different sets of points and wants both of you to find the distance between the two points.

    a. Your two points are $(5, 9)$ and $(2, 1)$. Find the distance between the two points.

    b. Your friend's two points are $(-5, -9)$ and $(-2, -1)$. Find the distance between the two points.

    c. Do you and your friend obtain the same answer? If possible, explain why.

    d. Give another example of this situation where the coordinates in the first set of points are a mixture of positive and negative values, and the second set of points have opposite values. Show that the distance is the same.

11. You are creating a flower garden in the triangular shape shown. You purchase edging to go around the flower garden. The edging costs $1.50 per foot. What is the cost of the edging? Round your lengths to the nearest whole number.

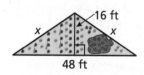

Name_____ Date_____

7.5 Enrichment and Extension

Classifying Triangles

Triangles can be classified as acute, right, or obtuse based on their angle measures.

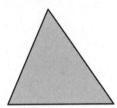 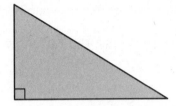 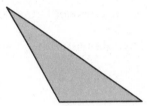

Acute triangle

3 acute angles

Right triangle

1 right angle and
2 acute angles

Obtuse triangle

1 obtuse angle and
2 acute angles

In a triangle where c is the longest side length and a and b are the two other side lengths:

If $a^2 + b^2 > c^2$, then the triangle is acute.

If $a^2 + b^2 = c^2$, then the triangle is right.

If $a^2 + b^2 < c^2$, then the triangle is obtuse.

Determine whether a triangle with the given side lengths is *acute*, *right*, or *obtuse*.

1. 9, 12, and 15

2. 10, 9, and 15

3. 10, 20, and 12

4. 15, 36, and 39

5. 7, 6, and 5

6. 26, 24, and 12

7. 8, 8, and 15

8. 45, 108, and 117

Use the distance formula to tell whether the three points form an *acute*, *right*, or *obtuse* triangle.

9. $(0, 0)$, $(-4, 5)$, $(2, 2)$

10. $(-2, 4)$, $(6, 0)$, $(-5, -2)$

11. $(0, 2)$, $(5, 1)$, $(1, -1)$

12. $(-7, 2)$, $(0, 1)$, $(-4, 4)$

7.5 Puzzle Time

What Comes After A Seahorse?

Write the letter of each answer in the box containing the exercise number.

Tell whether a triangle with the given side lengths is a right triangle.

1. 8 in., 9 in., 12 in.

    R. yes   **S.** no

2. 10 cm, 24 cm, 26 cm

    A. yes   **B.** no

3. 9 mm, 16 mm, 18 mm

    N. yes   **O.** no

Find the distance between the two points.

4. $(0, 0)$, $(6, 8)$

    D. 10   **E.** $\sqrt{300}$

5. $(2, 3)$, $(-3, -2)$

    Q. 5   **R.** $\sqrt{50}$

6. $(4, -7)$, $(5, -1)$

    D. 37   **E.** $\sqrt{37}$

7. During math class, your friend sits in the second row, third seat, which can be represented by the point $(2, 3)$. You sit in the fifth row, first seat, which can be represented by the point $(5, 1)$. What is the distance between your seats?

    G. 13   **H.** $\sqrt{13}$

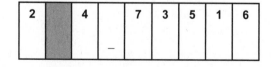

Name_____ Date_____

Technology Connection
For use after Section 7.3

Using the Pythagorean Theorem

The Pythagorean Theorem is one of the most famous theorems in mathematics partly because it can be used to solve so many types of problems. Although the theorem only applies to right triangles, right triangles themselves can be found within all rectangles and squares. Because of this, knowing how to find any side of a right triangle using the Pythagorean Theorem and a scientific calculator is an extremely useful skill.

EXAMPLE Use a scientific calculator to solve each right triangle.

a.

b.

SOLUTION

a. Because c is the hypotenuse, $c^2 = a^2 + b^2$. To solve for c, enter the following keystrokes on your calculator.

$$8\;\boxed{x^2}\;\boxed{+}\;15\;\boxed{x^2}\;\boxed{=}\;\boxed{\sqrt{}}\text{, or, }\boxed{\sqrt{}}\;\boxed{(}\;8\;\boxed{x^2}\;\boxed{+}\;15\;\boxed{x^2}\;\boxed{)}\;\boxed{=}$$

The display should show 17.

b. Because b is a leg, you can modify the Pythagorean Theorem and solve for b and find that $b^2 = c^2 - a^2$. Enter the following keystrokes on your calculator.

$$4.1\;\boxed{x^2}\;\boxed{-}\;1.68\;\boxed{x^2}\;\boxed{=}\;\boxed{\sqrt{}}\text{, or, }\boxed{\sqrt{}}\;\boxed{(}\;4.1\;\boxed{x^2}\;\boxed{-}\;1.68\;\boxed{x^2}\;\boxed{)}\;\boxed{=}$$

The display should show 3.74.

Use a scientific calculator to solve the right triangle.

1.
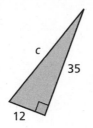

2.
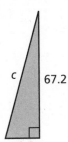

3.
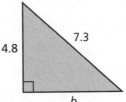

4.
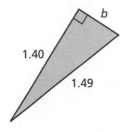

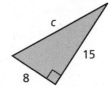
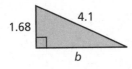

Chapter 8

Chapter 8 — Volume and Similar Solids

Dear Family,

Most families enjoy a movie and popcorn every once in a while. Maybe your family is no different. Have you ever wondered who eats the most popcorn? Maybe all your bowls are the same size, or maybe someone in your family likes to pull the biggest bowl out of the cupboard to fill it with popcorn!

This time, challenge your family to do some math before diving into the popcorn.

What you will need: 2 pieces of paper, tape, popcorn, and a ruler. Make two different cylinders with the two pieces of paper by taping the ends together with minimal overlap.

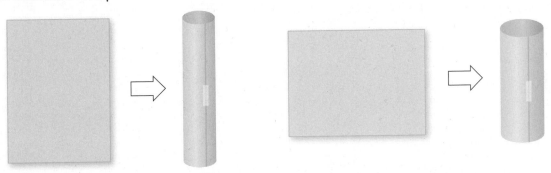

Measure the heights and the diameters of the cylinders you created. Which cylinder do you think holds more popcorn? Or, do you think they hold the same amount?

Experiment by filling the first cylinder with popcorn. Then carefully transfer the popcorn from the first cylinder to the second cylinder. Do they hold the same amount of popcorn? Which cylinder would you rather have your popcorn in while you watch the movie?

In this chapter, your student will learn how to calculate the volumes of cylinders, cones, and spheres. How is it beneficial to you to know the volume of a cylinder? Think about this as you watch your movie!

Nombre _____ Fecha _____

Volumen y sólidos similares

Estimada familia,

La mayoría de las familias disfrutan de ver una película y comer palomitas de maíz de vez en cuando. Puede que tu familia también lo haga. ¿Se han preguntado quién es el que más come palomitas de maíz? Puede que todos tus tazones sean del mismo tamaño, ¡peo a lo mejor alguien saca el tazón más grande de la alacena para llenarlo de palomitas de maíz!

Esta vez, reten a su familia a hacer un cálculo matemático antes de comer palomitas de maíz.

Lo que necesitarán: 2 hojas de papel, cinta pegante, palomitas de maíz, y una regla. Hagan dos cilindros diferentes usando las dos hojas de papel, pegando los bordes y evitando en lo posible que se traslapen.

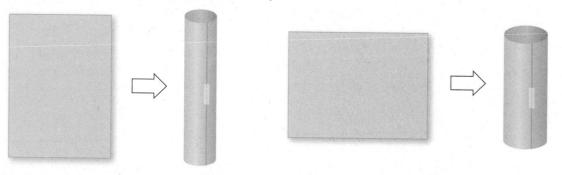

Midan las alturas y diámetros de los cilindros que hicieron. ¿En cuál cilindro creen que caben más palomitas de maíz? O, ¿creen que en ambos cabe la misma cantidad?

Hagan un experimento rellenando el primer cilindro con palomitas de maíz. Luego transfieran cuidadosamente las palomitas de maíz del primer cilindro al segundo. ¿Cabe la misma cantidad de palomitas de maíz en ambos cilindros? ¿En cuál de los dos cilindros preferirías colocar las palomitas de maíz mientras vez la película?

En este capítulo, su estudiante aprenderá a calcular el volumen de cilindros, conos y esferas. ¿De qué manera les beneficia conocer el volumen de un cilindro?

Give a real-life example of when knowing the volume of a cylinder would be useful.

Simplify.

1. 8^2 **2.** 14^2 **3.** 20^2

4. 18^2 **5.** 25^2 **6.** 21^2

Lesson 8.1

Start Thinking!
For use before Lesson 8.1

Explain to a partner how to find the volume of water a glass can hold.

Find the volume of the cylinder. Round your answer to the nearest tenth.

1.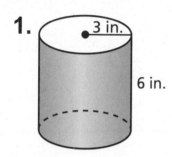

3 in.

6 in.

2.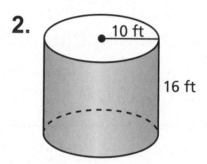

10 ft

16 ft

3.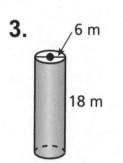

6 m

18 m

4.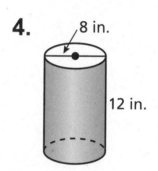

8 in.

12 in.

Name_____ Date_____

8.1 Practice A

Find the volume of the cylinder. Round your answer to the nearest tenth.

1.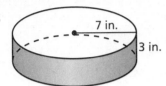
7 in.
3 in.

2.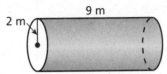
9 m
2 m

3.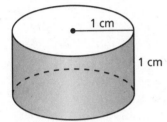
1 cm
1 cm

4.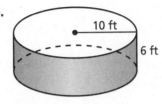
10 ft
6 ft

5.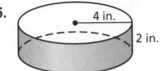
4 in.
2 in.

6.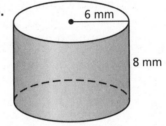
6 mm
8 mm

7. A water tank is in the shape of a cylinder with a diameter of 20 feet and a height of 20 feet. The tank is 70% full. About how many gallons of water are in the tank? Round your answer to the nearest whole number. $\left(1 \text{ ft}^3 \approx 7.5 \text{ gal}\right)$

8. A cylinder has a surface area of 339 square centimeters and a radius of 6 centimeters. Estimate the volume of the cylinder to the nearest whole number.

9. How does the volume of a cylinder change when its diameter is doubled? Explain.

Name _____ Date _____

Find the volume of the cylinder. Round your answer to the nearest tenth.

1.
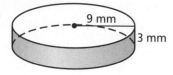

2.
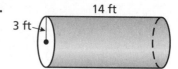

3.
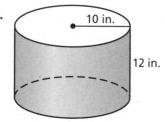

4.
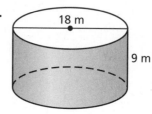

Find the missing dimension of the cylinder. Round your answer to the nearest whole number.

5. Volume = 550 in.³

6. Volume = 25,000 ft³

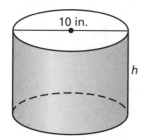

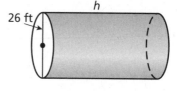

7. Your friend's swimming pool is in the shape of a rectangular prism, with a length of 25 feet, a width of 8 feet, and a height of 5 feet.

   a. What is the volume of your friend's swimming pool?

   b. Your swimming pool is in the shape of a cylinder with a diameter of 16 feet and has the same volume as your friend's pool. What is the height of your pool? Round your answer to the nearest whole number.

   c. While you were on vacation, 6 inches of water evaporated from your pool. About how many gallons of water evaporated from your pool? $\left(1 \text{ ft}^3 \approx 7.5 \text{ gal}\right)$ Round your answer to the nearest whole number.

Name_____ Date_____

8.1 Enrichment and Extension

Camouflage Packaging: Should we be concerned?

The shape and size of a product's packaging is often designed to make it look like you are getting more of the product than you actually are. This "camouflage" packaging may make a product more appealing to the consumer.

1. A deodorant container is approximately a rectangular prism that is 2.5 inches long, 1 inch wide, and 4.7 inches tall. The deodorant inside is only 2.4 inches tall.

   a. What percent of the container's volume is wasted? Round your answer to the nearest tenth of a percent.

   b. How many square inches of plastic would be saved with each container by making it the same height as the deodorant?

2. A box containing 10 chocolate-covered cherries is a rectangular prism that is 3.7 inches wide, 7.4 inches long, and 2.5 inches tall. The cherries are approximately spheres with a diameter of 1 inch.

   a. What percent of the container's volume is wasted? Round your answer to the nearest tenth of a percent. (*Hint:* The formula for the volume of a sphere is $V = \dfrac{4}{3}\pi r^3$.)

   b. The company decides to sell the cherries stacked on top of each other in a cylindrical cardboard container. What would be the smallest possible diameter, height, and volume of the container? How much cardboard would they save by using this packaging design? Explain.

3. What are some environmental consequences of camouflage packaging? Also, describe how camouflage packaging affects shipping and transportation and the effect that has on the environment.

4. Find your own example of camouflage packaging. Write a persuasive letter to the company supporting packaging designs that are less wasteful. Be sure to include the following things:

   • the percent of the current container's volume that is wasted space

   • a design for packaging that will have less wasted space and take less material to make

   • how much packaging material would be saved with your design

   • some of the environmental consequences from Exercise 3

Name_____ Date _____

8.1 Puzzle Time

Did You Hear About...

A	B	C	D	E	F
G	H	I	J	K	L
M	N				

Complete each exercise. Find the answer in the answer column. Write the word under the answer in the box containing the exercise letter.

63.6 cm³ **BECAUSE**	
356.9 in.³ **SO**	
128.4 cm **SEA**	
791.7 ft³ **SAILORS**	
88.9 ft **SHIP**	
549.8 cm³ **CARDS**	
22 in. **THE**	
2799.2 m³ **COULDN'T**	
435.7 m³ **HAD**	
593.8 ft³ **WAS**	
2 ft **ON**	

Find the volume of the cylinder. Round your answer to the nearest tenth.

A. $r = 12$ in.; $h = 4$ in.   **B.** $r = 6$ ft; $h = 7$ ft

C. $r = 3$ cm; $h = 13$ cm   **D.** $r = 9$ m; $h = 11$ m

E. $r = 8$ ft; $h = 15$ ft   **F.** $d = 10$ cm; $h = 7$ cm

G. $d = 3$ cm; $h = 9$ cm   **H.** $d = 8$ ft; $h = 15$ ft

I. $d = 14$ m; $h = 15$ m   **J.** $d = 6$ ft; $h = 21$ ft

Find the missing dimensions of the cylinder. Round your answer to the nearest whole number.

K. An official NHL hockey puck is shaped like a cylinder with a diameter of 3 inches and a volume of 7.1 cubic inches. What is the height of the hockey puck?

L. A water trampoline is shaped like a cylinder with a diameter of 11 feet and a volume of 190.1 cubic feet. What is the height of the trampoline?

M. A rolled-up sleeping bag is shaped like a cylinder with a radius of 5 inches and a volume of 1727.9 cubic inches. What is the height of the rolled-up sleeping bag?

N. A sports bottle is shaped like a cylinder with a height of 19 centimeters and a volume of 731.2 cubic centimeters. What is the diameter of the sports bottle?

7 cm **DECK**	
754.0 ft³ **THE**	
3015.9 ft³ **PLAY**	
1 in. **STANDING**	
65.7 ft³ **SITTING**	
521.6 in. **BOAT**	
2309.1 m³ **CAPTAIN**	
99.8 in.³ **WASN'T**	
1809.6 in.³ **THE**	
367.6 cm³ **WHO**	
131.4 in. **ARE**	

Start Thinking!
For use before Activity 8.2

Review with a partner the formulas for finding the area of the following figures:

square   rectangle

triangle   circle

Warm Up
For use before Activity 8.2

Find the area. Round your answer to the nearest tenth.

1.

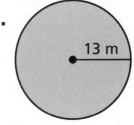

13 m

2.

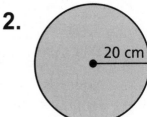

20 cm

3.

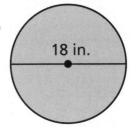

18 in.

4.

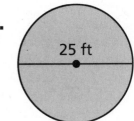

25 ft

Lesson 8.2 Start Thinking!
For use before Lesson 8.2

Explain which sugar cone can hold more ice cream:

Sugar cone 1: radius 3 cm; height 14 cm

Sugar cone 2: diameter 7 cm; height 13 cm

Lesson 8.2 Warm Up
For use before Lesson 8.2

Find the volume of the cone. Round your answer to the nearest tenth.

1.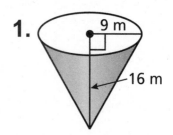

2.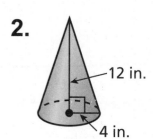

3.

4.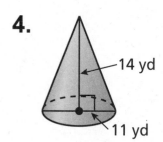

Name_____ Date_____

8.2 Practice A

Find the volume of the cone. Round your answer to the nearest tenth.

1.
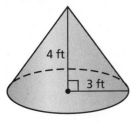

2.
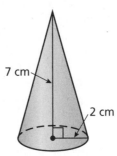

3.
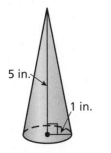

4.
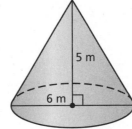

5.
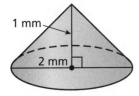

6.
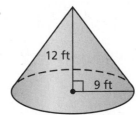

7. The volume of a cylinder is 24π cubic feet. What is the volume of a cone having the same base and same height?

8. A funnel is in the shape of a cone with a radius of 4 inches and a height of 10 inches.

   a. Find the volume of the funnel. Round your answer to the nearest tenth.

   b. The funnel is filled with oil. How many quarts of oil are in the funnel? $\left(1 \text{ qt} \approx 58 \text{ in.}^3\right)$ Round your answer to the nearest tenth.

Name _____ Date _____

Find the volume of the cone. Round your answer to the nearest tenth.

1.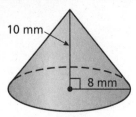
10 mm

8 mm

2.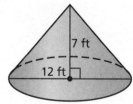
7 ft

12 ft

3.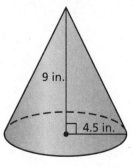
9 in.

4.5 in.

4.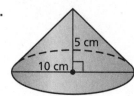
5 cm

10 cm

Find the missing dimension of the cone. Round your answer to the nearest tenth.

5. Volume = 100 in.^{3}

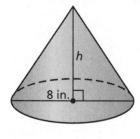
h

8 in.

6. Volume = 13.4 m^3

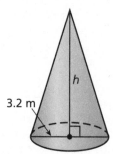
h

3.2 m

7. A paper cup is in the shape of a cone, with a diameter of 2 centimeters and a height of 5 centimeters.

   a. What is the volume of the paper cup?

   b. Water is running into the cup at a rate of 1.5 cubic centimeters per second. How long does it take for the cup to fill with water? Round your answer to the nearest tenth.

8. Cone A has the same radius but half the height of Cone B. What is the ratio of the volume of Cone A to the volume of Cone B?

8.2 Enrichment and Extension

I Scream…You Scream…We all Scream for Ice Cream…Cones!?!

Have you ever been at an ice cream shop and been faced with the question, "Would you like that in a cake cone or sugar cone?" You may or may not have a taste preference, but how do you know which one holds more?

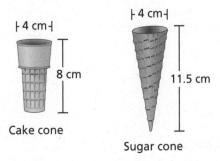

Cake cone

Sugar cone

1. Predict which of the two ice cream cones will hold more. Explain your reasoning.

2. The cake cone is approximately in the shape of a cylinder. Calculate the volume of both ice cream cones. Round your answers to the nearest tenth.

3. Was your prediction correct? Explain.

4. You order a medium soft serve frozen yogurt. Does it matter what kind of cone you choose? Will you get more ice cream if you choose the cake cone? What if you order two scoops of hard ice cream instead? Explain your reasoning.

5. The diameter of the sugar cone stays the same. How tall would the sugar cone have to be in order to have the same volume as the cake cone?

6. The box for the sugar cones has a recipe for a snack. It says that 1 chopped banana mixed with 1 cup chocolate pudding and $\frac{1}{4}$ cup chopped peanuts will fill 5 sugar cones. About how many batches of this recipe would it take to fill 5 of the cake cones pictured above?

7. The cake cone above is jumbo size. The box says they hold 50% more.

   a. How much do the regular size cake cones hold? Do the regular size cake cones still hold more than the sugar cones?

   b. The regular size cake cones have the same diameter as the jumbo size. How tall are they?

Name _____ Date _____

8.2 Puzzle Time

Who Took Tiny Pieces Of Mail Across Country Over A Hundred Years Ago?

Write the letter of each answer in the box containing the exercise number.

Find the volume of the cone. Round your answer to the nearest tenth.

1. $r = 3$ in.; $h = 5$ in.   2. $r = 4$ cm; $h = 6$ cm

3. $r = 5$ ft; $h = 12$ ft   4. $r = 3$ m; $h = 13$ m

5. $r = 7$ ft; $h = 7$ ft   6. $d = 10$ cm; $h = 6$ cm

7. $d = 14$ m; $h = 5$ m   8. $d = 8$ in.; $h = 7$ in.

9. $d = 12$ ft; $h = 9$ ft   10. $d = 15$ in.; $h = 8$ in.

Find the missing dimension of the cone. Round your answer to the nearest tenth.

11. A sorcerer's hat is shaped like a cone with a diameter of 8 inches and a volume of 301.6 cubic inches. What is the height of the sorcerer's hat?

12. A pine tree is shaped like a cone with a radius of 8 feet and a volume of 3887.2 cubic feet. What is the height of the pine tree?

13. A waterspout forms in the shape of a cone with a height of 35 meters and a volume of 229.1 cubic meters. What is the diameter of the waterspout?

14. Sand poured from a beach pail forms a cone with a height of 32 centimeters and a volume of 3351.0 cubic centimeters. What is the radius of the sand poured from a beach pail in the shape of a cone?

Answers
P. 256.6 m^3
E. 471.2 in.^{3}
S. 122.5 m^3
R. 18 in.
H. 359.2 ft^3
X. 5 m
E. 100.5 cm^3
T. 314.2 ft^3
P. 58 ft
Y. 157.1 cm^3
E. 117.3 in.^{3}
N. 47.1 in.^{3}
U. 10 cm
S. 339.3 ft^3

3	5	8		12	14	1	6		10	13	7	11	2	9	4

Review with a partner the formulas for the volumes of cylinders and cones.

How are the formulas similar? How are they different?

Activity 8.3 **Warm Up**
For use before Activity 8.3

Find the area of the circle. Round your answer to the nearest tenth.

1.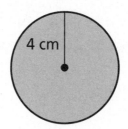
4 cm

2.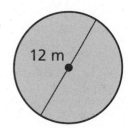
12 m

3.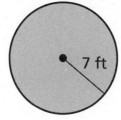
7 ft

4.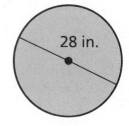
28 in.

Big Ideas Math Blue **265**
Resources by Chapter

Give a real-life example of how finding the volume of a sphere may be useful.

Find the volume of the sphere. Round your answer to the nearest tenth.

1.

r = 4 ft

2.

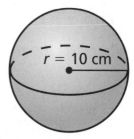

r = 10 cm

3.

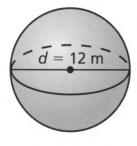

d = 12 m

4.

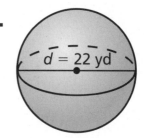

d = 22 yd

Name_____ Date _____

Find the volume of the sphere. Round your answer to the nearest tenth.

1.

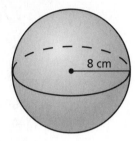

8 cm

2.

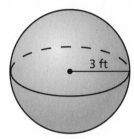

3 ft

3.

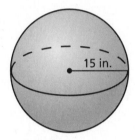

15 in.

4.

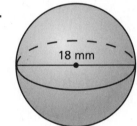

18 mm

Find the radius of the sphere with the given volume.

5. Volume $= 288\pi$ in.^{3}

6. Volume $= 562.5\pi$ cm^3

7. A fishing bobber has a radius of 0.5 inch. Find the volume of the fishing bobber. Round your answer to the nearest tenth.

Find the volume of the composite solid. Round your answer to the nearest tenth.

8.

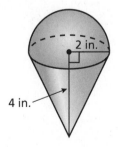

2 in.

4 in.

9.

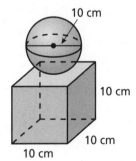

10 cm

10 cm

10 cm

10 cm

8.3 Practice B

Find the volume of the sphere. Round your answer to the nearest tenth.

1.

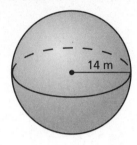

14 m

2.

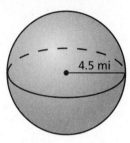

4.5 mi

3.

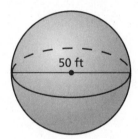

50 ft

4.

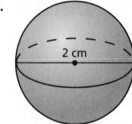

2 cm

Find the radius of the sphere with the given volume.

5. Volume = 2304π yd^3

6. Volume = 1543.5π mm^3

7. A spherical cabinet knob has a radius of 1.5 inches. Find the volume of the cabinet knob. Round your answer to the nearest tenth.

Find the volume of the composite solid. Round your answer to the nearest tenth.

8.

5 ft

5 ft

9.

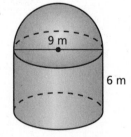

9 m

6 m

8.3 Enrichment and Extension

The Dodgeball Advantage

Dodgeball is a popular game among students. The object of the game is to pick up a rubber ball and throw it at members of the other team. If you hit them, they are out. But if a member of the other team catches the ball, you're out!

Frequently, games of dodgeball are played with multiple balls of different sizes. Which size is best for you?

1. Open your throwing hand (usually your right hand if you are right-handed, left hand if you are left-handed) and use a ruler to measure the distance from the tip of your thumb to the tip of your pinky finger. Record the measurement.

2. The circumference of a ball is the distance around the widest part of the ball. Find as many different-sized balls as you can, and measure the circumference of each. If you do not have a measuring tape you can get an inexact measurement with a yardstick by marking the ball and rolling it alongside the yardstick until you have made one full revolution. Record these measurements.

3. In order to grip a ball and be able to throw it with maximum velocity and accuracy, the ratio of your hand size to ball circumference must be greater than about $\frac{1}{3}$. Use this ratio to determine which of the balls meet this criteria.

4. Multiply your hand size by 3. This is about the maximum circumference a ball can have and still be thrown with the greatest velocity and accuracy. Record this measurement.

5. How do your answers to Exercises 2–4 help you during a game of dodgeball in which there are differen-sized balls?

6. What does it mean if the ratio from Exercise 3 is greater than 1?

7. Most balls used for dodgeball are rubber and can be squeezed. Use the information from Exercise 3 to explain why this helps you grip a larger ball.

8.3 Puzzle Time

What Is It That Never Asks Questions But Often Has To Be Answered?

Write the letter of each answer in the box containing the exercise number.

Find the volume of the sphere with the given radius or diameter. Round your answer to the nearest tenth.

1. $r = 16$ in.   **2.** $r = 9$ in.

3. $r = 8$ in.   **4.** $r = 10$ in.

5. $d = 26$ in.   **6.** $d = 22$ in.

Find the radius of the sphere with the given volume.

7. Volume $= 2304\pi$ in.^{3}

8. Volume $= 562.5\pi$ in.^{3}

9. Volume $= 18{,}432\pi$ in.^{3}

10. Volume $= 1543.5\pi$ in.^{3}

11. A snow globe consists of a pedestal in the shape of a cube with a sphere mounted on top of the pedestal. The pedestal has an edge length of 4 inches and the sphere has a diameter of 3 inches. What is the volume of the snow globe rounded to the nearest cubic inch?

Answers

E. 3053.6 in.^{3}

L. 7.5 in.

D. 78 in.^{3}

H. 9208.8 in.^{3}

O. 24 in.

E. 17,157.3 in.^{3}

R. 5575.3 in.^{3}

O. 2144.7 in.^{3}

T. 12 in.

B. 10.5 in.

L. 4188.8 in.^{3}

7	5	2		11	9	3	6	10	1	8	4

Start Thinking!
For use before Activity 8.4

Explain how a juice factory would use volume.

Warm Up
For use before Activity 8.4

Tell whether the ratios are equivalent.

1. $\dfrac{35}{20}, \dfrac{7}{4}$

2. $\dfrac{3}{8}, \dfrac{32}{12}$

3. $\dfrac{4}{8}, \dfrac{20}{24}$

4. $\dfrac{9}{2}, \dfrac{27}{6}$

5. $\dfrac{14}{18}, \dfrac{12}{21}$

6. $\dfrac{14}{20}, \dfrac{21}{30}$

Lesson 8.4 **Start Thinking!**
For use before Lesson 8.4

Explain to a partner how to determine if two figures are similar.

Lesson 8.4 **Warm Up**
For use before Lesson 8.4

1. All the dimensions of a cube increase by a factor of $\frac{5}{4}$.

   a. How many times greater is the surface area? Explain.

   b. How many times greater is the volume? Explain.

Name_____ Date_____

8.4 Practice A

Determine whether the solids are similar.

1.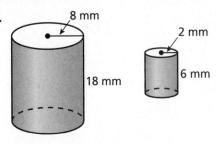
8 mm
2 mm
18 mm
6 mm

2.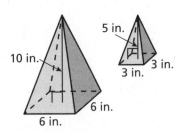
5 in.
10 in.
3 in.
3 in.
6 in.
6 in.

The solids are similar. Find the missing dimension(s).

3.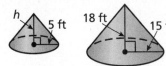
h
5 ft
18 ft
15 ft

4.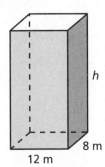
h
12 m
8 m
6 m
2 m
ℓ

The solids are similar. Find the surface area *S* or the volume *V* of the larger solid. Round your answer to the nearest tenth.

5. Volume = 250 mm³

3 mm

4 mm

6. Surface Area = 130 ft²

6 ft
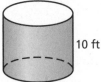
10 ft

7. The ratio of the corresponding linear measures of two similar cans of cat food is 4 : 3.

   a. The larger can has a surface area of 100 square inches. Find the surface area of the smaller can. Round your answer to the nearest tenth.

   b. The larger can has a volume of 150 cubic inches. Find the volume of the smaller can. Round your answer to the nearest tenth.

Name _____ Date _____

The solids are similar. Find the missing dimension(s).

1.

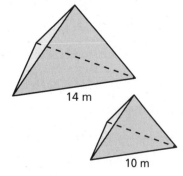

3 ft

9 ft

4 ft

r

2.

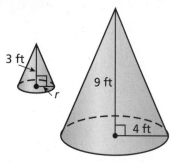

15 cm

w

5 cm

h

20 cm

12.5 cm

The solids are similar. Find the surface area *S* or the volume *V* of the smaller solid. Round your answers to the nearest tenth.

3. Surface Area = 294.7 m^2

14 m

10 m

4. Volume = 1500 ft^3

6 ft

3.2 ft

5. The ratio of the corresponding linear measures of two similar buckets of popcorn is 2 to 5. The larger bucket has a volume of 390 cubic inches. Find the volume of the smaller bucket. Round your answer to the nearest tenth.

6. A box of 60 tissues has a length of 11 centimeters, a width of 10.5 centimeters, and a height of 13.5 centimeters.

  a. Find the volume of the box of tissues. Round your answer to the nearest tenth.

  b. A similar box contains 100 tissues. The ratio of the corresponding linear measures of the two boxes is 3 : 5. Find the volume of the larger box. Round your answer to the nearest tenth.

  c. Find the dimensions of the larger box. Round your answers to the nearest tenth.

8.4 Enrichment and Extension

Logical Measuring

Example: You are making pasta out of a box that contains all the ingredients except for the water. You have to add exactly 2 cups of water. However, all you can find are two irregularly shaped containers. One holds 4 cups exactly, and the other holds 5 cups exactly. Neither one is marked, nor can they be marked. How can you use them to measure exactly 2 cups of water?

Step 1 Fill the 5-cup container. Pour it into the 4-cup container until the 4-cup container is full and there is exactly one cup left in the 5-cup container.

Step 2 Empty the 4-cup container. Pour the one cup from the 5-cup container into the 4-cup container.

Step 3 Refill the 5-cup container. Pour it into the 4-cup container until it is full. Because there is already one cup in the 4-cup container, there are exactly two cups left in the 5-cup container.

For each situation, the containers are irregular shapes and cannot be marked. Unless otherwise stated, you have unlimited access to more water. Answer each logic puzzle by giving the steps you would take. Try to do each with the least number of steps possible.

1. You have a 4-cup container and a 3-cup container. How can you use them to measure exactly 2 cups of water?

2. You have a 4-cup container and a 9-cup container. How can you use them to measure exactly 6 cups of water?

3. You have a 4-cup container and a 7-cup container. How can you use them to measure exactly 5 cups of water?

4. You have a 5-cup container and a 3-cup container. How can you use them to measure exactly 4 cups of water? There are two solutions to this one. See if you can find them both. Which one has less wasted water?

5. You have a 3-cup container, a 5-cup container, and an 8-cup container. The 8-cup container is exactly full with sugar, but the other two are empty. You want to split it evenly with a friend so you can both make the same recipe, which calls for 4 cups of sugar. Neither of you has any more sugar. How can you make it so that two of the containers have exactly 4 cups of sugar?

Name_____ Date _____

8.4 Puzzle Time

What Kind Of Seafood Do Weight Lifters Like Best?

Write the letter of each answer in the box containing the exercise number.

The solids are similar solids. Find the missing dimension.

1. Cylinder A: $r = 6$ in.; $h = 15$ in.   Cylinder B: $r = 8$ in.; $h = $ _?_

    R. 18 in.   **S.** 20 in.   **T.** 24 in.

2. Cone X: $h = 12$ ft; $r = 9$ ft   Cone Y: $h = 28$ ft; $r = $ _?_

    E. 21 ft   **F.** 27 ft   **G.** 36 ft

3. Pyramid F: $\ell = 7$ cm; $h = 10$ cm   Pyramid G: $\ell = 4.2$ cm; $h = $ _?_

    Q. 4 cm   **R.** 5 cm   **S.** 6 cm

The solids are similar. Find the missing surface area S or volume V.

4. Prism M: $w = 4$ mm; $S = 148$ mm^2 Prism N: $w = 6$ mm; $S = $ _?_

    J. 254 mm^2 **K.** 278 mm^2 **L.** 333 mm^2

5. Cone Y: $r = 3$ yd; $S = 36\pi$ yd^2 Cone Z: $r = 7$ yd; $S = $ _?_

    R. 182π yd^2 **S.** 196π yd^2 **T.** 204π yd^2

6. Cylinder J: $h = 13$ m; $V = 1300\pi$ m^3 Cylinder K: $h = 19.5$ m; $V = $ _?_

    U. 4387.5π m^3 **V.** 4597π m^3 **W.** 4775.5π m^3

7. Pyramid C: $h = 15$ in.; $V = 240$ in.^{3} Pyramid D: $h = 18$ in.; $V = $ _?_

    K. 396.14 in.^{3} **L.** 408.81 in.^{3} **M.** 414.72 in.^{3}

7	6	3	5	2	4	1

Name_____ Date_____

Finding Cube Roots

Because of its frequent use, even most simple calculators have a square root key,

$\boxed{\sqrt{}}$. To find a root higher than a square root (cube root, fourth root, etc.),

scientific calculators contain a "principal nth root" key, $\boxed{\sqrt[x]{}}$ or $\boxed{\sqrt[x]{y}}$, where x

(the *index* of the root) indicates the type of root to be found.

EXAMPLE Find the cube root of 100.

SOLUTION

The cube root of 100 can be written as $\sqrt[3]{100}$. On your calculator, enter

3 $\boxed{\text{2nd}}$ $\boxed{\sqrt[x]{}}$ 100 $\boxed{=}$. The answer is approximately 4.642.

EXAMPLE A standard size 5 soccer ball has a volume
of 333 cubic inches. What is the diameter
of the ball to the nearest tenth of an inch?
Let $\pi = 3.14$.

SOLUTION

Step 1 Substitute 333 into the formula for the volume of a sphere to

get $333 = \dfrac{4}{3}\pi r^3$.

Step 2 Solve the equation for r^3 and let $\pi = 3.14$ to find $r^3 \approx 79.54$.

Step 3 Solve for r by taking the cube root of both sides of the equation.
On your calculator, enter 3 $\boxed{\text{2nd}}$ $\boxed{\sqrt[x]{}}$ 79.54 $\boxed{=}$. Your display
should show approximately 4.3. This is the radius of the ball.

Step 4 Finally, double the radius to calculate the diameter of the ball.
Your solution is about 8.6 inches.

Use a scientific or graphing calculator to find the roots below.

1. $\sqrt[3]{512}$ **2.** $\sqrt[3]{-421.875}$ **3.** $\sqrt[4]{20,736}$

4. The volume of a men's basketball is about 434 cubic inches. If the volume
of a women's basketball is 43 cubic inches less than a men's ball, what is
the difference in diameters of the two sizes of basketballs? Let $\pi = 3.14$.
Round your answer to the nearest tenth.

Chapter 9

Name_____ Date_____

Dear Family,

Volunteering is a rewarding way to spend time with friends and family while helping your community.

Many charitable and non-profit organizations require a lot of management—as much as, or more than some businesses that operate for profit. Managers must raise money through donations and recruit volunteers—both of which involve convincing people of the value of supporting the organization. Organizations often use marketing campaigns and community presentations to promote their causes.

With your student, decide on a volunteer opportunity to explore. Take a look at a number of organizations. Do research on the Internet, attend community presentations, and view the organization's marketing material to learn as much as you can. Have your student analyze the data presented.

- What numerical data did the organization present? Are they the best measurements for the data?

- Did the organization use data displays? Did they use the best types of displays to make their point? If not, what would be a better display? Why?

- Does the volunteer opportunity fit your abilities and schedule?

If your analysis leaves you with questions, you and your student should contact the volunteer coordinator at the organization. After analyzing each organization, compare each opportunity to find one that is the best fit for you.

Not every volunteer effort requires a long-term commitment. Often, a community group will organize a neighborhood beautification or cleanup project. Talk with your student about how they would get such a project started. What kind of data would your student present to convince people to volunteer? Would your family like to put the plan into motion?

May you have a cause to celebrate!

Capítulo 9 · Análisis de datos y representaciones de datos

Estimada Familia:

El voluntariado es una manera gratificante de pasar tiempo con sus amigos y familia mientras ayuda a su comunidad.

Muchas organizaciones de caridad y sin fines de lucro requieren muchos recursos administrativos—tanto o más que los negocios en sí. Los administradores deben recaudar fondos a través de donaciones y reclutar voluntarios—ambos requieren convencer a las personas sobre la importancia de apoyar a la organización. Las organizaciones generalmente utilizan campañas de mercadeo y presentaciones a la comunidad para promover sus causas.

Con su estudiante, decidan explorar una oportunidad de voluntariado. Examinen un número de organizaciones. Hagan investigaciones en Internet, vayan a presentaciones en la comunidad y revisen el material de mercadeo de la organización para aprender lo más que puedan. Haga que su estudiante analice los datos presentados.

- ¿Qué datos numéricos presentó la organización? ¿Estas son las mejores medidas para los datos?

- ¿La organización utilizó representaciones de datos? ¿Usaron los mejores tipos de representaciones para explicar su mensaje? Si no, ¿qué representación sería mejor? ¿Por qué?

- ¿La oportunidad de voluntariado se ajusta a sus habilidades y horarios?

Si su análisis le deja interrogantes, usted y su estudiante deben contactar a la coordinador de voluntarios de la organización. Luego de analizar cada organización, comparen cada oportunidad para encontrar aquélla que mejor se adapte a ustedes.

No todos los voluntariados requieren un compromiso a largo plazo. A menudo un grupo en la comunidad organiza el embellecimiento del barrio o inicia un proyecto de limpieza. Hable con su alumno acerca de cómo ellos pueden iniciar un proyecto de esa naturaleza. ¿Qué tipo de información presentaría su estudiante para convencer a las personas para hacer un voluntariado? ¿A su familia le gustaría llevar a cabo esta iniciativa?

¡Que tengan una causa para celebrar!

Sketch a graph of the data shown in the table.
Choose appropriate titles.

Person	1	2	3	4	5	6
Number of Shoes	13	5	25	10	33	17

Plot the point in a coordinate plane.

1. $(1, 6)$ **2.** $(4, 3)$

3. $(0, 4)$ **4.** $(5, 2)$

5. $(3, 3)$ **6.** $(5, 0)$

Explain to a partner what it means for a scatter plot to have a *positive* relationship.

Explain to a partner what it means for a scatter plot to have a *nonlinear* relationship.

1. The table shows the average price (in dollars) of sweatshirts sold at different stores and the number of sweatshirts sold at each store in one month.

Average Price	25	38	32	35	50
Number Sold	150	90	142	115	75

   a. Write the ordered pairs from the table and plot them in a coordinate plane.

   b. Describe the relationship between the two data sets.

9.1 Practice A

Describe the relationship you would expect between the data. Explain.

1. age of the automobile and the odometer reading

2. time spent fishing and the amount of bait in the bucket

3. number of passengers in a car and the number of traffic lights on the route

4. The table shows the heights (in feet) of the waves at a beach and the numbers of surfers at the beach.

Wave Height	3	6	5	1
Number of Surfers	24	61	56	15

   a. Write the ordered pairs from the table and plot them in a coordinate plane.

   b. Describe the relationship between the two data sets.

5. The scatter plot shows the numbers of lawns mowed by a local lawn care business during one week.

   a. How many days does it take to mow 30 lawns?

   b. About how many lawns can be mowed in 1 day?

   c. Describe the relationship shown by the data.

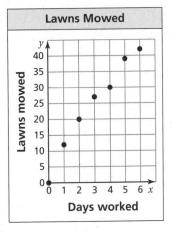

Describe the relationship between the data. Identify any outliers, gaps, or clusters.

6.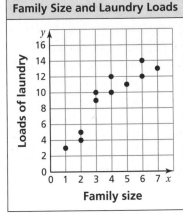

7.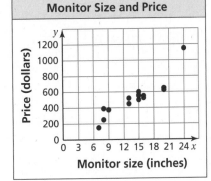

9.1 Practice B

1. The table shows the numbers of students remaining on an after-school bus and the numbers of minutes since leaving the school.

Number of students	56	45	39	24	17	6	0
Minutes	0	5	9	15	23	26	32

   a. Write the ordered pairs from the table and plot them in a coordinate plane.

   b. Describe the relationship between the two data sets.

2. The scatter plot shows the numbers of bushels filled and the numbers of apples picked.

   a. How many bushels are needed for 350 apples?

   b. About how many apples can be placed in 8 bushels?

   c. Describe the relationship shown by the data.

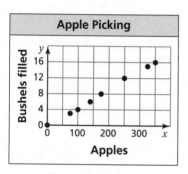

3. Describe a set of real-life data that has a positive linear relationship.

4. The scatter plot shows the numbers of yard sales in your neighborhood each month for a year.

   a. How many yard sales are during the month of February? June?

   b. During which month(s) are there no yard sales?

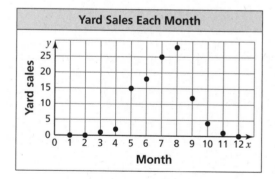

   c. What type of relationship do the data show?

   d. What type of climate might this neighborhood have?

   e. Identify any outliers, gaps, or clusters and explain why they might exist.

9.1 Enrichment and Extension

Hands and Feet

A person's hands and feet are measured many times throughout life for items such as boots and gloves. A foot is measured from the heel to the tip of the big toe. A hand is measured from the end of the wrist to the tip of the middle finger.

1. Do you think a person's hand size and foot size are related? Make a prediction about their relationship.

2. Use a ruler to measure the length of each student's feet and hands in your class. Round the measurements to the nearest centimeter.

3. Make a scatter plot containing the data with foot length on the x-axis and hand length on the y-axis.

4. Use the data to determine if your hypothesis in Exercise 1 is correct.

5. The Guinness World Record for largest feet ever is 47 centimeters. Based on your scatter plot, about how long would this person's hands have been?

6. The record holder's hand was measured at about 32 centimeters. Is this measurement close to your prediction in Exercise 5? Explain.

7. A person's feet measure 38 centimeters. Based on your scatter plot, about how long are the person's hands?

Name _____ Date _____

9.1 Puzzle Time

What Do You Call A Grouchy Person At The Beach?

Write the letter of each answer in the box containing the exercise number.

In Exercises 1–5, use the scatter plot.

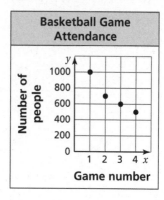

Answers	
N. 700	**E.** Game 1
R. Game 2	**T.** 600
D. Game 4	**M.** Game 3
C. 500	**I.** 1000
B. positive linear relationship	
A. negative linear relationship	
S. no relationship	

1. Which game did 500 people attend?

2. How many people attended Game 2?

3. Did more people attend Game 2 or Game 3?

4. How many more people attended Game 1 than Game 4?

5. Describe the relationship shown by the data.

Tell whether the data show a *positive*, a *negative*, or *no* relationship.

6.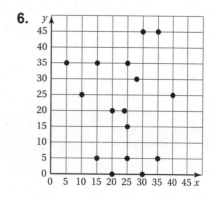

7.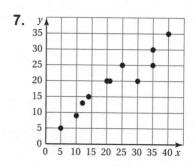

8.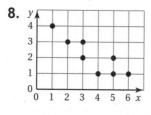

6	5	2	1	4	3	8	7

Research the population of your state each year for the past several years. You can find the information at *www.census.gov*. Record the results in a table.

Graph the data. Decide which units would be best and keep in mind that you may have to round to make graphing easier.

Is the graph linear? Can you use the graph to predict the population in future years?

Write an equation of the line that passes through the two points.

1. $(0, 4)$ and $(5, 3)$ **2.** $(0, 6)$ and $(2, 0)$

3. $(8, 3)$ and $(2, 6)$ **4.** $(1, 2)$ and $(5, 6)$

5. $(9, 3)$ and $(3, 1)$ **6.** $(4, 16)$ and $(2, 12)$

In which graph is the line shown most
representative of the data? Explain.

A   **B**   **C**

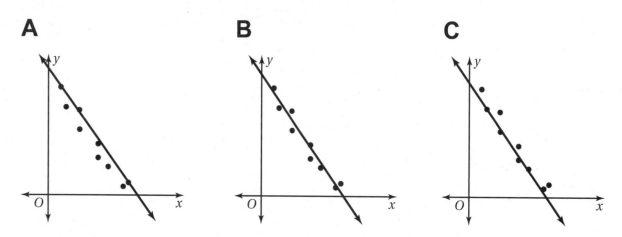

The table shows the weight y of x bananas.

Number of Bananas, x	0	1	2	3	4	5
Weight (ounces), y	0	5	8	14	17	20

1. Graph the data in the table.

2. Draw a line that you think best approximates
   the points.

3. Write an equation for your line.

4. Use the equation to predict the weight of
   10 bananas.

Name_____ Date_____

9.2 Practice A

1. The scatter plot shows the weights y of an infant from birth through x months.

   a. At what age did the infant weigh 11 pounds?

   b. What was the infant's weight at birth?

   c. Draw a line that you think best approximates the points.

   d. Write an equation for your line.

   e. Use the equation to predict the weight of the infant at 18 months.

   f. Does the data show a *positive*, a *negative*, or *no* relationship?

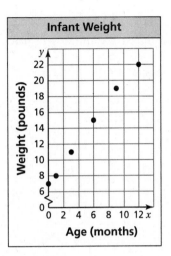

Infant Weight

2. The table shows the numbers of losses y a gamer has x weeks after getting a new video game.

Week, x	1	2	3	4	5	6	7
Losses, y	15	12	10	7	6	3	1

   a. Make a scatter plot of the data.

   b. Draw a line of fit.

   c. Write an equation of the line of fit.

   d. Does the data show a *positive*, a *negative*, or *no* relationship?

   e. Interpret the relationship.

3. The scatter plot shows the relationship between the numbers of girls and the numbers of boys in 10 different classrooms.

   a. What type of relationship, if any, does the data show?

   b. Is it possible to find the line of fit for the data? Explain.

   c. Is it reasonable to use this scatter plot to predict the number of boys in the classroom based on the number of girls? Explain.

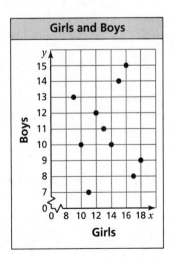

Girls and Boys

Name _____ Date _____

1. The scatter plot shows the costs y of bottles containing x fluid ounces of juice.

   a. How much does a gallon of juice cost?

   b. How many fluid ounces of juice can you purchase for $3?

   c. Draw a line that you think best approximates the points.

   d. Write an equation for your line.

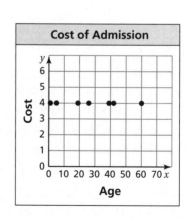

Cost of Juice

   e. Use the equation to predict the cost of a 256-fluid ounce container of juice.

   f. Does the data show a *positive*, a *negative*, or *no* relationship?

2. The table shows the mortgage interest rates y at a local bank for the years 2000 through 2008.

Year since 2000, x	0	1	2	3	4	5	6	7	8
Rate (%), y	7.6	6.8	6.2	6.0	5.2	5.8	6.1	5.9	5.5

   a. Make a scatter plot of the data.

   b. Draw a line of fit.

   c. Write an equation of the line of fit.

   d. Use the equation to predict the mortgage interest rate for the year 2010.

   e. Does the data show a *positive*, a *negative*, or *no* relationship?

   f. Interpret the relationship.

3. The scatter plot shows the relationship between the age of an individual x and the cost of admission y to a show.

   a. What type of relationship does the data show?

   b. Draw a line of fit.

   c. Write an equation of the line of fit.

   d. Interpret the relationship.

Cost of Admission

9.2   Enrichment and Extension

Correlation Coefficient

A scatter plot can reveal the relationship that exists between two sets of data. Are all relationships between data the same? Are some relationships stronger than others?

Calculate the correlation coefficient r to help determine the strength of the relationship between data. The correlation coefficient is a value between -1 and 1. When r is close to 1, the data share a strong positive relationship. When r is close to -1, the data share a strong negative relationship. If r is close to 0, the data do not share a relationship.

Analyzing the Relationship

The data in the table show the number of cubic meters x excavated during an archeological dig and the number y of artifacts found.

	x	y	xy	x^2	y^2
	1	1			
	2	3			
	3	4			
	4	5			
	5	6			
Sum	$A = 15$	$B =$	$C =$	$D =$	$F =$

1. Construct a scatter plot for the data. Draw a line of fit.

2. How many pairs of data are contained in the table? Use this number as your value for n.

3. Copy and complete the table.

4. Use the values in the table and a calculator to evaluate the formula to calculate the correlation coefficient. Round your answer to three decimal places.

$$r = \frac{n(C)-(A)(B)}{\sqrt{\left[n(D)-(A)^2\right]\left[n(F)-(B)^2\right]}}$$

5. What does the value of the correlation coefficient tell you about the relationship between the data? Does your scatter plot support your conclusion?

Name _____ Date _____

9.2 Puzzle Time

What Do Bumblebees Sing In The Shower?

Write the letter of each answer in the box containing the exercise number.

Write an equation of a line of fit for the data.

1. $(0, 10), (1, 10), (1, 25), (1, 20), (2, 30), (3, 40), (3, 50), (4, 40)$

    C. $y = -10x - 10$ **D.** $y = -10x + 10$ **E.** $y = 10x + 10$

2. $(0, 14), (1, 13), (2, 9), (3, 7), (4, 5), (5, 4), (6, 3), (6, 2), (7, 1)$

    B. $y = -2x + 14$ **C.** $y = 2x + 14$ **D.** $y = 2x - 14$

3. $(10, 5), (25, 20), (30, 30), (50, 35), (50, 40), (60, 50), (70, 75), (80, 60)$

    C. $y = \dfrac{22}{25}x + 2$ **D.** $y = -\dfrac{22}{25}x + 2$ **E.** $y = \dfrac{22}{25}x - 2$

4. $(40, 120), (50, 100), (70, 100), (80, 60), (100, 60), (110, 20), (120, 20), (130, 10)$

    A. $y = -\dfrac{5}{4}x - 170$ **B.** $y = -\dfrac{5}{4}x + 170$ **C.** $y = \dfrac{5}{4}x + 170$

Use a graphing calculator to find an equation of the line of best fit.

5. $(0, 1), (1, 1.5), (2, 2), (2, 2.5), (3, 2), (3, 3.75), (4, 3.5), (4, 4)$

    O. $y = 0.70x - 0.88$ **P.** $y = 0.70x + 0.88$ **Q.** $y = -0.70x + 0.88$

6. $(0, 1), (1, 1.5), (1.5, 1.25), (2, 1.5), (3, 2), (3, 2.5), (4.5, 4), (5, 5.25)$

    M. $y = -0.81x + 0.35$ **N.** $y = 0.81x - 0.35$ **O.** $y = 0.81x + 0.35$

4	3	1	2	6	5

Activity 9.3

Start Thinking!
For use before Activity 9.3

Use the double bar graph to complete the table.

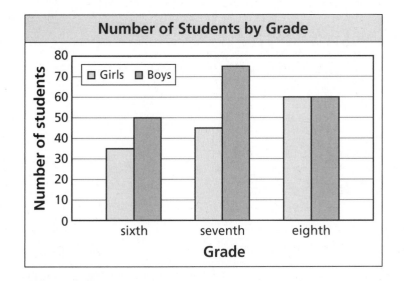

	Boys	Girls
6th grade		
7th grade		
8th grade		

Activity 9.3

Warm Up
For use before Activity 9.3

Use the table to complete the exercises.

		Been outside the U.S.?	
		Yes	No
Speak more than one language?	Yes	12	4
	No	18	12

1. How many people surveyed speak more than one language?

2. How many people surveyed have never traveled outside of the U.S.?

3. How many people only speak one language and have traveled outside of the U.S.?

Start Thinking!
For use before Lesson 9.3

Survey your class to determine the class's two most-watched television shows. Name the two shows.

Then complete the two-way table using data from your class.

		Watch show #1	
		Yes	No
Watch show #2	Yes		
	No		

Interpret the table.

Warm Up
For use before Lesson 9.3

You randomly survey students about country music. You display the two categories of data in the two-way table below.

		Like country music?	
		Yes	No
Student	Male	24	28
	Female	18	14

1. How many female students like country music?

2. How many male students do *not* like country music?

Name_____ Date_____

1. The two-way table shows the results of a football team's home games over the last five seasons and whether the stadium roof was open or closed.

		Stadium Roof	
		Open	**Closed**
Result	Win	25	7
	Loss	8	0

   a. How many home games did the team win?

   b. How many home games did the team lose with a closed roof?

   c. Find and interpret the marginal frequencies.

   d. What percent of the total home games did the team win with an open roof?

2. You randomly survey students in a school about whether they prefer cats or dogs as pets. The results are shown in the tally sheets. Make a two-way table including the totals of the rows and columns.

Male Students	
Pet	Tally
Dogs	ЖЖ ЖЖ ЖЖ II
Cats	ЖЖ III

Female Students	
Pet	Tally
Dogs	ЖЖ ЖЖ IIII
Cats	ЖЖ ЖЖ ЖЖ ЖЖ

3. You randomly survey people in the mall about whether or not they regularly use text messaging. The results are shown in the tally sheets.

Texts Regularly	
Age	Tally
20-29	ЖЖ ЖЖ ЖЖ ЖЖ ЖЖ
30-39	ЖЖ ЖЖ I
40-49	II

Does Not Text Regularly	
Age	Tally
20-29	ЖЖ II
30-39	ЖЖ ЖЖ III
40-49	ЖЖ ЖЖ

   a. Make a two-way table that includes the marginal frequencies.

   b. For each age group, what percent of the people in the survey text regularly? do not text regularly? Organize the results in a two-way table. Explain what one of the entries represents.

   c. Does the table in part (b) show a relationship between age and texting? Explain.

9.3 Practice B

1. Find and interpret the marginal frequencies.

		Number of doors	
		Two	Four
Number of Cylinders	Four	54	25
	Six	37	84

2. You randomly survey students in your school. You ask whether they spend more leisure time watching television, playing video games, or going online. You display your results in the two-way table.

   a. How many 11th-graders chose playing video games?

   b. Find and interpret the marginal frequencies for the survey.

   c. What percent of students in the survey are the 12th-graders who spend more time going online?

		Leisure Time		
		Television	Video games	Internet
Grade	10th	25	38	12
	11th	32	26	16
	12th	30	20	30

3. You randomly survey your classmates about the color of their hair. The results are shown in the tables.

   a. Make a two-way table.

   b. Find and interpret the marginal frequencies for the survey.

   c. For each hair color, what percent of the students in the survey are female? male? Organize the results in a two-way table.

Hair Color of Female Classmates			
Red	Blonde	Brunette	Black
3	15	41	33

Hair Color of Male Classmates			
Red	Blonde	Brunette	Black
4	21	30	27

9.3 Enrichment and Extension

Two-Way Tables

1. Students were polled about who they are planning to vote for in a student council election. The results are shown in the two-way table.

	Owen	Claire
Boys	35	27
Girls	18	46

    a. How many girls are planning to vote for Claire?

    b. How many boys were polled?

    c. How many students polled are planning to vote for Owen?

    d. Who do you think will win the election? Explain.

2. Out of a class of 20 students, 7 own a dog but not a cat, 5 own a cat but not a dog, and 3 own both a dog and a cat.

    a. Complete a two-way table for the situation.

    b. How many students in the class own a dog?

    c. How many students in the class own *neither* a dog *nor* a cat?

3. Two hundred people were surveyed about a book and the movie based on the book.

	Have read the book	Have not read the book
Have seen the movie	115	57
Have not seen the movie	7	?

    a. Complete the two-way table for the situation.

    b. How many people surveyed have seen the movie?

    c. What percent of people surveyed have not read the book?

4. In a class of 25 students, there are 10 girls who play soccer and 4 boys who do not. How many boys play soccer if there are 14 girls in the class? Make a two-way table to help you answer the question.

9.3 Puzzle Time

What Do You Get When You Cross A Snake And A Kangaroo?

Write the letter of each answer in the box containing the exercise number.

You randomly survey students in your school about whether they have access to the Internet at home. You display the two categories of data in the two-way table.

		Internet	
		Yes	No
Grade	6th	30	6
	7th	28	3
	8th	35	7

Answers	
U.	6
M.	3
P.	42
T.	28
R.	93
O.	30
J.	16
P.	31
U.	36
E.	35
D.	7

1. How many sixth-graders have access to the Internet at home?

2. How many seventh-graders do not have access to the Internet at home?

3. How many eighth-graders have access to the Internet at home?

4. What is the marginal frequency for the number of sixth-graders surveyed?

5. What is the marginal frequency for the number of seventh-graders surveyed?

6. What is the marginal frequency for the number of eighth-graders surveyed?

7. What is the marginal frequency for the number of students surveyed who have access to the Internet at home?

8. What is the marginal frequency for the number of students surveyed who do not have access to the Internet at home?

8	4	2	6		7	1	5	3

List all of the different ways you know to display data.

Which can be used to display a list of values?

Which can be used to display information divided into categories?

Which can be used to display the relationship between two sets of data?

Make a circle graph of the data.

1. A middle school has 390 sixth-graders, 310 seventh-graders, and 300 eighth-graders.

2. The results of a survey in which 20 people were asked to name their favorite color are shown in the table.

Color	blue	red	green	pink	other
People	7	4	3	2	4

Start Thinking!
For use before Lesson 9.4

How are a bar graph and a histogram similar?
How are they different?

How are a line graph and a dot plot similar?
How are they different?

How are a stem-and-leaf plot and box-and-whisker plot similar? How are they different?

Warm Up
For use before Lesson 9.4

1. Analyze and display the data in a way that best describes the data. Explain your choice of display.

Student's Quiz Scores						
Quiz	1	2	3	4	5	6
Grade	82	77	91	88	100	84

9.4 Practice A

Choose an appropriate data display for the situation. Explain your reasoning.

1. the price of a stock over the last 5 years

2. the numbers of breads, rolls, muffins, and cookies baked this week

3. the number of runners in each 10-year age bracket

4. the comparison of city population and the number of fire stations

Explain why the data set is misleading.

5.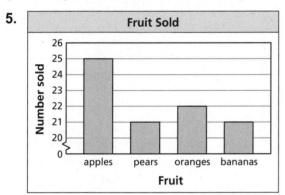

6.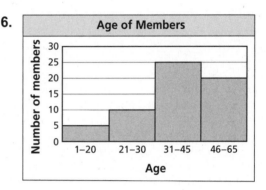

7. An EMT wants to use a data display to show students the relationship between the speed of the vehicle and the number of accidents. Choose an appropriate data display for the situation. Explain your reasoning.

8. What type of data display is appropriate for showing the averages of data over a period of time?

9. The home insurance industry wants to use a data display to show the variability in the costs of insurance for a $200,000 home. Choose an appropriate data display for the situation. Explain your reasoning.

10. A nutritionist wants to use a data display to show kindergarteners the recommended amounts of fruits, vegetables, breads, meats, and dairy that should be consumed each day. Choose an appropriate data display for the situation. Explain your reasoning.

11. The Smithsonian has been collecting data over the last 60 days. They want to use a data display to both put the data in order and to display how the data is distributed. Choose an appropriate data display for the situation. Explain your reasoning.

9.4 Practice B

Choose an appropriate data display for the situation. Explain your reasoning.

1. the heights of girls in grades 6 through 12

2. the numbers of computers offered within $100 price ranges

3. the comparison of the number of students and the number of office staff

4. the percentages of income budgeted for food, utilities, housing, gas, and education

Explain why the data set is misleading.

5.

6.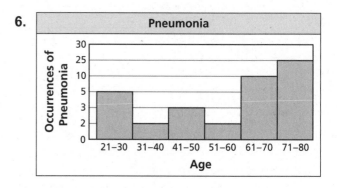

7. You spin a spinner 20 times and want to use a data display to show the number of times each of the numbers 1 through 5 occurs. Choose an appropriate data display for the situation. Explain your reasoning.

8. What type of data display is appropriate for showing the median of the data values?

9. A professor wants to use a data display to show the relationship between class sizes and passing rates for college students. Choose an appropriate data display for the situation. Explain your reasoning.

10. A dentist wants to use a data display to show the percentages of clients using different types of toothbrushes. Choose an appropriate data display for the situation. Explain your reasoning.

11. The new executive was making a presentation to the Board of Directors. He used a pictograph to show the weekly profits made by his department during the last 3 months.

    a. Explain why this would be an inappropriate use of a data display.

    b. Choose an appropriate data display for his situation.

9.4   Enrichment and Extension

Misleading Statistics

When someone quotes a statistic and says, "The average number of …," the word "average" can refer to any of the measures of center, not necessarily the mean of the data.

1. The graph shows the hourly wages of 10 employees in a company. Find the mean, median, and mode of the data set.

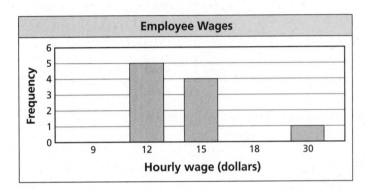

2. The company advertises that the average pay rate for its employees is $15 per hour.

   a. Which measure of center is the company using?

   b. Why do you think the company used this measure of center?

3. A competitor claims that the average pay rate is only $12 per hour, and a newspaper reports that the average pay rate is $13.50 per hour.

   a. Which measure of center is each one using?

   b. Why do you think each one chose the measure of center that was used?

4. Which measure of center best represents the data set?

5. The company has 100 employees. The sample used to gather data was the 10 employees who had been working at the company the longest. Is the sample a good representation of the population as a whole? Explain.

Name _____ Date _____

What Do You Call A Boomerang That Doesn't Come Back?

Write the letter of each answer in the box containing the exercise number.

Choose an appropriate display for the situation.

1. the outcomes of rolling a number cube with sides labeled 1, 2, 3, and 4

2. the percent of votes that each soda received during a taste testing contest

3. the number of students on the cross country team each year

Explain why the data display is misleading.

4.

5.

Answers
T. line graph
K. circle graph
I. The break in the vertical axis makes the differences appear to be greater.
S. Pictures are of different sizes.
C. dot plot

4	3	5	1	2

Name_____ Date_____

Linear Regression, Interpolation, and Extrapolation

In the Chapter 6 Technology Connection, you learned how to use a spreadsheet to display scatter plots. By including a few additional formulas in your spreadsheet, you can find the line of best fit for the data. With this line, you can then predict a value outside the data range (*extrapolation*) or a value within the data range that was not measured (*interpolation*).

EXAMPLE   Use a spreadsheet to find the line of best fit for the data and then predict the values of *y* when *x* = 3 and *x* = 12.

(−3, 10), (−1, 7), (1, 4), (2, 1),
(4, −2), (6, −5), (7, −5), (9, −8)

SOLUTION

Step 1   In a spreadsheet, starting in cells A1 and B1, enter the values of *x* in column A and the values of *y* in column B.

Step 2   To find the line of best fit, you need to find the slope and *y*-intercept that best describes the data. To find the slope, in cell C1 enter the formula =SLOPE(B1:B8, A1:A8) and then press Enter. The cell should display −1.5331.

Step 3   To find the *y*-intercept, in cell D1 enter the formula =INTERCEPT(B1:B8, A1:A8). The cell should display 5.041. So, the line of best fit is $y = -1.5331x + 5.041$.

Step 4   Substitute the *x*-values of 3 and 12 into the equation to interpolate the point (3, 0.4417) and extrapolate the point (12, −13.3562).

In Exercises 1–3, use a spreadsheet.

The chart below shows the number of points *y* scored in a basketball after *x* minutes.

Minutes, *x*	2	5	12	18	20	24	26
Points, *y*	2	6	8	12	16	18	20

1. What is the line of best fit for the data?

2. How many points would you expect after 14 minutes?

3. How many points would you expect after 30 minutes?

Chapter 10

Chapter 10 Exponents and Scientific Notation

Dear Family,

People shop on the Internet, talk to one another using email, and keep digital photo and video albums. Computers represent all this information using numbers.

The number system that computers use is based on powers of 2 and is called the *binary system*. For example, the number 45 is represented as $32 + 8 + 4 + 1 = 2^5 + 2^3 + 2^2 + 2^0$. Try this with your student.

- Find the first eight powers of two, starting with $2^0 = 1$. Write these values on the blanks under the powers of two in the table.

Power	$2^7 =$ _____	$2^6 =$ _____	$2^5 =$ _____	$2^4 =$ _____	$2^3 =$ _____	$2^2 =$ _____	$2^1 =$ _____	$2^0 =$ 1
Digit (0 or 1)								

- Pick any number from 0 to 255. Find the sum of the powers of two that equal your number.

- Put a 1 in the "Digit" row if the power of two is in your number; put a 0 in the "Digit" row if the power of two is not in your number. For example, the digits for 45 are shown below because $45 = 2^5 + 2^3 + 2^2 + 2^0$.

Power	2^7	2^6	2^5	2^4	2^3	2^2	2^1	2^0
Digit	0	0	1	0	1	1	0	1

- Write your number as a binary number. For example, 45 is 00101101.

Computer storage and file sizes are often recorded in kilobytes. A kilobyte is equal to 2^{10} bytes = 1024 bytes. People often round this to 1000 bytes. Ask your student to research what powers of two correspond to megabyte, gigabyte, and terabyte. Find the following information on the Internet or in the library.

- How many kilobytes does a typical page of text use?

- How many megabytes does a typical digital photo use?

- How many gigabytes does one minute of video typically use? How does video compare to audio?

Understanding powers helps make computer terms a *bit* more familiar!

Capítulo 10 — Exponentes y Notación Científica

Estimada Familia:

Las personas compran por Internet, conversan entre sí usando el correo electrónico y tienen álbumes de videos y fotos digitales. Las computadoras representan toda esta información usando números.

El sistema numérico que las computadoras usan se basa en potencias de 2 y se llama *sistema binario*. Por ejemplo, el número 45 se representa como $32 + 8 + 4 + 1 = 2^5 + 2^3 + 2^2 + 2^0$. Intente hacer esto con su estudiante.

- Encuentren las primeras ocho potencias de dos, empezando con $2^0 = 1$. Escriban estos valores en los espacios en blanco bajo las potencias de dos en la tabla

Potencia	$2^7 =$ ___	$2^6 =$ ___	$2^5 =$ ___	$2^4 =$ ___	$2^3 =$ ___	$2^2 =$ ___	$2^1 =$ ___	$2^0 =$ 1
Dígito (0 ó 1)								

- Escojan cualquier número entre 0 y 255. Encuentren la suma de las potencias de dos que equivalen a su número.

- Coloquen un 1 en la fila de "Dígito" si la potencia de dos se encuentra en su número; coloquen un 0 en la fila de "Dígito" si la potencia de dos no se encuentra en su número. Por ejemplo, los dígitos de 45 se muestran a continuación porque $45 = 2^5 + 2^3 + 2^2 + 2^0$.

Potencia	2^7	2^6	2^5	2^4	2^3	2^2	2^1	2^0
Dígito	0	0	1	0	1	1	0	1

- Escriban su número como número binario. Por ejemplo, 45 es 00101101.

La capacidad de almacenamiento de una computadora y los tamaños de los archivos a menudo se registran en kilobytes. Un kilobyte equivale a 2^{10} bytes = 1024 bytes. A menudo, la gente redondea esto a 1000 bytes. Pida a su estudiante que investigue qué potencias de dos corresponden a megabyte, gigabyte y terabyte. Encuentren la siguiente información en la Internet o en la biblioteca.

- ¿Cuántos kilobytes usa una hoja de texto común?

- ¿Cuántos megabytes usa una fotografía digital común?

- ¿Cuántos gigabytes usa un minuto de video común? ¿Cómo se puede comparar el video con el audio?

¡Comprender las potencias permitirá que se familiaricen un *poco* más con los términos de computación!

When have you used exponents before?

What is another way to say "x to the second power?" Why do you think it is called that?

What is another way to say "x to the third power?" Why do you think it is called that?

Find the product.

1. $5 \times 5 \times 5$

2. $10 \times 10 \times 10$

3. $(-3) \times (-3) \times (-3)$

4. $10 \times 10 \times 10 \times 10 \times 10$

5. $4 \times 4 \times 4 \times 4$

6. $(-2) \times (-2) \times (-2) \times (-2)$

Use the nursery rhyme on page 411 of your textbook to guide you in writing your own "power poem."

Lesson 10.1 Warm Up
For use before Lesson 10.1

Write the product using exponents.

1. $2 \cdot 2 \cdot 2$

2. $(-7) \cdot (-7)$

3. $\dfrac{2}{3} \cdot \dfrac{2}{3} \cdot \dfrac{2}{3} \cdot \dfrac{2}{3} \cdot \dfrac{2}{3}$

4. $\left(-\dfrac{1}{6}\right) \cdot \left(-\dfrac{1}{6}\right) \cdot \left(-\dfrac{1}{6}\right)$

5. $11 \cdot 11 \cdot 11 \cdot 11 \cdot 11 \cdot 11 \cdot 11$

6. $\left(-\dfrac{1}{4}\right) \cdot \left(-\dfrac{1}{4}\right) \cdot \left(-\dfrac{1}{4}\right) \cdot \left(-\dfrac{1}{4}\right)$

Name_____ Date_____

10.1 Practice A

Write the product using exponents.

1. $6 \cdot 6 \cdot 6 \cdot 6 \cdot 6$

2. $(-2) \cdot (-2) \cdot (-2)$

3. $\dfrac{2}{3} \cdot \dfrac{2}{3} \cdot \dfrac{2}{3} \cdot \dfrac{2}{3}$

4. $(-1.2) \cdot (-1.2) \cdot (-1.2)$

5. $\dfrac{1}{5} \cdot \dfrac{1}{5} \cdot x \cdot x \cdot x$

6. $10 \cdot 10 \cdot (-n) \cdot (-n) \cdot (-n)$

7. $(-5) \cdot (-5) \cdot (-5) \cdot (-5) \cdot y \cdot y \cdot y \cdot y \cdot y$

Evaluate the expression.

8. 9^2

9. -5^4

10. $(-3)^4$

11. $\left(\dfrac{1}{4}\right)^3$

12. Write the prime factorization of 500 using exponents.

Evaluate the expression.

13. $7 + (-2) \cdot 3^2$

14. $\left(15^2 - 5 \cdot 4^2\right) \div 5$

15. $\left| \dfrac{1}{3}\left(2^3 - \dfrac{10^2}{5}\right) \right|$

16. $\dfrac{3}{2}\left(4^3 - 2^2 \cdot 3^2\right)$

17. There are 5 posts supporting the guard rail for the steps to your home. The tallest post is 3 feet tall. The height of each of the other posts is $\dfrac{5}{6}$ the height of the next larger post.

    a. Write an expression for the height of the shortest post.

    b. What is the height of the shortest post?

18. You ran 4 miles. Rob ran half as far as you. Tim ran half as far as Rob. Nicole ran half as far as Tim.

    a. Write an expression for how far Nicole ran.

    b. How far did Nicole run?

Name_____ Date _____

Write the product using exponents.

1. $4 \cdot 4 \cdot 4 \cdot 4 \cdot 4 \cdot 4$

2. $(-12) \cdot (-12) \cdot (-12) \cdot (-12) \cdot (-12)$

3. $-\dfrac{3}{7} \cdot \dfrac{3}{7} \cdot \dfrac{3}{7}$

4. $\left(-\dfrac{3}{7}\right) \cdot \left(-\dfrac{3}{7}\right) \cdot \left(-\dfrac{3}{7}\right)$

5. $(-9) \cdot (-9) \cdot (-9) \cdot (-9) \cdot x \cdot x \cdot x$

6. $25 \cdot 25 \cdot 25 \cdot 25 \cdot (-p) \cdot (-p) \cdot (-p) \cdot (-p) \cdot (-p)$

7. $(-2) \cdot (-2) \cdot x \cdot x \cdot x \cdot y \cdot y \cdot y \cdot y$

Evaluate the expression.

8. 7^3

9. -4^4

10. $(-4)^4$

11. $\left(\dfrac{2}{5}\right)^3$

12. Write the prime factorization of 1323 using exponents.

Evaluate the expression.

13. $280 - (-3) \cdot (-5)^3$

14. $\left(20^2 - 3^3 \cdot 8^2\right) \div 16$

15. $\dfrac{2}{3}\left(16^2 - 17^2\right)$

16. $\left| \dfrac{1}{5}\left(\dfrac{6^3}{3^3} - 2^3 \right) \right|$

17. Bed A is 7 feet long. Bed B is $\dfrac{7}{8}$ as long as bed A. Bed C is $\dfrac{7}{8}$ as long as bed B. Bed D is $\dfrac{7}{8}$ as long as bed C.

    a. Write an expression for the length of bed D.

    b. What is the length of bed D?

10.1 Enrichment and Extension

The Sierpinski Triangle

A geometric pattern is formed by multiplying by the same number at each step. For example, the numbers 1, 2, 4, 8, 16, … form a geometric pattern because each number is twice the previous number.

The Sierpinski Triangle is constructed using the pattern below.

Start

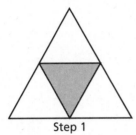
Step 1

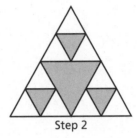
Step 2

•••

1. Describe the pattern between steps.

2. Draw the next step in the pattern.

3. Complete the table.

Step	White Triangles	Gray Triangles
0	1	0
1	3	1
2		
3		
4		

4. Describe the pattern in the number of white triangles at each step.

5. Describe the pattern in the number of gray triangles at each step.

6. How many white triangles will there be at the ninth step? Write your answer using exponents.

Name _____ Date _____

10.1 Puzzle Time

How Does A Bee Part His Hair?

Write the letter of each answer in the box containing the exercise number.

Evaluate the expression.

1. 3^3

2. -4^5

3. $(-2)^5$

4. $(-7)^4$

5. $\left(\dfrac{1}{5}\right)^3$

6. $\left(-\dfrac{1}{3}\right)^5$

7. $-\left(\dfrac{1}{4}\right)^3$

8. $\left|-\left(\dfrac{1}{6}\right)^3\right|$

9. $7^3 - 5^4$

10. $4 \cdot 3^4 + 6$

11. $2\left(11^3 - 10^3\right)$

12. $\dfrac{1}{8}\left(4^6 - 4^3\right)$

13. $\left|6^3 - 7^3\right|$

14. $\left|9^2 + (-9)^3\right|$

15. You are sending a package in the mail. The box is a cube measuring 14 inches on all sides. How many cubic inches is the package?

16. You sent an email to 8 friends. They each forwarded the email to 8 friends. And those friends each forwarded the email to 8 friends. The chain of emails is represented by the expression $8 + 8^2 + 8^3$. How many people were sent your email?

Answers

S. $-\dfrac{1}{243}$

T. -282

C. 584

I. -1024

E. 662

O. $\dfrac{1}{125}$

I. 27

O. 504

H. 330

B. 2744

W. $\dfrac{1}{216}$

H. 2401

H. 127

Y. 648

M. $-\dfrac{1}{64}$

N. -32

8	2	9	4		10	1	6		13	5	3	11	14	16	12	7	15

314 Big Ideas Math Blue
Resources by Chapter

Activity 10.2 Start Thinking!

For use before Activity 10.2

Explain why exponents are a useful convention.

Give an example of a variable expression that is much easier to write using exponents than not using them.

Activity 10.2 Warm Up

For use before Activity 10.2

Evaluate the expression.

1. 3^5

2. 5^4

3. 10^6

4. $(-4)^3$

5. $(-3)^2$

6. $(-2)^5$

In Activity 10.2, you found the rule for finding the product of powers: $a^m \cdot a^n = a^{m+n}$.

Which of the following expressions can be simplified using the product of powers rule?

$2^6 \cdot 2^7$ $3^2 \cdot 4^2$ $(-2)^2 \cdot (-2)^{12}$

$c^3 \cdot c^4$ $x^3 \cdot y^1$ $a^2 \cdot 4^2$

Simplify the expression. Write your answer as a power.

1. $2^4 \cdot 2^3$

2. $7^5 \cdot 7^7$

3. $\left(\dfrac{1}{2}\right)^2 \cdot \left(\dfrac{1}{2}\right)^5$

4. $\left(-\dfrac{3}{5}\right)^3 \cdot \left(-\dfrac{3}{5}\right)^3$

5. $x^5 \cdot x^{11}$

6. $y^3 \cdot y$

Name_____ Date _____

Simplify the expression. Write your answer as a power.

1. $2^3 \cdot 2^2$

2. $9^6 \cdot 9^8$

3. $(-7)^3 \cdot (-7)^5$

4. $\left(\dfrac{5}{8}\right)^{10} \cdot \left(\dfrac{5}{8}\right)^2$

5. $c \cdot c^5$

6. $q^4 \cdot q^4$

7. $\left(-\dfrac{4}{9}\right)^2 \cdot \left(-\dfrac{4}{9}\right)^5$

8. $(4.7)^3 \cdot (4.7)^2$

9. $\left(3^2\right)^3$

10. $\left(k^5\right)^{10}$

11. $\left(\left(\dfrac{1}{2}\right)^4\right)^3$

12. $\left((9.2)^3\right)^6$

Simplify the expression.

13. $(4n)^2$

14. $(-2w)^5$

15. $\left(\dfrac{1}{3}p\right)^4$

16. $(2.5j)^3$

17. $(ab)^{18}$

18. $3^2\left(3 \cdot 3^4\right)$

19. Is $3^2 \cdot 4^2 = 12^4$? Evaluate each side of the equation to explain your answer.

20. The volume of a sphere is $V = \dfrac{4}{3}\pi r^3$ and the relationship between

   the radius r and the diameter d is $r = \dfrac{d}{2}$.

   a. Find the volume of the sphere in terms of the diameter d and simplify the expressions.

   b. What is the volume of the sphere when the diameter is $\dfrac{2}{3}$ centimeter?

10.2 Practice B

Simplify the expression. Write your answer as a power.

1. $8^3 \cdot 8^7$

2. $(-16)^5 \cdot (-16)^{21}$

3. $\left(-\dfrac{5}{9}\right)^5 \cdot \left(-\dfrac{5}{9}\right)^5$

4. $\left(\dfrac{1}{15}\right)^{12} \cdot \left(\dfrac{1}{15}\right)$

5. $q^7 \cdot q^9$

6. $(13.2)^6 \cdot (13.2)^2$

7. $(-7.4)^9 \cdot (-7.4)^{12}$

8. $\left(9^3\right)^3$

9. $\left(d^2\right)^6$

10. $\left(2.9^3\right)^6$

11. $\left(\left(\dfrac{5}{8}\right)^2\right)^3$

12. $\left(\left(-\dfrac{2}{9}\right)^3\right)^5$

Simplify the expression.

13. $(-2p)^4$

14. $\left(\dfrac{1}{5}k\right)^3$

15. $(1.4c)^3$

16. $(mn)^8$

17. $\left(3^2\right)^4 - 3^5 \cdot 3$

18. $10\left(\dfrac{1}{5}v\right)^3$

19. The volume of a right circular cylinder is $V = \pi r^2 h$. The relationship between the height h of a given right circular cylinder and the radius r is
$r = \dfrac{2}{3}h.$

   a. Find the volume of the right circular cylinder in terms of the height h and simplify the expression.

   b. What is the volume of the right circular cylinder when the height is $\dfrac{3}{4}$ inch?

Find the value of x in the equation without evaluating the power.

20. $3^2 \cdot 3^x = 3^{12}$

21. $\left(5^x\right)^4 = 5^{24}$

10.2 Enrichment and Extension

Compound Exponents

Compound exponents have the form a^{m^n}. They are evaluated from the top down.

Example: Simplify 4^{3^2}.

$$4^{3^2} = 4^{\left(3^2\right)} \qquad \text{Rewrite.}$$
$$= 4^9 \qquad \text{Simplify.}$$
$$= 262{,}144 \qquad \text{Evaluate.}$$

Simplify the expression.

1. x^{4^3} **2.** y^{3^4} **3.** a^{11^2} **4.** b^{9^3}

Compound exponents are used in Fermat numbers. Fermat numbers have the form $2^{2^n} + 1$ and are used in number theory and computational algorithms.

5. Complete the table.

n	2^n	2^{2^n}	Fermat number
1	2	4	5
2			
3			
4			

6. What pattern do you notice in the 2^{2^n} column?

7. Would 3^{2^n} have the same pattern? Explain.

8. Which do you think would grow faster, 2^{2^n} or 2^{n^2}?

10.2 Puzzle Time

Did You Hear About...

A	B	C	D	E	F
G	H	I	J	K	L
M	N				

Complete each exercise. Find the answer in the answer column. Write the word under the answer in the box containing the exercise letter.

$-4c^5$ **NOTES**
2058 **KEYS**
$-1024c^5$ **BECAUSE**
3^{24} **HOW**
6^{10} **PIANO**
$8a^3$ **DOOR**
$\left(\dfrac{4}{5}\right)^8$ **WHO**
$\dfrac{16}{81}m^4$ **OF**
$6 \cdot 10^7$ **STUCK**
$(-8)^{30}$ **THE**

Simplify the expression. Write your answer as a power.

A. $4 \cdot 4^5$

B. $6^3 \cdot 6^7$

C. $(-3)^8 \cdot (-3)^3$

D. $\left(\dfrac{4}{5}\right)^2 \cdot \left(\dfrac{4}{5}\right)^6$

E. $\left(7^3\right)^5$

F. $\left((-8)^{10}\right)^3$

Simplify the expression.

G. $(8a)^3$

H. $(-4c)^5$

I. $(1.5r)^2$

J. $\left(\dfrac{2}{3}m\right)^4$

K. $3^2 \cdot 3^4 - 4^4$

L. $7 \cdot \left(7^3 - 7^2\right)$

M. $\left(\dfrac{1}{3}\right)^4 \cdot \left(9^3\right)^2$

N. The budget for a remake of a movie is 100 times the budget of the original movie. The original movie's budget was $6 \cdot 10^5$ dollars. What is the budget of the remake? Express your answer as a power.

$2.25r^2$ **ONE**
$(-3)^{11}$ **TEACHER**
$1.5r^2$ **CLASS**
7^{15} **CALLED**
6561 **GOT**
$512a^3$ **LOCKSMITH**
$\dfrac{2}{3}m^4$ **SHE**
$\left(\dfrac{4}{5}\right)^{12}$ **ARE**
4^6 **THE**
473 **HER**

Activity 10.3 Start Thinking!

For use before Activity 10.3

You have learned about the Product of Powers Property. What does the property state?

There is a related property called the Quotient of Powers Property. What do you think it might state?

Activity 10.3 Warm Up

For use before Activity 10.3

Write the power as repeated multiplication.

1. 5^4

2. 7^3

3. 6^7

4. $(-4)^3$

5. $(-3)^5$

6. $(-1)^3$

Start Thinking!
For use before Lesson 10.3

Scott learned about the Quotient of Powers Property in math class, but he is not convinced that it is helpful. For example, he thinks that it is just as easy to simplify $\dfrac{2^5}{2^2}$ by calculating $2^5 = 32$ and dividing by $2^2 = 4$ to get 8. Do you agree or disagree with Scott? Give reasons to support your answer.

Lesson 10.3

Warm Up
For use before Lesson 10.3

Simplify the expression. Write your answer as a power.

1. $\dfrac{5^9}{5^6}$

2. $\dfrac{4^8}{4^4}$

3. $\dfrac{2.5^5}{2.5^2}$

4. $\dfrac{10.1^7}{10.1^3}$

5. $\dfrac{(-5)^{12}}{(-5)^{10}}$

6. $\dfrac{(-2)^7}{(-2)^6}$

10.3 Practice A

Simplify the expression. Write your answer as a power.

1. $\dfrac{3^8}{3^6}$

2. $\dfrac{10^{11}}{10^3}$

3. $\dfrac{(-4)^5}{(-4)^4}$

4. $\dfrac{(5.6)^{15}}{(5.6)^9}$

5. $\dfrac{p^{13}}{p^{11}}$

6. $\dfrac{(-0.7)^{25}}{(-0.7)^{12}}$

7. $\dfrac{s^{28}}{s^7}$

8. $\dfrac{\pi^6}{\pi}$

9. A personal computer developed in the 1980s had approximately 2^{18} bytes of memory. Today a laptop has 1 gigabyte $= 2^{30}$ bytes of memory. How many times more memory does today's laptop have than the personal computer from the 1980s?

Simplify the expression. Write your answer as a power.

10. $\dfrac{6^3 \bullet 6^7}{6^4}$

11. $\dfrac{3^4 \bullet 3^5}{3 \bullet 3^2}$

12. $\dfrac{(-0.5)^8 \bullet (-0.5)^5}{(-0.5)^6 \bullet (-0.5)^2}$

13. $\dfrac{m^{14}}{m^{10}} \bullet \dfrac{m^5}{m^2}$

Simplify the expression.

14. $\dfrac{5^4 \bullet n^4}{5^2}$

15. $\dfrac{x^5 \bullet z^4}{x^2 \bullet z^2}$

16. $\dfrac{c^6 \bullet d^{10} \bullet 2^6}{d^5 \bullet 2^3}$

17. $\dfrac{a^{12}b^8}{a^{10}b^5}$

Find the value of *x* in the equation without evaluating the power.

18. $\dfrac{5^9}{5^x} = 625$

19. $\dfrac{3^7 \bullet 3^x}{3^6} = 9$

10.3 Practice B

Simplify the expression. Write your answer as a power.

1. $\dfrac{12^{20}}{12^{9}}$

2. $\dfrac{7.6^{13}}{7.6^{3}}$

3. $\dfrac{(-9)^{15}}{(-9)^{3}}$

4. $\dfrac{(-8.5)^{11}}{(-8.5)^{10}}$

5. $\dfrac{u^{33}}{u^{11}}$

6. $\dfrac{\pi^{9}}{\pi^{4}}$

7. $\dfrac{(-1000)^{13}}{(-1000)^{8}}$

8. $\dfrac{t^{21}}{t^{19}}$

9. One kilometer equals 10^{3} meters. One terameter equals 10^{12} meters. How many times larger is a terameter than a kilometer?

Simplify the expression. Write your answer as a power.

10. $\dfrac{11^{7} \bullet 11^{10}}{11^{4} \bullet 11^{2}}$

11. $\dfrac{2.5^{8} \bullet 2.5^{3}}{2.5 \bullet 2.5^{4}}$

12. $\dfrac{(-7.9)^{15} \bullet (-7.9)^{9}}{(-7.9)^{12} \bullet (-7.9)^{7}}$

13. $\dfrac{b^{35}}{b^{20}} \bullet \dfrac{b^{15}}{b^{10}}$

Simplify the expression.

14. $\dfrac{4^{8} \bullet m^{7} \bullet n^{4}}{4^{5} \bullet m^{2}}$

15. $\dfrac{r^{12} \bullet s^{7} \bullet t^{9}}{r^{9} \bullet s^{3}}$

16. $\dfrac{p^{18} q^{11}}{p^{10} q^{8}}$

17. $\dfrac{3^{5} a^{17} b^{21}}{3^{4} a^{15} b^{12}}$

Find the value of x in the equation without evaluating the power.

18. $\dfrac{9^{7}}{9^{x}} = 729$

19. $\dfrac{2^{12} \bullet 2^{x}}{2^{10}} = 32$

Name_____ Date_____

10.3 Enrichment and Extension

Number Search

Émile Borel was a French mathematician who studied probability theory and randomness. He developed a theory that if monkeys randomly hit the keys of typewriters, over a long period of time, one would eventually by chance type the play *Hamlet* by William Shakespeare.

Evaluate each expression. Circle the corresponding answer in the grid. Answers may read vertically, horizontally, diagonally, backwards, or forwards, but always in a straight line. When you have finished, put the unused numbers in the blanks in order, reading left to right and top to bottom.

Question: What is the probability of one monkey randomly typing *Hamlet* on the first try?

5	7	8	1	9	4	3
3	2	6	0	7	6	2
1	4	5	3	5	8	1
5	0	6	2	9	0	4
2	7	7	0	4	8	1
8	0	4	3	6	7	9
7	9	1	2	4	0	5

Answer: About __ in (__ __)¯¯¯¯¯

1. $2^3 + 3^2 + 753$

2. $(2^2)^2 \cdot 5^2 + 6^2$

3. $95^2 + 10^2 - 1^2$

4. $31^2 - 3^2 \cdot 2$

5. $26^2 + 27^2 + 3^2 - 2$

6. $3^4 + 2^2$

7. $7^3 + 3$

8. $5(5)^3 + 2(5^3)$

9. $\dfrac{9^4 + 19 - (-7)^3}{7}$

10. $\dfrac{1}{2}(6^4 - 9^2 - 1)$

11. $(7 \cdot 2^2)^2 \cdot 10 - 15$

12. $\dfrac{10^5 + 10^4}{2} + 2 \cdot 10^3 + 21^2 - 3 \cdot 2^2 - 2^2$

Name _____ Date _____

10.3 Puzzle Time

What Do You Give A Dog That Loves Computers?

Write the letter of each answer in the box containing the exercise number.

Simplify the expression. Write the answer as a power.

1. $\dfrac{8^{12}}{8^6}$

2. $\dfrac{3^{24}}{3^{15}}$

3. $\dfrac{(-7)^{14}}{(-7)^4}$

4. $\dfrac{2.8^7}{2.8^4}$

5. $\dfrac{\pi^{12}}{\pi^5}$

6. $\dfrac{x^8}{x^3}$

7. $\dfrac{3^4 \cdot 3^5}{3^2 \cdot 3^2}$

8. $\dfrac{8^{15}}{8^7 \cdot 8}$

9. $\dfrac{\pi^5 \cdot \pi^9}{\pi^3 \cdot \pi^3}$

10. $\dfrac{x^{14} \cdot x^5}{x^7}$

11. $\dfrac{(-7)^3 \cdot (-7)^9}{(-7)^2 \cdot (-7)}$

12. $\dfrac{2.8^{15} \cdot 2.8^8}{2.8^9 \cdot 2.8^6}$

13. There are about $4 \cdot 10^5$ known species of beetles. The number of known species of caddis flies is about 10^4. How many times more species of beetles are there than caddis flies?

14. The area of the Pacific Ocean is approximately $6.4 \cdot 10^7$ square miles. The area of the Gulf of Mexico is approximately 10^5 square miles. How many times greater is the area of the Pacific Ocean than the area of the Gulf of Mexico?

Answers

Y. 2.8^3

D. x^{12}

I. π^7

D. $(-7)^9$

E. x^5

E. 3^9

T. 40

G. 8^7

O. $(-7)^{10}$

S. π^8

S. 8^6

K. 640

T. 3^5

G. 2.8^8

11	3	8	12	4		10	5	9	14	6	7	13	2	1

What do you think it means for a number to be raised to the **zero power**?

Use your calculator to see if you are right.

Simplify the expression. Write your answer as a power.

1. $\dfrac{5^4 \cdot 5^2}{5^3}$

2. $\dfrac{2^{11} \cdot 2^5}{2^{13}}$

3. $\dfrac{4^5 \cdot 4^3}{4^2}$

4. $\dfrac{a^{13} \cdot a^{11}}{a^{12}}$

5. $\dfrac{c^9 \cdot c^5}{c^{10}}$

6. $\dfrac{n^7 \cdot n^{14}}{n^{11}}$

Can a number raised to a negative power ever be greater than 1? If so, give an example. If not, explain why not.

Can a number raised to a negative power ever be less than 0? If so, give an example. If not, explain why not.

Evaluate the expression.

1. $\dfrac{3^6}{3^6}$

2. $7^0 \cdot 7^2$

3. $\dfrac{-2^6}{-2^6}$

4. $5^3 \cdot 5^{-3}$

5. $9^0 \cdot 9^3$

6. $(-3)^3 \cdot (-3)^{-3}$

10.4 Practice A

Evaluate the expression.

1. 3^{-4}

2. 32^0

3. $\dfrac{8^3}{8^5}$

4. $\dfrac{(-9)^4}{(-9)^7}$

5. $5^{-12} \cdot 5^{12}$

6. $\dfrac{1}{4^{-5}} \cdot \dfrac{1}{4^8}$

7. $6^{-1} \cdot 6^{-2}$

8. $\dfrac{2^6}{2^{-8} \cdot 2^{10}}$

9. One terameter equals 10^{12} meters. One micrometer equals 10^{-6} meter. One nanometer equals 10^{-9} meter.

   a. Find the product of one terameter and one micrometer, using only positive exponents.

   b. Find the quotient of one terameter and one micrometer, using only positive exponents.

   c. Find the product of one terameter and one nanometer, using only positive exponents.

   d. Find the quotient of one terameter and one nanometer, using only positive exponents.

   e. Find the quotient of one nanometer and one terameter, using only positive exponents.

   f. Find the quotient of one nanometer and one micrometer, using only positive exponents.

   g. Find the product of one nanometer and one micrometer, using only positive exponents.

Simplify. Write the expression using only positive exponents.

10. $8x^{-3}$

11. $5^{-3} \cdot m^6$

12. $\dfrac{7p^5}{p^{-1}}$

13. $\dfrac{10t^{-5}}{t^{-2}}$

14. $\dfrac{15d^4}{3d^9}$

15. $6w^{-2} \cdot 4w^2$

10.4 Practice B

Evaluate the expression.

1. 5^{-3}

2. $(-8)^0$

3. $\dfrac{6^{-3}}{6^{-5}}$

4. $\dfrac{15^{-4}}{15^{-4}}$

5. $10^{-1} \cdot 10^{-2}$

6. $\dfrac{1}{3^{-4}} \cdot \dfrac{1}{3^6}$

7. $27^{-18} \cdot 27^{18}$

8. $\dfrac{4^{-7}}{4^2 \cdot 4^{-5}}$

9. One millimeter equals 10^{-3} meter. One picometer equals 10^{-12} meter. One femtometer equals 10^{-15} meter.

    a. Find the product of one millimeter and one picometer, using only positive exponents.

    b. Find the quotient of one picometer and one millimeter, using only positive exponents.

    c. Find the product of one millimeter and one femtometer, using only positive exponents.

    d. Find the quotient of one femtometer and one picometer, using only positive exponents.

    e. Find the quotient of one picometer and one femtometer, using only positive exponents.

    f. Find the quotient of one millimeter and one femtometer, using only positive exponents.

    g. Find the product of one picometer and one femtometer, using only positive exponents.

Simplify. Write the expression using only positive exponents.

10. $\dfrac{14u^{-4}}{7u^8}$

11. $\dfrac{18w^{-8}}{w^{-5}}$

12. $y^5 \cdot z^{-3}$

13. $\dfrac{2^{-3} \cdot a^0 \cdot b^5}{b^{-4}}$

10.4 Enrichment and Extension

Exponential Graphs

An exponential equation has the form $y = a^x$,
where a is a positive number. For example,

$y = 2^x$ and $y = \left(\dfrac{3}{4}\right)^x$ are exponential equations.

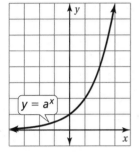

$y = a^x$

1. Is the graph of $y = 2^x$ linear? Explain your reasoning.

2. What is the y-intercept of $y = 2^x$?

3. Does $y = 2^x$ have an x-intercept?

4. Copy and complete the table for

   $y = \left(\dfrac{1}{2}\right)^x$ and plot the points to graph it.

   Describe how the graph of $y = \left(\dfrac{1}{2}\right)^x$

   compares to the graph of $y = 2^x$.

5. What is the y-intercept of $y = \left(\dfrac{1}{2}\right)^x$?

6. Will all exponential equations have the
   same y-intercept? Explain your reasoning.

7. What value of a will make the graph linear?

x	y
−3	
−2	
−1	
0	
1	
2	
3	

Name _____   Date _____

 **10.4 Puzzle Time**

What Happened When The Tree Saw The Ghost?

Circle the letter of each correct answer in the boxes below. The circled letters
will spell out the answer to the riddle.

Evaluate the expression.

1. $7^{-5} \cdot 7^3$

2. $5^2 \cdot 5^{-6}$

3. $\dfrac{2^7}{2^{10}}$

4. $\dfrac{6^0}{6^3}$

5. $\dfrac{(-8)^3}{(-8)^5}$

6. $\dfrac{(2.2)^7}{(2.2)^9}$

7. $\dfrac{4^5}{4^4} \cdot \dfrac{4^8}{4^{13}}$

8. $\dfrac{(-9)^3}{(-9)^7 \cdot (-9)^{-2}}$

Simplify the expression using only positive exponents.

9. $3^{-2} a^4$

10. $12^{-1} t^{-3}$

11. $\dfrac{b^4}{5^{-2} b^8}$

12. $\dfrac{14 r^8}{2 r^{15}}$

13. $\dfrac{x^5 \cdot y^6}{2^{-2} \cdot x^0 \cdot y^9}$

14. $\dfrac{6 \cdot f^{-4} \cdot g^2}{2 \cdot f^{-4} \cdot g^{-1}}$

H	A	I	S	T	R	M	E	W	L	A	N	S	U	V	D	Y
8	$\dfrac{4x^4}{y^2}$	$\dfrac{1}{12t^3}$	$\dfrac{1}{16}$	$\dfrac{1}{49}$	$\dfrac{1}{9a^4}$	$\dfrac{1}{36}$	$7r^7$	$\dfrac{1}{4.84}$	$3fg^3$	$\dfrac{1}{216}$	81	$\dfrac{1}{625}$	$\dfrac{x^5}{4y^3}$	$\dfrac{25}{b^2}$	49	$-\dfrac{1}{64}$

I	P	T	E	G	T	R	O	I	S	F	Q	I	K	E	B	D
$\dfrac{12}{t^3}$	$3g^3$	$\dfrac{1}{125}$	$\dfrac{1}{8}$	4.84	$\dfrac{25}{b^4}$	$\dfrac{1}{81}$	-8	$\dfrac{a^4}{9}$	64	$\dfrac{4x^5}{y^3}$	$\dfrac{3}{fg}$	$\dfrac{1}{64}$	-16	$\dfrac{1}{256}$	$\dfrac{t^3}{12}$	$\dfrac{7}{r^7}$

Activity 10.5 **Start Thinking!**
For use before Activity 10.5

Explain how a scientist might use negative exponents.

Activity 10.5 **Warm Up**
For use before Activity 10.5

Evaluate the expression.

1. 10^3 **2.** 10^{-4} **3.** 10^5

4. 10^{-2} **5.** 10^{10} **6.** 10^{-5}

Use the Internet to find the mass of an electron and the mass of Earth.

Before you begin your research, do you expect that the masses will be given in scientific notation? Why or why not?

Were you correct?

Lesson 10.5 **Warm Up**
For use before Lesson 10.5

Write the number shown on the calculator display in standard form.

1.

4.3E10

2.

1.2E-3

3.

7.33E18

4.

9.365E-14

10.5 Practice A

Write the number shown on the calculator display in standard form.

1.

6.21ᴇ10

2.

5.17ᴇ16

Tell whether the number is written in scientific notation. Explain.

3. 4.375×10^{-8}

4. 62.9×10^{14}

5. 9.897×10^{-15}

6. 0.451×10^{-12}

7. 25×10^{18}

8. 5.1786×10^{-25}

Write the number in standard form.

9. 8×10^{6}

10. 9×10^{-2}

11. 2×10^{3}

12. 5.3×10^{-4}

13. 1.2×10^{8}

14. 7.86×10^{5}

15. The average distance from Earth to the Sun is about 1.5×10^{11} meters. The average distance from Earth to the Moon is about 3.84×10^{8} meters.

   a. Write the distance from Earth to the Sun in standard form.

   b. Write the distance from Earth to the Moon in standard form.

   c. Which is closer to Earth, the *Sun* or the *Moon*?

16. A day is about 8.64×10^{4} seconds.

   a. How many seconds are in 5 days? Write your answer in standard form.

   b. How many seconds are in 1 month (30 days)? Write your answer in standard form.

   c. How many seconds are in 1 year (365 days)? Write your answer in standard form.

   d. How many seconds are in 1 leap year (366 days)? Write your answer in standard form.

   e. What is the difference (in seconds) between 1 year and 1 leap year? Write your answer in both standard form and scientific notation.

10.5 Practice B

Write the number shown on the calculator display in standard form.

1.

8.6E-10

2.

4.39E12

Tell whether the number is written in scientific notation. Explain.

3. 17×10^{15}

4. 3.712×10^{-8}

5. 7.54×10^{21}

6. 0.999×10^{-15}

7. 125.42×10^{-12}

8. 7.65×10^{25}

Write the number in standard form.

9. 5×10^{-4}

10. 1.54×10^{5}

11. 1.78×10^{-6}

12. 9.876×10^{-4}

13. 2.08×10^{7}

14. 3.555×10^{8}

15. The radius of Earth is about 6.38×10^{6} meters. The radius of the Moon is about 1.74×10^{6} meters. The radius of the Sun is about 7×10^{8} meters.

    a. Which is the largest, *Earth*, the *Moon,* or the *Sun*?

    b. Which is the smallest, *Earth*, the *Moon,* or the *Sun*?

    c. Write the radius of Earth in standard form.

    d. Write the radius of the Moon in standard form.

    e. Write the radius of the Sun in standard form.

16. A year is about 3.156×10^{7} seconds.

    a. How many seconds are in 5 years? Write your answer in standard form.

    b. How many seconds are in half a year? Write your answer in standard form.

    c. How many seconds are in 1 month? Write your answer in standard form.

10.5 Enrichment and Extension

Different Bases

The decimal system is a base 10 system. Each place value represents 10 to a power. Computers often use a binary or base 2 system, where each place value represents a power of 2. Some systems use a base 8 or a base 16 system.

To convert a number from a given base into base 10, write the number as a sum of powers of the base and evaluate the expression.

1. Write 30,275 as a sum of powers of 10.

$$\underline{\quad} \bullet 10^4 + \underline{\quad} \bullet 10^3 + \underline{\quad} \bullet 10^2 + \underline{\quad} \bullet 10^1 + \underline{\quad} \bullet 10^0$$

2. The number 1001010 is in base 2. Write the number as a sum of powers of 2.

$$\underline{\quad} \bullet 2^6 + \underline{\quad} \bullet 2^5 + \underline{\quad} \bullet 2^4 + \underline{\quad} \bullet 2^3 + \underline{\quad} \bullet 2^2 + \underline{\quad} \bullet 2^1 + \underline{\quad} \bullet 2^0$$

3. Evaluate the expression in Exercise 2 to convert 1001010 from base 2 to base 10.

4. The number 331 is in base 4.

    a. Powers of what number should appear in your sum?

    b. How many terms will there be in your sum?

    c. Write and evaluate an expression to convert 331 from base 4 into base 10.

5. Use powers of the given base to write each number as a sum of powers of the base. Then evaluate the expression to convert the number to base 10.

    a. The number 22012 is in base 3.

    b. The number 3004 is in base 8.

    c. The number 501 is in base 6.

    d. The number 312 is in base 16.

6. Write 41 in base 2. (A base 2 system uses the digits 0 and 1.)

10.5 Puzzle Time

What Position Did The Ghost Play On The Hockey Team?

Write the letter of each answer in the box containing the exercise number.

1. Which number is written in scientific notation?

   H. 1.8×8^{-5} **I.** 4.2×10^{-8} **J.** 6.5×9^{7}

2. Which number is *not* written in scientific notation?

   S. 5.3×10^{-6} **T.** 6×10^{-6} **U.** 45×10^{8}

3. Which number is *not* written in scientific notation?

   E. 0.9×10^{12} **F.** -8.2×10^{10} **G.** 1×10^{-13}

4. Write 3.54×10^{6} in standard form.

   N. 0.00000354   **O.** 3,540,000   **P.** 354,000,000

5. Write -1.92×10^{-4} in standard form.

   H. −0.000192   **I.** −19,200   **J.** −0.0000192

6. The distance to the Sun is about 9.3×10^{7} miles. What is the distance to the Sun in standard form?

   K. 9,300,000 mi   **L.** 93,000,000 mi   **M.** 930,000,000 mi

7. The population of a country is about 1.32×10^{9}. What is the population of the country in standard form?

   E. 13,200,000,000 people   **F.** 132,000,000 people   **G.** 1,320,000,000 people

7	5	4	2	6	1	3

Start Thinking!
For use before Activity 10.6

Choose a number greater than 1,000,000. Write it in standard form.

Write a list of steps that describe how you would write the number in scientific notation.

Repeat the process for a number less than 0.0009.

Activity 10.6

Warm Up
For use before Activity 10.6

Write the number in standard form.

1. 6×10^3

2. 4×10^{-4}

3. 2×10^5

4. 2.6×10^{-2}

5. 5.25×10^{10}

6. 8.52×10^{-5}

Estimate the population of the world.

Go to *www.census.gov* to find the actual world population.

Write the population in scientific notation. How did you choose to round the number and why?

Write the number in scientific notation.

1. 0.00034

2. 6,750,000

3. 0.00000007

4. 125,000

5. 15,200,000,000

6. 0.000000000917

10.6 Practice A

Write the number in scientific notation.

1. 350,000

2. 0.0004

3. 0.000000000000527

4. 12,500,000

5. 1,900,000,000

6. 0.0000001

7. 5,000,000,000,000

8. 0.00006524

Order the numbers from least to greatest.

9. 3.6×10^8, 6.3×10^8, 3.26×10^8

10. 9.8×10^{-12}, 1.23×10^{-11}, 5.05×10^{-13}

11. 6.18×10^7, 5.6×10^{-7}, 6.8×10^7

12. 4.81×10^{-5}, 4.27×10^{-5}, 4.7×10^{-5}

13. The number of stars in the Milky Way Galaxy has been approximated to be between 200 billion and 400 billion. Write these numbers in scientific notation.

14. The ångström is a unit of length defined to be 0.1 nanometer or 0.0000000001 meter. Write this number in scientific notation.

15. In 2013, the net worth of a businessman was $59,000,000,000.

   a. Write $59,000,000,000 in scientific notation.

   b. As of 2012, the businessman had given over $28,000,000,000 to charity. Write $28,000,000,000 in scientific notation.

   c. In 2002, the businessman's wealth briefly surpassed $101,000,000,000. Write $101,000,000,000 in scientific notation.

16. A pipette is a laboratory instrument that is used to transport a measured volume of liquid. A pipette that dispenses between 1 and 1000 microliters is called a micropipette.

   a. A microliter is equivalent to 0.000001 liter. Write 0.000001 in scientific notation.

   b. One thousand microliters is equivalent to 0.001 liter. Write 0.001 in scientific notation.

Order the numbers from least to greatest.

17. $\dfrac{16}{5}$, 322, 3.2×10^2, 3.2%

18. 5.89×10^3, $\dfrac{589}{1000}$, 0.58

Name _____ Date _____

10.6 Practice B

Write the number in scientific notation.

1. 0.000085

2. 410,000,000

3. 0.0143

4. 134,750,000,000

5. 7,000,000,000,000,000

6. 0.00000000000199

7. 52,400,000,000,000

8. 0.00000006133

Order the numbers from least to greatest.

9. $4.15 \times 10^{14}, 5.4 \times 10^{14}, 4.5 \times 10^{14}$

10. $2.8 \times 10^{-20}, 7.22 \times 10^{-22}, 3.11 \times 10^{-19}$

11. $4.118 \times 10^{-3}, 4.1 \times 10^{-5}, 4.181 \times 10^{-5}$

12. $6.7 \times 10^{-32}, 3.72 \times 10^{32}, 6.17 \times 10^{-32}$

13. The atomic mass of carbon-12 is 0.00000000000000000000001992 kilogram. Write this number in scientific notation.

14. Approximately how many moons would be needed side-by-side to span across the Sun?

Sun

1.392 × 10⁶ km

Moon

3.475 × 10³ km

not drawn to scale

15. Most golf balls have about 250 to 450 dimples. The record holder is a ball with 1070 dimples.

    a. Write 1070 in scientific notation.

    b. In a recent year, it was estimated that 540,000,000 golf balls were sold. Using an average of 350 dimples, how many dimples were on the golf balls sold in that year? Write your answer in scientific notation.

16. The population of a country is about 6,940,000.

    a. Write 6,940,000 in scientific notation.

    b. There are about 17,251 people per square mile in the country. What is the area of the country (in square miles)? Round your answer to the nearest whole number.

Order the numbers from least to greatest.

17. $5\frac{3}{8}, 0.00538, 0.53\%, \frac{538}{1000}$

18. $8.19 \times 10^{-2}, \frac{270}{330}, 0.0082$

10.6 Enrichment and Extension

Avogadro's Number

The mass of an atom is too small to measure with grams or milligrams. Scientists use *atomic mass units* (amu) to describe the mass of an atom. The number of atomic mass units in one gram is a constant known as Avogadro's number.

$$1 \text{ g} \approx 6.022 \times 10^{23} \text{ amu}$$
$$1.661 \times 10^{-24} \text{ g} \approx 1 \text{ amu}$$

1. Copy and complete the table.

Element	Chemical Symbol	Mass (amu)	Mass (g)
Silver	Ag	1.26×10^{25}	
Oxygen	O		28
Platinum	Pt	9.64×10^{24}	
Helium	He	3.01×10^{22}	
Nitrogen	N		34

2. Arrange the chemical symbols in order of increasing mass. What word do the symbols spell?

Name _____ Date _____

10.6 Puzzle Time

If A Man Wears Pajamas What Does A Woman Wear?

Write the letter of each answer in the box containing the exercise number.

1. Write 102,800,000 in scientific notation.

   A. 1.028×10^8 **B.** 1028×10^5 **C.** 1×10^8

2. Write 0.0000522 in scientific notation.

   Q. 5.22×10^5 **R.** 5.22×10^{-4} **S.** 5.22×10^{-5}

3. Write −0.32 in scientific notation.

   A. -3.2×10^{-1} **B.** -3.2×10^0 **C.** -32×10^{-2}

4. Write 420,000,000,000 in scientific notation.

   L. 42×10^{10} **M.** 4.2×10^{11} **N.** 4.2×10^{12}

5. Write 0.000006 in scientific notation.

   A. 6×10^{-6} **B.** 6×10^{-7} **C.** 6×10^{-8}

6. A movie earned $1,845,000,000 at the box office. What is the dollar amount written in scientific notation?

   J. 1.845×10^9 **K.** 18.45×10^8 **L.** 1.845×10^6

7. The volume of a cylinder with radius $r = 1.5 \times 10^{-4}$ inch and height $h = 2.4 \times 10^{-3}$ inch is 0.00000000017 cubic inch. Write the volume of the cylinder in scientific notation.

   L. 1.7×10^{-9} cubic inch   **M.** 1.7×10^{-10} cubic inch   **N.** 1.7×10^{-11} cubic inch

7	5	6	3	4	1	2

Copy the following two numbers.

0.00000001492

1.492×10^{-8}

Which number is easier to copy?

The second number is written in scientific notation. What are some benefits of using scientific notation to write very large or very small numbers?

Tell whether the number is written in scientific notation. Explain.

1. 4.64×10^9 **2.** 0.12×10^{-4}

3. $1.06 \times 10^{0.2}$ **4.** 12.94×10^1

Explain how to write a number in scientific notation. Why is scientific notation used to write numbers?

Evaluate the expression using two different methods. Write your answer in scientific notation.

1. $\left(3.1 \times 10^4\right) + \left(2.3 \times 10^4\right)$

2. $\left(4 \times 10^6\right) + \left(1.7 \times 10^5\right)$

3. $\left(7.5 \times 10^7\right) \times \left(4 \times 10^7\right)$

4. $\left(6.6 \times 10^4\right) \times \left(5 \times 10^3\right)$

Name_____ Date_____

10.7 Practice A

Find the sum or difference. Write your answer in scientific notation.

1. $\left(2 \times 10^{4}\right) + \left(5 \times 10^{4}\right)$

2. $\left(3.5 \times 10^{-3}\right) + \left(1 \times 10^{-3}\right)$

3. $\left(8.3 \times 10^{-5}\right) - \left(4.4 \times 10^{-5}\right)$

4. $\left(7.2 \times 10^{9}\right) - \left(5.8 \times 10^{9}\right)$

5. $\left(7.4 \times 10^{-6}\right) + \left(5 \times 10^{-6}\right)$

6. $\left(7.13 \times 10^{12}\right) + \left(8.04 \times 10^{12}\right)$

Find the product or quotient. Write your answer in scientific notation.

7. $\left(1 \times 10^{5}\right) \times \left(4 \times 10^{2}\right)$

8. $\left(8 \times 10^{5}\right) \div \left(4 \times 10^{5}\right)$

9. $\left(2 \times 10^{-4}\right) \times \left(3 \times 10^{7}\right)$

10. $\left(9 \times 10^{7}\right) \div \left(3 \times 10^{2}\right)$

11. $\left(6 \times 10^{-12}\right) \times \left(7 \times 10^{-9}\right)$

12. $\left(8 \times 10^{5}\right) \times \left(8 \times 10^{5}\right)$

13. $\left(2 \times 10^{-3}\right) \times \left(1.1 \times 10^{2}\right)$

14. $\left(9 \times 10^{-7}\right) \times \left(2.5 \times 10^{3}\right)$

Find the area of the figure. Write your answer in scientific notation.

15.

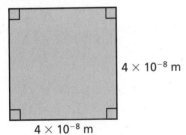

4×10^{-8} m

4×10^{-8} m

16.

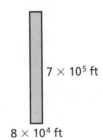

7×10^{5} ft

8×10^{4} ft

17. The table shows the volumes of the three largest giant sequoia trees. Which tree has the greatest volume? How much greater is its volume than each of the other two trees?

Tree Name	Volume (cubic feet)
General Grant	4.66×10^{4}
General Sherman	5.25×10^{4}
Washington	4.785×10^{4}

10.7 Practice B

Find the sum or difference. Write your answer in scientific notation.

1. $\left(1.4 \times 10^2\right) - \left(1.1 \times 10^2\right)$

2. $\left(5.2 \times 10^{-4}\right) - \left(4.58 \times 10^{-4}\right)$

3. $\left(6.4 \times 10^{-2}\right) + \left(4.7 \times 10^{-3}\right)$

4. $\left(5.92 \times 10^{14}\right) - \left(3 \times 10^{12}\right)$

Find the product or quotient. Write your answer in scientific notation.

5. $\left(6 \times 10^{-4}\right) \times \left(4 \times 10^7\right)$

6. $\left(8.4 \times 10^{-4}\right) \div \left(2.1 \times 10^{-6}\right)$

7. $\left(7.5 \times 10^{-5}\right) \div \left(3 \times 10^{-3}\right)$

8. $\left(9 \times 10^8\right) \times \left(3 \times 10^3\right)$

9. $\left(5 \times 10^{-3}\right) \times \left(1.3 \times 10^6\right)$

10. $\left(2.3 \times 10^6\right) \div \left(4.6 \times 10^{-9}\right)$

11. $\left(6.8 \times 10^{-14}\right) \div \left(8.5 \times 10^{10}\right)$

12. $\left(6.1 \times 10^{-6}\right) \times \left(3 \times 10^{-1}\right)$

13. $\left(6 \times 10^{-8}\right) \times \left(3.1 \times 10^{12}\right)$

14. $\left(4 \times 10^{10}\right) \times \left(2.5 \times 10^3\right)$

Find the area of the figure. Write your answer in scientific notation.

15.

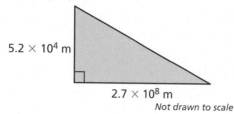

5.2×10^4 m

2.7×10^8 m

Not drawn to scale

16.

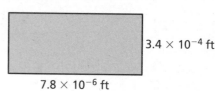

3.4×10^{-4} ft

7.8×10^{-6} ft

Not drawn to scale

17. How many times greater is the total area of Russia than the total area of Finland?

Finland
Total Area $\approx 3.4 \times 10^5$ km^2

Russia
Total Area $\approx 1.7 \times 10^7$ km^2

10.7 Enrichment and Extension

Engineering Notation

Engineering notation is similar to scientific notation except the power of ten can only be a multiple of three. As a result, the factor must be greater than or equal to 1 and less than 1000.

Example: $650,000,000 = 650 \times 10^6$

Example: $0.00000001 = 10 \times 10^{-9}$

You can use the same rules to perform arithmetic operations on numbers written in engineering notation as you did with scientific notation.

$$\textbf{Example: } \left(5.5 \times 10^{-3}\right) - \left(4.8 \times 10^{-3}\right) = (5.5 - 4.8) \times 10^{-3}$$
$$= 0.7 \times 10^{-3}$$
$$= 700 \times 10^{-6}$$

Example: $\left(4.3 \times 10^3\right) \times \left(6.0 \times 10^4\right) = 25.8 \times 10^7 = 258 \times 10^6$

Write the number in engineering notation.

1. 20,500,000

2. 0.000000048

3. 3.41×10^5

4. 8.15×10^{-7}

Evaluate the expression. Write your answer in engineering notation.

5. $\left(17 \times 10^{12}\right) + \left(255 \times 10^{12}\right)$

6. $\left(7.545 \times 10^8\right) + \left(4.55 \times 10^7\right)$

7. $\left(340 \times 10^{-6}\right) - \left(285 \times 10^{-6}\right)$

8. $\left(8.7 \times 10^7\right) - \left(5.5 \times 10^6\right)$

9. $\left(4.8 \times 10^2\right) \times \left(6.9 \times 10^5\right)$

10. $\left(9.2 \times 10^{-4}\right) \times \left(5.7 \times 10^{12}\right)$

11. $\left(4.8 \times 10^4\right) \div \left(2.5 \times 10^7\right)$

12. $\left(7.2 \times 10^8\right) \div \left(1.6 \times 10^{-3}\right)$

13. What is one advantage of expressing numbers in engineering notation?

14. What is one disadvantage of expressing numbers in engineering notation?

10.7 Puzzle Time

What Happened When The Rubber Duckie Fell Into The Bathtub?

Write the letter of each answer in the box containing the exercise number.

Find the sum or difference. Write your answer in scientific notation.

1. $\left(4 \times 10^7\right) + \left(6.1 \times 10^7\right)$

2. $\left(3.12 \times 10^{-5}\right) - \left(1.79 \times 10^{-5}\right)$

3. $\left(5.8 \times 10^{-9}\right) + \left(2.67 \times 10^{-9}\right)$

4. $\left(2.3 \times 10^4\right) - \left(1.1 \times 10^4\right)$

5. $\left(7 \times 10^{-8}\right) + \left(3.48 \times 10^{-5}\right)$

6. $\left(9.6 \times 10^{-3}\right) - \left(7.7 \times 10^{-4}\right)$

Find the product or quotient. Write your answer in scientific notation

7. $\left(6.3 \times 10^{-3}\right) \times \left(2 \times 10^2\right)$

8. $\left(4.1 \times 10^8\right) \div \left(8.2 \times 10^8\right)$

9. $\left(5.7 \times 10^{-6}\right) \times \left(3 \times 10^{-4}\right)$

10. $\left(9.2 \times 10^5\right) \div \left(1.6 \times 10^7\right)$

11. A rectangular table located in the lobby of a middle school has a length of 2.24×10^3 millimeters and a width of 1.54×10^2 millimeters. Find the area of the rectangular table top.

Answers
K. 5.75×10^{-2}
I. 1.33×10^{-5}
P. 5×10^{-1}
E. 8.47×10^{-9}
U. 1.01×10^8
Q. 3.4496×10^5
D. 1.26×10^0
A. 3.487×10^{-5}
U. 1.71×10^{-9}
T. 1.2×10^4
C. 8.83×10^{-3}

2	4		11	9	5	6	10	3	7		1	8

Name_____ Date_____

Operations with Scientific Notation

You can use your calculator and scientific notation to perform operations on large or small numbers.

EXAMPLE Multiply: $63{,}000{,}000{,}000 \times 204$

SOLUTION

Step 1 Rewrite the first number using scientific notation.

$63{,}000{,}000{,}000 = 6.3 \times 10^{10}$

Step 2 Enter the product. Press 6.3 ⌑2nd⌑ [EE] 10 ☒ 204.

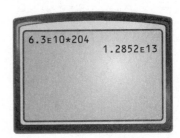

Step 3 Press ⌑ENTER⌑. The product is equal to
1.2852×10^{13} or $12{,}852{,}000{,}000{,}000$.

Find the sum, difference, product, or quotient.

1. $310{,}000{,}000 \times 56{,}000$

2. $0.00000009 \div 0.0005$

3. $\left(5.6 \times 10^{7}\right) + \left(6.6 \times 10^{4}\right)$

4. $\left(1.3 \times 10^{-4}\right) - \left(5.1 \times 10^{-5}\right)$

5. $0.0000075 \times 230{,}000$

6. $44{,}600{,}000{,}000 + 5{,}600{,}000{,}000$

7. $0.00000000558 - 0.0000000026$

8. $\left(9.8 \times 10^{12}\right) \div \left(3.2 \times 10^{3}\right)$

9. When does your calculator display answers using standard notation? When does it display answers using scientific notation? Give examples to support your answers.

Projects

Name_____ Date_____

Objective Draw and analyze similar triangles to predict your height from your stride.

Materials Yardstick, ruler, protractor, calculator

Investigation
- Work in a group of 3. Measure the length of your leg from the ground to your hip.

- Take one normal step and "freeze." Have a member of your group measure the length from the toe on the back foot to the toe on the front foot. This is your *walking stride length*.

- Take one running stride and have someone measure your running stride length.

- Record two measurements for each person in the group.

Data Analysis
1. Sketch an isosceles triangle to represent the length of your legs and your walking stride. Choose a scale, such as 10 inches (actual stride length) to 2 centimeters (stride length in drawing.)

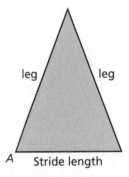

2. Measure $\angle A$.

3. Repeat Steps 1 and 2 for your running stride length.

4. Calculate the ratio $\dfrac{\text{my height}}{\text{leg length}}$. Share your ratio with the members of your group. Find the mean of your group ratios, rounded to the nearest tenth.

5. Gather the measures of $\angle A$ for the walking stride length from the members of your group. Find the mean of these angle measures. Repeat this for the measures of $\angle A$ for the running stride length.

6. You will receive two sets of footprints. Measure the stride lengths. Use the stride lengths, the mean of $\angle A$, and the mean of your group's height : leg length ratio to make a scale drawing for these stride lengths.

7. Measure the leg length on the drawing with a ruler and use your scale to find the actual leg length for these footprints. Calculate the approximate height of the person who left the footprints.

Make a Poster Explain the Investigation. Display your data, scale drawings, and calculations. Describe how you determined the height of the person who made the "mystery" footprints.

Project   Student Grading Rubric
For use after Chapter 2

	Student Score	Teacher Score

Cover Page 10 points

    a. Name (4 points) _____ _____

    b. Class (2 points) _____ _____

    c. Project Name (2 points) _____ _____

    d. Due Date (2 points) _____ _____

Investigation 20 points

    a. Measurements for leg length, walking stride length, and running stride length are shown. (20 points) _____ _____

Data Analysis 120 points

    a. Includes all scale drawings. Drawing are labeled correctly and drawn to scale. (30 points) _____ _____

    b. Measured $\angle A$. (15 points) _____ _____

    c. Shows height : leg length ratios and means. (15 points) _____ _____

    d. Finds the mean of $\angle A$ for walking stride lengths and running stride lengths. (15 points) _____ _____

    e. Accurately measures stride length of footprints and makes accurate scale drawings. (30 points) _____ _____

    f. Calculates a reasonable height for the person who made the footprints. (15 points) _____ _____

Poster 50 points

    a. Includes a description of the investigation, all data, all scale drawings, and calculations. (25 points) _____ _____

    b. Describes the process for estimating the height of the person who made the footprints. (15 points) _____ _____

    c. Poster is neat and well laid out. (10 points) _____ _____

FINAL GRADE _____ _____

Materials Yardstick, ruler, protractor, calculator; You will need to provide the students with a running and walking stride length for another person, such as yourself. Prepare these ahead of time and have enough for each group. For added interest, you can draw actual footprints representing the stride length on newsprint or poster board.

Alternatives Students who are on crutches or unable to walk could measure the strides of others. They might also measure the strides of a jointed doll or a cooperative pet. Are the triangles formed by the stride lengths for a dog the same as for a small human, or different? Could you use them to estimate the size of a bear from its tracks?

Determining size from footprints is used in both forensic medicine and paleontology. The class project might focus on one of these, e.g. "Who left the footprints running away from the crime scene?" or "How tall was the bipedal dinosaur who left these walking footprints?"

Common Errors Small children have shorter legs and arms proportionate to their size than adults and adolescents. If students are looking for a shorter stride to use in their measurements, they should not use very small children. You can illustrate this by drawing two stick figures on the board who are the same height, but one with a larger head, longer torso, and shorter legs, and ask which represents an adult and which a toddler. This could spark a discussion about using proportion in drawing.

Note that the actual height of the mystery strider may be more or less than the height students calculate using their model.

Suggestions Explain to students that the footprints of walkers and runners vary: runners, for example, have a deeper imprint at the ball of the foot. You can illustrate this if you have access to sand or soft dirt that two students can cross.

Students use the mean angle measures and ratios to create a model triangle. Then, given a stride length and information as to whether the strider is walking or running, they assume that the unknown strider's triangle is similar to their model triangle. A class discussion prior to the project about how models are similar (in the mathematical sense) to what they represent will help students grasp the different ways similar figures are (and are not) used in this application.

Cover Page   10 points

    a. Name (4 points)

    b. Class (2 points)

    c. Project Name (2 points)

    d. Due Date (2 points)

Scoring Rubric	
A	179–200
B	159–178
C	139–158
D	119–138
F	118 or below

Investigation   20 points

    a. Measurements for leg length, walking stride length, and running stride length are shown. (20 points)

Data Analysis   120 points

    a. Includes all scale drawings. Drawing are labeled correctly and drawn to scale. (30 points)

    b. Measured $\angle A$. (15 points)

    c. Shows height : leg length ratios and means. (15 points)

    d. Finds the mean of $\angle A$ for walking stride lengths and running stride lengths. (15 points)

    e. Accurately measures stride length of footprints and makes accurate scale drawings. (30 points)

    f. Calculates a reasonable height for the person who made the footprints. (15 points)

Poster   50 points

    a. Includes a description of the investigation, all data, all scale drawings, and calculations. (25 points)

    b. Describes the process for estimating the height of the person who made the footprints. (15 points)

    c. Poster is neat and well laid out. (10 points)

Name_____ Date_____

Objective Analyze data from an experiment.

Materials Rope or clothesline (90 centimeters); meter stick

Investigation Work in a group of 3. Choose one person to tie knots in the rope, one person to measure the rope, and one person to record the results.

Measure the length of the rope in centimeters. This is the length of the rope when the number of knots is zero. Record the length in the table below.

Number of Knots	0	1	2	3	4	5	6	7	8
Length of Rope (cm)									

Tie a knot in the rope. Measure the length of the rope after the knot is tied. Record this length in the table. Tie another knot with the same tightness in the rope. Measure the length of the rope and record this length in the table. Repeat this process until you complete the table.

Data Analysis
- What happens to the length of the rope as the number of knots increases?

- By how many centimeters does the length of the rope change from zero knots to one knot? one knot to two knots? Is the change relatively consistent?

- Let the input be the number of knots and the output be the length of the rope. Make a mapping diagram of your data. Write ordered pairs to represent the data and then graph the ordered pairs. What does the *y*-intercept represent in this situation?

- Write an equation that gives the length of the rope in terms of the number of knots tied. Use your equation to estimate the length of the rope after 10 knots have been tied. Tie two more knots in the rope. How does the length of the rope compare with the estimate you found using your equation?

- Compare your equation and graph with those of other groups in your class. Do you have the same slopes? *y*-intercepts? equations? Explain.

- Write three inequalities to show how your slope compares to the slopes of three other groups in your class.

- What effect, if any, do each of these things have on the data: the tightness of each knot; the space between the knots; the thickness of the rope?

Written Summary Write a report in which you describe your data and analyze the results. Include comparisons of your data to the class data. Include all equations, mapping diagrams, and graphs. Be sure to include the answers to the questions above.

Name _____ Date _____

	Student Score	Teacher Score
Cover Page 10 points		
a. Name (4 points)	_____	_____
b. Class (2 points)	_____	_____
c. Project Name (2 points)	_____	_____
d. Due Date (2 points)	_____	_____
Investigation 40 points		
a. Table is complete. (30 points)	_____	_____
b. Data is carefully measured and recorded. (10 points)	_____	_____
Data Analysis 130 points		
a. All questions are answered completely. (30 points)	_____	_____
b. Mapping diagram and ordered pairs are correct. (30 points)	_____	_____
c. Equation is correctly written. (15 points)	_____	_____
d. Graph is clearly labeled and correct. (20 points)	_____	_____
e. Meaning of graph is well explained. (10 points)	_____	_____
f. Inequalities are correctly written. (10 points)	_____	_____
g. Effect of knot tightness, space between knots, and thickness of rope is accurately addressed. (15 points)	_____	_____
Written Summary 30 points		
a. Method of investigation is described. (15 points)	_____	_____
b. Table and data analysis are clearly presented. (15 points)	_____	_____
FINAL GRADE	_____	_____

Teacher's Project Notes

For use after Chapter 4

Materials
A 90-centimeter rope, such as clothesline, and a meter stick for each group; Cut a piece of rope for every three students. You cannot reuse the rope from one class to another because of the knots, so be sure to cut enough rope for all the classes doing the project.

Alternatives
For greater variety in the data, you can give each group a rope with a different thickness.

For a more guided version, this could be done as a class project, in which students take turns in front of the class tying knots in different types of ropes. The data the class gathers should be recorded in separate tables for each type of rope. Then the data can be compared.

Common Errors
Students may measure carelessly. Make sure they hold the rope straight and measure carefully so that they get accurate data.

Make sure students tie their knots about the same tightness; they should not have some tight and some loose. This may make their measurements less consistent.

When students graph their ordered pairs, they may mistakenly connect the points. If they do this, ask students what an x-value of 2.5 represents in this situation. Guide students to see that it doesn't make sense to have 2.5 knots.

Suggestions
If the rope is thinner than clothesline, students may have difficulty measuring the change in length. Avoid giving students rope that is too thin or too thick.

Instead of a written summary, you may want students to do a poster to present all the data, graphics, and data analysis.

Cover Page   10 points

    a. Name (4 points)

    b. Class (2 points)

    c. Project Name (2 points)

    d. Due Date (2 points)

Scoring Rubric	
A	179–200
B	159–178
C	139–158
D	119–138
F	118 or below

Investigation   40 points

    a. Table is complete. (30 points)

    b. Data is carefully measured and recorded. (10 points)

Data Anaylsis   130 points

    a. All questions are answered completely. (30 points)

    b. Mapping diagram and ordered pairs are correct. (30 points)

    c. Equation is correctly written. (15 points)

    d. Graph is clearly labeled and correct. (20 points)

    e. Meaning of graph is well explained. (10 points)

    f. Inequalities are correctly written. (10 points)

    g. Effect of knot tightness, space between knots, and thickness of rope is accurately addressed. (15 points)

Written summary   30 points

    a. Method of investigation is described. (15 points)

    b. Table and data analysis are clearly presented. (15 points)

Name_____ Date _____

Objective Analyze and model how your ability to make a basket changes with distance.

Materials Graph paper, a yardstick, a wastebasket, and paper wadded-up to form a ball

Investigation • Work with two other people. One person will shoot baskets, one will measure the distance from the basket, and one should record the number of baskets made.

• Stand 0 yards from the wastebasket. Shoot your paper ball into the basket 10 times and record the number of shots that go into the basket.

Distance from Basket (yd)	Number of Shots That Go into the Basket (out of 10 shots)
0	
1	
2	

• Step back 1 yard. Shoot your paper ball into the basket 10 times from this distance and record the number of balls that go into the basket. Step back another yard and shoot again. Repeat until you reach a distance where none of your shots go into the basket.

• After one person finishes shooting baskets, switch roles and repeat the experiment until everyone has a chance to shoot baskets. (There should be one table of data for each person.)

Data Analysis 1. Write the ordered pairs represented by your data. Use the distance from the basket as the input.

2. Describe the input and output of the function represented by your data.

3. Graph the ordered pairs on a graph.

4. Describe the relationship between x and y. Is the relationship *linear* or *nonlinear*? Explain.

5. Use two of the ordered pairs you wrote to write an equation of a line to represent your data. Graph the equation on the same graph as the ordered pairs. Do you think your line represents the data well? Why or why not?

6. Predict how many shots you can sink from 2.5 yards. Test your prediction.

Written Report Write a report about your experiment that includes your data, graph, models, and explanations.

Name _____ Date _____

Project **Student Grading Rubric**
For use after Chapter 6

Cover Page 10 points

    a. Name (4 points) _____ _____

    b. Class (2 points) _____ _____

    c. Project Name (2 points) _____ _____

    d. Due Date (2 points) _____ _____

Investigation 20 points

    a. Complete the table until the number of shots that
    go into the basket is zero. (20 points) _____ _____

Data Analysis 130 points

    a. Write the ordered pairs represented by your data.
    (20 points) _____ _____

    b. Describe the input and output of the function.
    (20 points) _____ _____

    c. Graph the ordered pairs. (30 points) _____ _____

    d. Describe the relationship between x and y and
    explain if the relationship is linear or nonlinear.
    (20 points) _____ _____

    e. Write an equation of a line to represent the data.
    Graph the equation. Explain whether the line
    represents the data well. (30 points) _____ _____

    f. Make and test a reasonable prediction. (10 points) _____ _____

Written Report 40 points

    a. Report includes data, graphs, models, and
    explanations. (30 points) _____ _____

    b. Report is neat and clearly written. (10 points) _____ _____

FINAL GRADE _____ _____

Materials Graph paper, a yardstick, enough wastebaskets for every three students, scrap paper to use as a ball

Alternatives You could do the investigation with a real basketball and net, but the starting point should be a little further away. The data with a real basketball and net will not be as consistent as with the wastebasket model, as it requires more ability.

After completing the wastebasket investigation, you can ask students to predict their results for a real basketball and net. Then repeat the experiment using a real basketball and net.

Common Errors Students may write the ordered pairs in the opposite order. Make sure they realize the number of baskets is *dependent* on the distance from the wastebasket, so the distance from the wastebasket is the input.

Students may think that the inputs of the function are integers, because they only found integer distances from the wastebasket. Ask them if fractional distances make sense in this situation.

Suggestions You may want to have the students in a group combine their data and analyze the impact this has on the data. Does it change the answers to any of their questions?

You may want to work with the class to find a linear model and an exponential model for a set of data using the regression feature of a graphing calculator. Ask students which model they think best fits the data and why.

The 3-point line in basketball is related to the difficulty of making the shot. Ask students to relate this to their results. Where would they place the 3-point line from the wastebasket? Should there be a 1-point line because close wastebasket shots are very easy?

Grading Rubric

For use after Chapter 6

Cover Page   10 points

     a. Name (4 points)

     b. Class (2 points)

     c. Project Name (2 points)

     d. Due Date (2 points)

Scoring Rubric	
A	179–200
B	159–178
C	139–158
D	119–138
F	118 or below

Investigation   20 points

     a. Complete the table until the number of shots that go into the basket is zero. (20 points)

Data Analysis   130 points

     a. Write the ordered pairs represented by your data. (20 points)

     b. Describe the input and output of the function. (20 points)

     c. Graph the ordered pairs. (30 points)

     d. Describe the relationship between x and y and explain if the relationship is linear or nonlinear. (20 points)

     e. Write an equation of a line to represent the data. Graph the equation. Explain whether the line represents the data well. (30 points)

     f. Make and test a reasonable prediction. (10 points)

Written Report   40 points

     a. Report includes data, graphs, models, and explanations. (30 points)

     b. Report is neat and clearly written. (10 points)

Name_____ Date_____

Astronomy
For use after Chapter 10

Objective   **Use scientific notation to answer questions about astronomy.**

Materials   Internet or other resource with astronomical data, calculator

Investigation   Use a resource such as http://solarsystem.nasa.gov/planets/index.cfm to find the masses and distances needed to answer the following questions.

Round your answers to 3 significant digits. (For example, $3.68241 \times 10^{11} \approx 3.68 \times 10^{11}$.) Use scientific notation to represent your distances.

1. Find a list of the planets that have at least two moons. Choose one of these planets.

2. Find the average distance from the Sun to your planet and from the Sun to Earth.

3. Model the orbits as circles (even though the orbit is really a flat ellipse). Find the smallest possible distance between your planet and Earth. Find the greatest possible distance between your planet and Earth. Write inequalities to represent the distances between the planets.

4. You want to launch a high-speed probe from Earth to take images of your planet. The probe travels at 250,000 kilometers per hour. What would be the shortest possible time it would take the probe to travel to your planet? Explain.

5. List the names of the moons of your planet. For each moon, find the mass, radius, and the distance from the planet. Write these numbers in scientific notation. Order the moons from least to greatest mass, least to greatest radius, and least to greatest distance from the planet. Is there a pattern?

Make a Poster   Make a poster to organize all the information you have learned from your research and calculations. Include visuals and descriptions of your work.

Name _____ Date _____

	Student Score	Teacher Score

Poster Information 10 points

    a. Name (4 points) _____ _____

    b. Class (3 points) _____ _____

    c. Due Date (3 points) _____ _____

Investigation 160 points

    a. Distance from Earth to the Sun is correct and written in scientific notation. (15 points) _____ _____

    b. Distance from the chosen planet to the Sun is correct and is written in scientific notation. (15 points) _____ _____

    c. The smallest possible distance from the planet to Earth is visualized and calculated. (20 points) _____ _____

    d. The greatest possible distance from the planet to Earth is visualized and calculated. (20 points) _____ _____

    e. The inequalities correctly represent the distances between the planets. (10 points)

    f. The shortest possible time needed for the probe to travel to the planet is accurate. (30 points) _____ _____

    g. Names of moons for the planet are listed. Mass, radii, and the distance from the planet are written in scientific notation. The moons are listed from least to greatest by mass, radius, and distance from the planet. Patterns are described. (50 points) _____ _____

Poster 30 points

    a. Includes calculations, visuals, inequalities, and answers to all questions. (20 points) _____ _____

    b. Poster is neat and organized well. (10 points) _____ _____

FINAL GRADE _____ _____

Materials Internet or other resource with astronomical data, calculator
The NASA site is a good source:
http://solarsystem.nasa.gov/planets/index.cfm

Alternatives Students could write a fictional story in which they use each of the items they calculated.

A possible extension for advanced students is *escape velocity*. Given the average radius and mass of a planet or moon, calculate the *escape velocity*, the velocity an object would need to escape the body's gravitational pull.

$$V_{\text{Escape}} = \sqrt{\frac{2\left(6.67 \times 10^{-11}\dfrac{m^3}{\text{kg} \cdot \text{sec}^3}\right)\left(m_{\text{planet}}\right)}{r_{\text{planet}}}}$$

The escape velocity is in kilometers per hour, the mass is in kilograms, and the radius is in kilometers.

You could focus the discussion on rocket speeds, and work out how long it would take to reach various objects: How long does sunlight take to reach Pluto? How long would a Saturn V rocket take to reach Jupiter?

Common Errors A review of unit analysis can help students check their work—e.g. a formula that will result in a speed in square kilometers is wrong.

Students may find it easiest to multiply and divide the decimals, then use the rules of exponents on the 10^x factors.

Make sure students write the numbers in scientific notation correctly to make the calculations a bit easier.

Suggestions At the start of the project, talk with the class about what it means to write a number to three significant digits.

Discuss that scientific notation can be used with any numbers, but it is most often used when discussing very small or very large numbers, such as those used in astronomy.

You may want students to work in pairs and turn in one poster for the pair. Students can work together on the calculations or do the calculations separately and compare their answers.

Planets that have at least two moons are Mars, Jupiter, Saturn, Uranus, and Neptune.

Grading Rubric

For use after Chapter 10

Poster Information 10 points

    a. Name (4 points)

    b. Class (3 points)

    c. Due Date (3 points)

Investigation 160 points

    a. Distance from Earth to the Sun is correct and written in scientific notation. (15 points)

    b. Distance from the chosen planet to the Sun is correct and written in scientific notation. (15 points)

    c. The smallest possible distance from the planet to Earth is visualized and calculated. (20 points)

    d. The greatest possible distance from the planet to Earth is visualized and calculated. (20 points)

    e. The inequalities correctly represent the distances between the planets. (10 points)

    f. The shortest possible time needed for the probe to travel to the planet is accurate. (30 points)

    g. Names of moons for the planet are listed. Mass, radii, and the distance from the planet are written in scientific notation. The moons are listed from least to greatest by mass, radius, and distance from the planet. Patterns are described. (50 points)

Poster 30 points

    a. Includes calculations, visuals, lists, inequalities, and answers to all questions. (20 points)

    b. Poster is neat and well organized. (10 points)

Credits

8 Gallant, Morrie. *Awesome Riddle Book*. Sterling, December 1999; **14** Singleton, Glen. *1001 Cool Jokes*. Hinkler Books Pty Ltd., 2003; **20** Rissinger, Matt and Philip Yates. *Totally Terrific Jokes*. Sterling, June 2001; **26, 36, 42, 48** Singleton, Glen. *1001 Cool Jokes*. Hinkler Books Pty Ltd., 2003; **54** *The Youth Online Club –101 Jokes for Kids*. [Cited 12 January 2009] Available from *www.youthonline.ca/101thingstodo/jokes61-70.shtml*; **60, 66** Adapted from Singleton, Glen. *1001 Cool Jokes*. Hinkler Books Pty Ltd., 2003; **72** Rissinger, Matt and Philip Yates. *Greatest Giggles Ever*. Sterling, 2002; **82** Horsfall, Jacqueline. *Kids' Silliest Jokes*. Sterling, March 2003; **88** Rosenbloom, Joseph. *Biggest Riddle Book in the World*. Sterling Publishing Company, 1976; **94, 100** Horsfall, Jacqueline. *Kids' Silliest Jokes*. Sterling, March 2003; **110** Rissinger, Matt and Philip Yates. *Totally Terrific Jokes*. Sterling, June 2001; **116** Gallant, Morrie. *Awesome Riddle Book*. Sterling, December 1999; **124** Rosenbloom, Joseph. *Biggest Riddle Book in the World*. Sterling Publishing Company, 1976; **130, 136** Adapted from Rissinger, Matt and Philip Yates. *Totally Terrific Jokes*. Sterling, June 2001; **142** Rissinger, Matt and Philip Yates. *Totally Terrific Jokes*. Sterling, June 2001; **148** Hall, Katy. *Really, Really Bad Sports Jokes*. Candlewick, August 1998; **158** Dahl, Michael. *Chewy Chuckles*. Picture Window Books, 2003; **164, 170, 176** Chmielewski, Gary. *The Sports Zone*. Norwood House Press, 2008; **188** O'Donnell, Rosie. *Kids are Punny: Jokes Sent By Kids to The Rosie O'Donnell Show*. Warner Books, June 1997; **194** Rosenbloom, Joseph. *Biggest Riddle Book in the World*. Sterling Publishing Company, 1976; **200** Rissinger, Matt and Philip Yates. *Totally Terrific Jokes*. Sterling, June 2001; **206** Singleton, Glen. *1001 Cool Jokes*. Hinkler Books Pty Ltd., 2003; **212** Cunningham, Bronnie. *The Best Book of Riddles, Puns, & Jokes*. Doubleday & Company., 1973; **222** Gallant, Morrie. *Awesome Riddle Book*. Sterling, December 1999; **228** Cunningham, Bronnie. *The Best Book of Riddles, Puns, & Jokes*. Doubleday & Company., 1973; **234** Gallant, Morrie. *Awesome Riddle Book*. Sterling, December 1999; **240** Adapted from Gallant, Morrie. *Awesome Riddle Book*. Sterling, December 1999; **248** LE Holland & Howell. *The Usborne Book of Animal Jokes*. Usborne Publishing Company, 2003; **258** Adapted from Helmer, Marilyn and Jane Kurisu. *Funtime Riddles*. Kids Can Press, Ltd., February 2004; **264** Walton, Rick. *Really, Really Bad School Jokes*. Candlewick, August 1998; **270** Cunningham, Bronnie. *The Best Book of Riddles, Puns, & Jokes*. Doubleday & Company., 1973; **276** Hall, Katy. *Really, Really Bad Sports Jokes*. Candlewick, August 1998; **286** O'Donnell, Rosie. *Kids are Punny: Jokes Sent By Kids to The Rosie O'Donnell Show*. Warner Books, June 1997; **292** Horsfall, Jacqueline. *Kids' Silliest Jokes*. Sterling Publishing Company, 2002; **298** Phunny, U. R. *More Animal Jokes*. ABDO Company, 2005; **304** O'Donnell, Rosie. *Kids are Punny: Jokes Sent By Kids to The Rosie O'Donnell Show*. Warner Books, June 1997; **314** Gallant, Morrie. *Awesome Riddle Book*. Sterling, December 1999; **320** Adapted from Gallant, Morrie. *Awesome Riddle Book*. Sterling, December 1999; **326, 332** Rissinger, Matt and Philip Yates. *Totally Terrific Jokes*. Sterling, June 2001; **338** Rissinger, Matt and Philip Yates. *Totally Terrific Jokes*. Sterling, June 2001; **344** Gallant, Morrie. *Awesome Riddle Book*. Sterling, December 1999; **350** Horsfall, Jacqueline. *Kids' Silliest Jokes*. Sterling Publishing Company, 2002

Answers

Chapter 1

1.1 Start Thinking!
For use before Activity 1.1

Answers will vary.

1.1 Warm Up
For use before Activity 1.1

1. $118°$ **2.** $57°$ **3.** $90°$

4. $101°$ **5.** $16°$ **6.** $77°$

1.1 Start Thinking!
For use before Lesson 1.1

The Subtraction Property of Equality states that you can subtract the same number from both sides of an equation. The Multiplication Property of Equality states that you can multiply each side of an equation by the same number. The Division Property of Equality states that you can divide each side of an equation by the same nonzero number. *Sample situation:* If you are preparing two plates of food, you add the same amount of various foods to each plate so they remain equal servings (Addition Property of Equality).

1.1 Warm Up
For use before Lesson 1.1

1. 30   **2.** 46   **3.** 20   **4.** 53

1.1 Practice A

1. $x = 7$ **2.** $n = 34$ **3.** $k = -3$

4. $d = 3\pi$ **5.** $y = -1.3$ **6.** $w = \dfrac{19}{10}$

7. $49 = s + 19$; 30 points

8. $y = 8$ **9.** $d = -18$ **10.** $b = -0.4$

11. $x = -8.2$ **12.** $p = \dfrac{3}{2}$ **13.** $k = 3.75$

14. $7.50x = 33.75$; 4.5 hours

15. $s = 11.3$ **16.** $p = -8$ **17.** greater than

18. 13π cm^2 **19.** $20 + A = 44$; 24 in.^{2}

1.1 Practice B

1. $x = -12$ **2.** $h = 26\pi$ **3.** $m = 1.75$

4. $a = \dfrac{17}{12}$ **5.** $p = -\dfrac{1}{4}$ **6.** $c = -2.8$

7. $p - 9.75 = 64$; \$73.75

8. $x = -5$ **9.** $h = 8.6\pi$ **10.** $j = 10$

11. $t = -4$ **12.** $q = -3$ **13.** $w = -\dfrac{28}{3}$

14. $4.5\ell = 55.8$; 12.4 in.

15. $r = 22$ **16.** $n = \dfrac{49}{12}$

17. *Sample answer:* $x + 15 = 10$; $3x = -15$

18. 40 pieces of fruit   **19.** \$4, \$12, \$24

1.1 Enrichment and Extension

Red	Blue	Yellow	Yellow	Blue	Red
Blue	Yellow	Green	Green	Yellow	Blue
Yellow	Green	Red	Red	Green	Yellow
Yellow	Green	Red	Red	Green	Yellow
Blue	Yellow	Green	Green	Yellow	Blue
Red	Blue	Yellow	Yellow	Blue	Red

1. yes; Blue squares result from dividing each side of the equation by the same number. Instead of dividing each side, you can multiply each side by a fraction. Then you would be using the Multiplication Property of Equality and all the blue squares would now be red.

2. yes; Green squares result from subtracting the same number from each side of an equation. Instead of subtracting the same number from each side, you can add a negative number to each side of the equation. Then you would be using the Addition Property of Equality and all the green squares would now be yellow.

1.1 Puzzle Time

THE MAN WHO PUT SOAP IN HIS SOUP SO HE COULD WASH IT DOWN WITH SOMETHING

1.2 Start Thinking!
For use before Activity 1.2

Sample answer: Checking your answers can help you detect and avoid arithmetic errors. On exams, checking answers can help you catch mistakes and improve your score. In real-life, in construction work, checking answers can help avoid costly mistakes.

Answers

1.2 Warm Up
For use before Activity 1.2

1. $5n + 5$ 2. $-3x - 7$ 3. $11f$

4. $3m + 16$ 5. $4t + 8$ 6. $3y + 2$

1.2 Start Thinking!
For use before Lesson 1.2

Sample answer: For the situation described,
$\text{cost} = 80x + 60$. To solve, you use two inverse
operations: first *subtract* 60 from each side, and then
divide each side by 80. *Sample scenario:* the enrollment
fee plus monthly rate for a gym membership

1.2 Warm Up
For use before Lesson 1.2

1. 33; 74°, 73°, 33°

2. 60; 120°, 60°, 120°, 60°

3. 97; 107°, 97°, 59°, 97°

4. 25; 106°, 106°, 113°, 90°, 125°

1.2 Practice A

1. $y = 2$ 2. $m = 5$ 3. $k = 10$

4. $z = -1$ 5. $x = 3$ 6. $x = -22$

7. 22 ft

8. $70 + 2x = 360$; $x = 145$

9. $3x + 1.75 = 9.25$; $2.50

10. $1.50n + 2n = 10.50$; 3 magazines

11. a. $2x + 5x + 4 = 25$; $x = 3$

    b. 6 ft and 15 ft

12. $\dfrac{14 + 19 + x}{3} = 17$; 18 points

13. $26 - 3.5x = 8.5$; 5 pens

1.2 Practice B

1. $k = 20$ 2. $p = -14$ 3. $y = 21$

4. $x = 2$ 5. $h = 9$ 6. $x = -3$

7. $44 + (x + 20) + 3x = 180$; $x = 29$

8. a. 42 ft

    b. $x + 3x + 2x = 42$; $x = 7$

    c. 7 ft by 50 ft; 21 ft by 50 ft; 14 ft by 50 ft

9. $58.40

10. $18 + x + (4x - 1) = 42$; 19 in.

11. $4x + 2.5 = 14.3$; $2.95

1.2 Enrichment and Extension

Reading down each column, the solutions to the
equations are:

$x = 10$	$x = 6$	$x = -3$
$x = 2$	$x = 2$	$x = 5$
$x = 4$	$x = -3$	$x = 7$
$x = -3$	$x = 7$	$x = 6$
$x = 4$	$x = 1$	$x = 4$
$x = 1$	$x = 5$	$x = 4$

1.2 Puzzle Time

AT THE BOTTOM

1.3 Start Thinking!
For use before Activity 1.3

2 chips

1.3 Warm Up
For use before Activity 1.3

1. 4 m   2. 10 cm   3. 10 in.   4. 10 ft

1.3 Start Thinking!
For use before Lesson 1.3

Subtraction Property of Equality; no; You are still
left with the two-step equation $2x = 12x - 20$;
Subtracting $2x$ from each side is a better first step.

1.3 Warm Up
For use before Lesson 1.3

1. 5 ft   2. 12 in.

1.3 Practice A

1. $x = 3$ 2. $x = 1.5$ 3. $y = -4$

4. $n = 3$ 5. $q = 15$ 6. $d = 5$

7. $h = -3$ 8. $b = -5$

9. $15 + 0.25m = 20 + 0.05m$; 25 minutes

Answers

10. $\frac{1}{3}x = x - 22; \; x = 33$

11. 150
12. $0.6p = p - 32; \; \$80$

13. no solution
14. no solution

15. infinitely many solutions

16. infinitely many solutions

17. $x = \frac{1}{2}$
18. $x = -\frac{1}{4}$

1.3 Practice B

1. $x = 15$
2. $x = 8$
3. $y = 4$

4. $m = 21$
5. $p = 4$
6. $s = 3$

7. $t = -6$
8. $n = -\frac{27}{8}$

9. The solver did not distribute 0.2 to both terms.

$0.4x = 0.2(x - 8)$

$0.4x = 0.2x - 1.6$

$0.2x = -1.6$

$x = -8$

10. no solution
11. no solution

12. $x = 3$
13. $x = 0$

14. infinitely many solutions

15. infinitely many solutions

16. $0.6p = 0.8(p - 40); \; \$160$

1.3 Enrichment and Extension

1. $d = \frac{4}{3}$
2. $e = 4$
3. $t = -1.5$

4. $a = -1$
5. $a = \frac{1}{3}$
6. $y = 0$

7. $r = 1$
8. $a = -5$
9. $s = 2$

10. $a = 2.25$
11. $\ell = 3$

Answer: at a yard sale

1.3 Puzzle Time

IT'S TOAD AWAY

1.4 Start Thinking!
For use before Activity 1.4

Check students' sketches. *Sample answer:*

Square: $P = 4s; \; A = s^2$

Rectangle: $P = 2\ell + 2w; \; A = \ell w$

Parallelogram: $A = bh$

Triangle: $P = a + b + c; \; A = \frac{1}{2}bh$

Circle: $C = 2\pi r; \; A = \pi r^2$

Trapezoid: $A = \frac{1}{2}h(b_1 + b_2)$

1.4 Warm Up
For use before Activity 1.4

1. 30 ft^3
2. 48 m^3

3. 147 in.^3
4. 640 cm^3

1.4 Start Thinking!
For use before Lesson 1.4

Sample answer: When you solve the literal equation $5x + 4y = 14$ for x, you first subtract $4y$ from each side, and then divide by 5. When you solve the one-variable equation $5x + 20 = 14$ for x, you first subtract 20 from each side, and then divide by 5. The steps are almost identical.

1.4 Warm Up
For use before Lesson 1.4

1. a. $A = bh$ **b.** $b = \dfrac{A}{h}$ **c.** 16 m

2. a. $V = Bh$ **b.** $B = \dfrac{V}{h}$ **c.** 48 m^2

1.4 Practice A

1. $y = 7 - \dfrac{2}{5}x$
2. $y = 4 - \dfrac{2}{3}x$

3. $y = -6 + 10x$
4. $y = 3\pi - \dfrac{1}{2}x$

5. a. $r = \dfrac{d}{2}$ **b.** 65 mi/h

6. $R = P - C$
7. $X = pN$

8. $h = \dfrac{3V}{\pi r^2}$
9. $b = \dfrac{2A}{h}$

Answers

10. a. $d = \dfrac{C}{\pi}$ **b.** $\dfrac{8}{\pi}$ in. **c.** 3 in.

11. a. $c = \dfrac{2A}{d}$ **b.** 7 ft **c.** 8 ft

1.4 Practice B

1. $y = 8 + 12x$

2. $y = \dfrac{3\pi}{4} - \dfrac{5}{8}x$

3. $y = \dfrac{3}{2} + 0.8x$

4. $y = -3.6 + 3x$

5. a. $w = \dfrac{V}{\ell h}$ **b.** 7 ft

6. $B = \dfrac{T}{2} - \dfrac{hP}{2}$

7. $x = \dfrac{C}{80} - 12.5$

8. $h = \dfrac{S}{2\pi r} - \dfrac{r}{2}$

9. $P = \dfrac{2A}{a}$

10. a. $C = \dfrac{5}{9}(F - 32)$ **b.** 100°C **c.** 26.7°C

11. a. $m = \dfrac{360A}{\pi r^2}$ **b.** 143.2°

c. greater than; The numerator will be larger.

1.4 Enrichment and Extension

1. The height is about 4.11 feet using both methods.

2. *Sample answer:* Method 2; Because you can do all of the calculations in one step.

1.4 Puzzle Time

A RIVER

Technology Connection

1. $x = 2$ **2.** $x = -2$ **3.** $x = \dfrac{3}{2}$ or 1.5

Chapter 2

2.1 Start Thinking!
For use before Activity 2.1

Check students' sketches.

2.1 Warm Up
For use before Activity 2.1

1. $1\dfrac{1}{2}$ in., $1\dfrac{1}{2}$ in., $1\dfrac{1}{2}$ in. **2.** $1\dfrac{5}{8}$ in., $1\dfrac{3}{16}$ in., 2 in.

3. $1\dfrac{3}{8}$ in., $1\dfrac{1}{16}$ in., $2\dfrac{1}{16}$ in. **4.** $2\dfrac{1}{8}$ in., $1\dfrac{13}{16}$ in., $1\dfrac{3}{8}$ in.

2.1 Start Thinking!
For use before Lesson 2.1

1. yes; Consider two equilateral triangles, one with 1-inch sides and another with 2-inch sides. Both have three 60° angles, but they are not congruent because the corresponding sides are not congruent.

2. no; Consider two triangles made from toothpicks that have side lengths of 5 centimeters, 6 centimeters, and 7 centimeters. No matter how you arrange each set of toothpicks, they will always form two congruent triangles.

2.1 Warm Up
For use before Lesson 2.1

1. not congruent **2.** not congruent **3.** not congruent

4. congruent **5.** not congruent **6.** congruent

2.1 Practice A

1. congruent **2.** not congruent

3. Corresponding angles: $\angle A$ and $\angle D$, $\angle B$ and $\angle E$, $\angle C$ and $\angle F$

Corresponding sides: side AB and side DE, side BC and side EF, side CA and side FD

4. Corresponding angles: $\angle G$ and $\angle K$, $\angle H$ and $\angle L$, $\angle I$ and $\angle M$, $\angle J$ and $\angle N$

Corresponding sides: side GH and side KL, side HI and side LM, side IJ and side MN, side JG and side NK

5. not congruent; Corresponding side lengths are not congruent.

6. congruent; Corresponding side lengths and corresponding angles are congruent.

7. The corresponding sides are not congruent, so the two figures are not congruent.

8. no; Congruent polygons have congruent angles. Thus, both polygons would have a right angle.

2.1 Practice B

1. Corresponding angles: $\angle A$ and $\angle J$, $\angle B$ and $\angle K$, $\angle C$ and $\angle L$, $\angle D$ and $\angle M$

Corresponding sides: side AB and side JK, side BC and side KL, side CD and side LM, side DA and side MJ

Answers

2. Corresponding angles: $\angle P$ and $\angle V$, $\angle Q$ and $\angle W$, $\angle R$ and $\angle X$, $\angle S$ and $\angle Y$, $\angle T$ and $\angle Z$

Corresponding sides: side PQ and side VW, side QR and side WX, side RS and side XY, side ST and side YZ, side TP and side ZV

3. not congruent; Corresponding side lengths are not congruent.

4. congruent; Corresponding side lengths and corresponding angles are congruent.

5. a. 10 in. **b.** $\angle L$ **c.** 24 in.

6. a. true; They have the same mark.

b. false; side MN is congruent to side ED.

c. false; $\angle B$ corresponds to $\angle P$.

d. true; $\angle B$ corresponds to $\angle P$ and $\angle C$ corresponds to $\angle O$. So, side BC is congruent to side PO.

e. true; $m\angle A = 90°$.
$m\angle B = m\angle C = m\angle O = 130°$.
$m\angle D = m\angle N = 120°$. So, the sum is
$90° + 130° + 130° + 70° + 120° = 540°$.

f. false; $\angle B \cong \angle C$ and $m\angle C = 130°$. So, $m\angle B = 130°$.

2.1 Enrichment and Extension

1. The lengths of the sides in Triangle B are 5 times larger than the lengths of the sides in Triangle A.

2. 12 cm **3.** 60 cm

4. The perimeter of Triangle B is 5 times larger than the perimeter of Triangle A. In Exercise 1, it was observed that each length in Triangle B was 5 times larger than that of Triangle A.

5. 6 cm^2 **6.** 150 cm^2

7. The area of Triangle B is 25 times larger than the area of Triangle A.

8. The side lengths of Triangle B are 5 times larger than the side lengths of Triangle A. Because area is a two dimensional measurement, you can predict that the area of Triangle B will be $5 \cdot 5$ or $(5)^2$ or 25 times larger than the area of Triangle A.

9. 162 cm^2

10. no; If all the sides did not increase by the same factor, you could not predict the total change in perimeter or area.

2.1 Puzzle Time

BAKED BEINGS

2.2 Start Thinking!
For use before Activity 2.2

Sample answer: architect, engineer, interior designer

2.2 Warm Up
For use before Activity 2.2

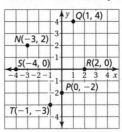

2.2 Start Thinking!
For use before Lesson 2.2

Sample answer: Bathroom tile because the tile fits together without space.

2.2 Warm Up
For use before Lesson 2.2

1. no **2.** yes **3.** no **4.** yes

2.2 Practice A

1. yes **2.** no

3. $P'(-2, 2)$, $Q'(1, 5)$, $R'(3, 3)$

4. 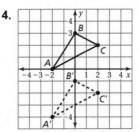 **5.**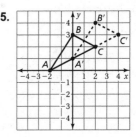

6. 3 units left and 4 units down

7. 3 units right and 4 units up

2.2 Practice B

1. no **2.** yes

3. $T'(1, 3)$, $U'(4, 4)$, $V'(4, -1)$, $W'(1, -1)$

4. 2 units left and 4 units down

5. 7 units up

6. a. 1 unit right and 7 units down

b. 1 unit left and 7 units up

Answers

7. a. yes **b.** no **c.** yes

2.2 Enrichment and Extension

1. A: right 1 and down 5; B: right 1 and down 4;
C: right 1 and down 3; D: right 1 and down 5;
E: down 5; F: left 2 and down 3; G: left 2 and
down 5

2. A: left 4 and down 4; B: left 4 and up 1;
C: left 5 and down 2; D: left 4 and up 4;
E: left 5 and up 3; F: left 5 and up 5;
G: left 5 and up 2

3. A: down 4; B: left 1 and down 4; C: down 5;
D: left 4 and down 4; E: left 6 and down 6;
F: left 4.5 and down 2; G: left 6 and up 1; or
A: down 3; B: left 1 and down 3; C: down 4;
D: left 4 and down 5; E: left 6 and down 4;
F: left 4.5 and down 2; G: left 6

4–5. A: right 7 and up 5; B: right 6 and up 3;
C: right 5 and up 8; D: right 1 and up 5;
E: up 4; F: right 1 and up 7; G: up 5; or
A: right 6 and up 4; B: right 6 and up 3;
C: right 5 and up 8; D: right 1 and up 5;
E: right 1 and up 5; F: left 1 and up 5;
G: up 5

6. *Answer should include, but is not limited to:* The
puzzle should have seven tans that can form the
shape without overlapping the tans. Some puzzles
will have more than one solution.

2.2 Puzzle Time

DARKNESS

2.3 Start Thinking!
For use before Activity 2.3

Sample answer: An airplane glides out of its gate then
down the runway. It travels from one point to the next.
When it reaches its destination it lands on the runway
and taxis to the gate.

2.3 Warm Up
For use before Activity 2.3

1.

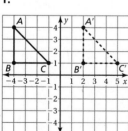

2.

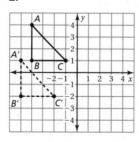

2.3 Start Thinking!
For use before Lesson 2.3

Sample answer: radar and civic; Palindromes like mom
are reflections. Palindromes like pop are not reflections.

2.3 Warm Up
For use before Lesson 2.3

1. no   **2.** yes   **3.** no   **4.** yes

2.3 Practice A

1. yes   **2.** no

3.

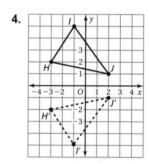

$E'(0, -2), F'(3, -1), G'(4, -3)$

4.

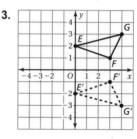

$H'(-3, -2), I'(-1, -5), J'(2, -1)$

5.

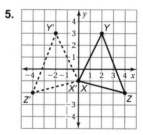

$X'(0, -1), Y'(-2, 3), Z'(-4, -2)$

6.

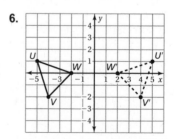

$U'(5, 1), V'(4, -2), W'(2, 0)$

Answers

7. WOW   **8.** y-axis   **9.** x-axis

10.

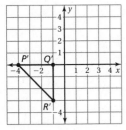

11. Quadrant III

2.3 Practice B

1. no   **2.** yes

3.

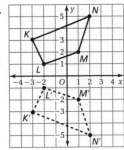

$K'(-3, -3), L'(-2, -1), M'(1, -2), N'(2, -5)$

4.

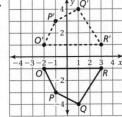

$O'(-2, 1), P'(-1, 3), Q'(1, 4), R'(3, 1)$

5.

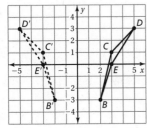

$B'(-2, -3), C'(-3, 1), D'(-5, 3), E'(-3, 0)$

6.

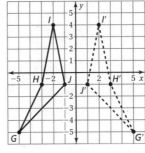

$G'(5, -5), H'(3, -1), I'(2, 4), J'(1, -1)$

7. bob   **8.** x-axis   **9.** y-axis

10.

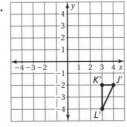

11. a. $A''(2, 1), B''(-4, -2), C''(-2, 2)$

     b. Each coordinate in the resulting triangle is the opposite of its corresponding coordinate in $\triangle ABC$.

2.3 Enrichment and Extension

Figures B and H cannot be created using the Master.

Sample answer:

A: 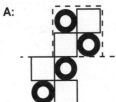   C: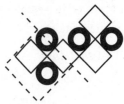

D: 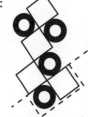   E: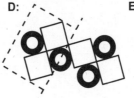

F: 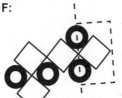   G: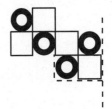

Answers

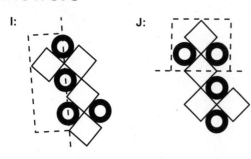

I: **J:**

2.3 Puzzle Time

A COAT OF PAINT

2.4 Start Thinking!
For use before Activity 2.4

Yes, the 50-yard line. *Sample answer:* A football field is a reflection of itself over the 50-yard line.

2.4 Warm Up
For use before Activity 2.4

1. $D'(-5\ 4)$, $E'(-5, 2)$, $F'(-1, 2)$, $G'(-1, 4)$

2. $H'(2, -1)$, $I'(2, -5)$, $J'(4, -4)$, $K'(4, -2)$

2.4 Start Thinking!
For use before Lesson 2.4

Sample answer: translation: how the players move down the court; reflection: the basketball court; rotation: a player using his pivot foot when he has the ball.

2.4 Warm Up
For use before Lesson 2.4

1. translation   2. reflection   3. rotation

2.4 Practice A

1. yes; 180° clockwise   2. no

3. $A'(-1, -4)$, $B'(-2, -2)$, $C'(-1, -1)$

4. $A'(-1, -4)$, $B'(-2, -2)$, $C'(-1, -1)$

5. $A'(-4, 1)$, $B'(-5, 3)$, $C'(-4, 4)$

6. $A'(2, 1)$, $B'(0, 0)$, $C'(-1, 1)$

7. yes   8. no

2.4 Practice B

1. no

2. yes; 90° counterclockwise

3. $A'(1, -1)$, $B'(2, -2)$, $C'(2, -4)$, $D'(1, -5)$

4. $A'(1, -1)$, $B'(2, -2)$, $C'(2, -4)$, $D'(1, -5)$

5. $A'(1, 1)$, $B'(2, 0)$, $C'(2, -2)$, $D'(1, -3)$

6. $A'(9, 1)$, $B'(8, 0)$, $C'(6, 0)$, $D'(5, 1)$

7. no   8. yes

2.4 Enrichment and Extension

1. *Sample answer:* Rotate 90 degrees clockwise about the origin. Reflect in the *x*-axis. Translate 2 units left and 2 units up. Rotate 180 degrees about the origin.

2. Translate 3 units down. Rotate 180 degrees about the origin. Reflect in the *y*-axis. Rotate 90 degrees counterclockwise about the origin. Translate 1 unit right.

3. *Sample answer:* Rotate 90 degrees clockwise about the origin. Reflect in the *y*-axis. Reflect in the *x*-axis. Rotate 90 degrees counterclockwise about the origin. Translate 3 units down.

4. *Sample answer:* Translate 2 units up. Reflect in the *x*-axis. Rotate 180 degrees about the origin. Translate 3 units left. Rotate 90 degrees counterclockwise about the origin. Reflect in the *y*-axis.

2.4 Puzzle Time

A TRAFFIC JAM

2.5 Start Thinking!
For use before Activity 2.5

Sample answer: Drawing a sketch of your garden that is proportional to the actual garden will help you buy the correct number of seeds to plant.

2.5 Warm Up
For use before Activity 2.5

1. yes   2. no   3. no

4. no   5. yes   6. yes

2.5 Start Thinking!
For use before Lesson 2.5

Sample answer: Two figures are similar if their sides are proportional.

2.5 Warm Up
For use before Lesson 2.5

1. yes; The sides are proportional.

2. no; The sides are not proportional.

3. yes; The sides are proportional.

4. yes; The sides are proportional.

Answers

2.5 Practice A

1. Corresponding angles: $\angle A$ and $\angle D$, $\angle B$ and $\angle E$, $\angle C$ and $\angle F$

   Corresponding sides: side AB and side DE, side BC and side EF, side AC and side DF

2. yes; Corresponding angles are congruent and the ratio of the lengths of corresponding sides is $\frac{3}{4}$.

3. no   **4. a.** no **b.** yes

5. 2 in. by 5 in.; 1 in. by 2.5 in.

2.5 Practice B

1.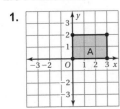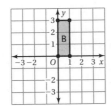

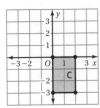

A and C; Corresponding sides and corresponding angles are congruent.

2. yes

3. Corresponding angles: $\angle P$ and $\angle T$, $\angle Q$ and $\angle U$, $\angle R$ and $\angle V$

   Corresponding sides: side PQ and side TU, side QR and side UV, side PR and side TV

4. 110°   **5.** 70°   **6.** 70°   **7.** 70°

8. **a.** no **b.** yes **c.** no **d.** yes

9. no; The angles will be corresponding, so the triangles will be similar.

10. **a.** *Sample answer:* 2, 3, and 4
    b. *Sample answer:* 12, 18, and 24 **c.** yes

2.5 Enrichment and Extension

1. *Sample answer:* A house or other object might be blocking the path of your character. So, you could use a laser to shrink it so that you can get to a prize or safety. You might use a laser to enlarge a supply of food or other supplies.

2. **a.** $A(1, 4)$, $B(1, -5)$, $C(13, -5)$

   b. $A(1, 3)$, $B(1, 1)$, $C\left(3\frac{2}{3}, 1\right)$

3. **a.** $A(0, 3)$, $B\left(4\frac{1}{2}, -1\frac{1}{2}\right)$, $C\left(3, -1\frac{1}{2}\right)$, $D(3, -6)$,

   $E(-3, -6)$, $F\left(-3, -1\frac{1}{2}\right)$, $G\left(-4\frac{1}{2}, -1\frac{1}{2}\right)$

   b. $A(2, 1)$, $B(3, 0)$, $C\left(2\frac{2}{3}, 0\right)$, $D\left(2\frac{2}{3}, -1\right)$,

   $E\left(1\frac{1}{3}, -1\right)$, $F\left(1\frac{1}{3}, 0\right)$, $G(1, 0)$

4. **a.** $A(-2, 1)$, $B(-7, -9)$, $C(-17, -9)$,

   $D\left(-9\frac{1}{2}, -16\frac{1}{2}\right)$, $E(-12, -29)$, $F\left(-2, -21\frac{1}{2}\right)$,

   $G(8, -29)$, $H\left(5\frac{1}{2}, -16\frac{1}{2}\right)$, $I(13, -9)$, $J(3, -9)$

   b. $A\left(-2\frac{1}{2}, 0\right)$, $B(-3, -1)$, $C(-4, -1)$,

   $D\left(-3\frac{1}{4}, -1\frac{3}{4}\right)$, $E\left(-3\frac{1}{2}, -3\right)$, $F\left(-2\frac{1}{2}, -2\frac{1}{4}\right)$,

   $G\left(-1\frac{1}{2}, -3\right)$, $H\left(-1\frac{3}{4}, -1\frac{3}{4}\right)$, $I(-1, -1)$,

   $J(-2, -1)$

5. The area of the enlarged triangle is 9 times larger, which is 3 squared. Because area is in square units, the factors are squared. So, if the base and height are 3 times larger, you square that factor to find how much bigger the area is.

2.5 Puzzle Time

THE BICYCLE THAT KEPT FALLING OVER BECAUSE IT WAS TWO TIRED

2.6 Start Thinking!
For use before Activity 2.6

Sample answer: You need to find the area of your room by measuring the length and width.

2.6 Warm Up
For use before Activity 2.6

1. $P = 32$ in.; $A = 63$ in.^{2}

2. $P = 60$ cm; $A = 225$ cm^2

3. $P = 12$ cm; $A = 6$ cm^2

4. $P = 48$ in.; $A = 130$ in.^{2}

Answers

2.6 Start Thinking!
For use before Lesson 2.6

When your neighbor doubles the side lengths of the deck, the perimeter of the deck will double in size.

2.6 Warm Up
For use before Lesson 2.6

1. The perimeter will quadruple.

2. The area will double.

3. The perimeter will triple.

4. The perimeter will double.

2.6 Practice A

1. Perimeter: 5 : 9; Area: 25 : 81

2. Perimeter: 3 : 7; Area: 9 : 49

3. Multiplies it by 4.

4. a. 4 : 5   b. 16 : 25   c. 35.2 ft

5. $x = \dfrac{50}{3}$

6. a. B b. 2 in.   c. 4 : 7   d. 31.36 : 49

2.6 Practice B

1. Perimeter: 5 : 13; Area: 25 : 169

2. Multiplies it by 3.   3. $x = 10.5$

4. a. 9 : 14   b. 81 : 196   c. 70 ft

5. a. 2.56 times greater   b. 12.5 ft^2 c. 15 ft

6. a. 4 : 25   b. 2 : 5   c. 5π

2.6 Enrichment and Extension

1. $32.73

2. 80 in.

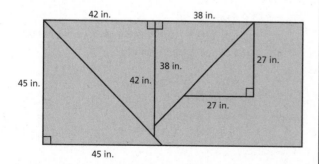

3. $8.87   4. 2981 in.^{2} 5. 619 in.^{2} 6. 17%

7. *Sample answer:* Cutting straight rectangles is easy to do, and then they do not have to find a use for the left over material that is oddly shaped.

8. *Sample answer:* She could make more frames that are smaller. She could use the material as a rag for household cleaning. She could use it as a drop cloth to protect small surfaces near where she is painting or doing other crafts.

2.6 Puzzle Time

TO THE WASPITAL

2.7 Start Thinking!
For use before Activity 2.7

Sample answer: photos

2.7 Warm Up
For use before Activity 2.7

1. 8   2. −20   3. −3

4. −1.5   5. 2   6. 4

2.7 Start Thinking!
For use before Lesson 2.7

Sample answer: A photographer may need to enlarge or reduce a photo to fit a specific spot in a magazine.

2.7 Warm Up
For use before Lesson 2.7

1.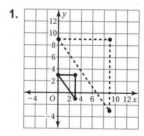
The triangles are similar.

2.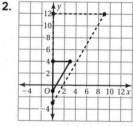
The triangles are similar.

2.7 Practice A

1.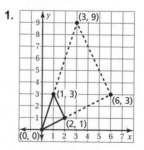
The triangles are similar.

2.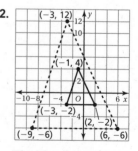
The triangles are similar.

Answers

3. yes   **4.** no

5.

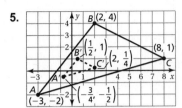

reduction

6.

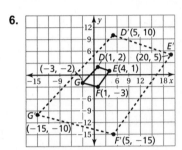

enlargement

7. reduction; $k = \dfrac{1}{2}$ **8.** enlargement; $k = 3$

9. 12

10. $P''(6, 1), Q''(10, 5), R''(2, 9)$

2.7 Practice B

1.

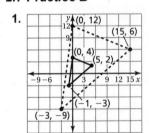

The triangles are similar.

2.

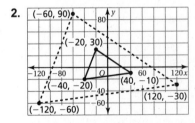

The triangles are similar.

3. no   **4.** yes

5.

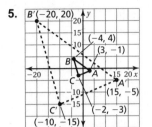

enlargement

6.

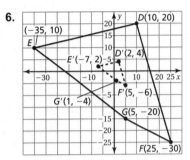

reduction

7. reduction; $k = \dfrac{1}{3}$ **8.** enlargement; $k = \dfrac{5}{2}$

9. 360°; 360°; perimeter of image is 2 times larger

10. $\dfrac{1}{6}$

2.7 Enrichment and Extension

1. no; Dilating an object changes its size but not its orientation. Flipping the surfboard would require a reflection.

2. 5 inches wide, 11.25 inches long

3. 3 inches wide, 6.75 inches long

4. a. scale factor = 4   **b.** 300% increase

5. a. scale factor = $\dfrac{1}{2}$ **b.** 50% decrease

6. The scale factor used to increase the width is different from the scale factor used to increase the length.

2.7 Puzzle Time

A DOC-TOPUS

Technology Connection

1. The reflected triangle also moves so that it is still a mirror image of the original triangle.

2. The dilated triangle is a different size than the original triangle, but it is similar to the original triangle.

Big Ideas Math Blue **A11**
Answers

Answers

3. The closer the center of rotation is to $\triangle DEF$, the closer the rotation.

Chapter 3

3.1 Start Thinking!
For use before Activity 3.1

Sample answers: vertical window blinds, lines formed by floor tiles, top and bottom of walls, the edges of rectangular objects

3.1 Warm Up
For use before Activity 3.1

1. $x = 48$ 2. $x = 12.5$ 3. $x = 10$

4. $x = 5.5$ 5. $x = 32$ 6. $x = \dfrac{15}{8}$

3.1 Start Thinking!
For use before Lesson 3.1

yes; You know that three of the angles are congruent to the given angle. The other four angles are supplementary to the given angle (or congruent angles) because they form straight angles.

3.1 Warm Up
For use before Lesson 3.1

1. k and ℓ 2. m 3. 8

4. $\angle 1 \cong \angle 3 \cong \angle 6 \cong \angle 8$; $\angle 2 \cong \angle 4 \cong \angle 5 \cong \angle 7$

3.1 Practice A

1. $m\angle 1 = 115°$; $m\angle 2 = 65°$

2. $m\angle 1 = 106°$; $m\angle 2 = 74°$

3. $m\angle 1 = m\angle 3 = 139°$ (supplementary)
   $m\angle 2 = 41°$ (vertical)
   $m\angle 4 = m\angle 6 = 139°$ (corresponding)
   $m\angle 5 = m\angle 7 = 41°$ (corresponding)

4. $m\angle 6 = m\angle 7 = 63°$ (supplementary)
   $m\angle 5 = 117°$ (vertical)
   $m\angle 1 = m\angle 3 = 117°$ (corresponding)
   $m\angle 2 = m\angle 4 = 63°$ (corresponding)

5. $160°$; $\angle 1$ and $\angle 5$ are corresponding angles.

6. $37°$; $\angle 6$ and $\angle 4$ are vertical angles.

7. $98°$; *Sample answer:* $\angle 8$ and $\angle 4$ are corresponding angles, and $\angle 4$ and $\angle 3$ are supplementary angles.

8. $120°$; $\angle 4$ and $\angle 5$ are supplementary angles.

9. $\angle 2$ is congruent to $\angle 4$. $\angle 4$ is congruent to $\angle 8$. So, $\angle 2$ is congruent to $\angle 8$.

10. $\angle 6$ is supplementary to $\angle 3$. $\angle 3$ is congruent to $\angle 1$. So, $\angle 6$ is supplementary to $\angle 1$.

3.1 Practice B

1. $m\angle 6 = m\angle 7 = 32°$ (supplementary)
   $m\angle 5 = 148°$ (vertical)
   $m\angle 1 = m\angle 3 = 148°$ (corresponding)
   $m\angle 2 = m\angle 4 = 32°$ (corresponding)

2. $m\angle 1 = 90°$ (vertical)
   $m\angle 2 = m\angle 3 = 90°$ (supplementary)
   $m\angle 6 = m\angle 4 = 90°$ (corresponding)
   $m\angle 5 = m\angle 7 = 90°$ (corresponding)

3. $130°$; $\angle 1$ and $\angle 8$ are corresponding angles.

4. $127°$; *Sample answer:* $\angle 5$ and $\angle 4$ are corresponding angles, and $\angle 4$ and $\angle 3$ are supplementary angles.

5. $109°$; $\angle 7$ and $\angle 3$ are supplementary angles.

6. $115°$; *Sample answer:* $\angle 4$ and $\angle 5$ are corresponding angles, and $\angle 5$ and $\angle 6$ are supplementary angles.

7. always; They are vertical angles.

8. sometimes; They are supplementary if they are right angles.

9. never; They are supplementary.

10. never; They are adjacent angles.

11. always; Angles 2 and 6 are congruent because they are corresponding angles. Angles 6 and 8 are congruent because they are vertical angles. So, angles 2 and 8 are congruent.

12. no; Any two adjacent angles will be supplementary and two acute angles cannot be supplementary.

3.1 Enrichment and Extension

1. $2°$, $89°$, $89°$

2. yes; One angle is $2°$ because of vertical angles, and the other two are $89°$ because of alternate interior angles.

Answers

3. 4 : 1

4. focal length of eyepiece: 5 cm; focal length of objective lens: 20 cm

5. 5 times

6. decrease; The focal length of the eyepiece would be longer, so $\dfrac{250}{f}$ would be smaller.

3.1 Puzzle Time
IT DIDN'T WANT TO GET ITS HARE WET

3.2 Start Thinking!
For use before Activity 3.2

Sample answer: A yield sign is an equilateral triangle.

3.2 Warm Up
For use before Activity 3.2

1. right **2.** acute **3.** straight **4.** obtuse

3.2 Start Thinking!
For use before Lesson 3.2

Sample answer: construction, bridge building

3.2 Warm Up
For use before Lesson 3.2

1. 40° **2.** 45° **3.** 41°

4. 36° **5.** 63° **6.** 60°

3.2 Practice A

1. $x = 72$ **2.** $x = 65$ **3.** $x = 120$ **4.** $x = 52$

5. no; 35.9°, 110.4°, 33.7°

6. yes

7. a. 45, 90, 45

   b. Every triangle has one 90° angle and two 45° angles.

   c. An isosceles right triangle has two 45° angles.

3.2 Practice B

1. $x = 102$ **2.** $x = 60$ **3.** $x = 28$ **4.** $x = 12$

5. $x = 135$ **6.** $k = 155$ **7.** 118 **8.** 155

9. 18°, 72°, 90° **10.** yes; 20°, 90°

3.2 Enrichment and Extension

1. $\dfrac{56}{65}$ **2.** $\dfrac{72}{65}$ **3.** $\dfrac{33}{65}$

4. $\dfrac{56}{33}$ **5.** $\dfrac{72}{97}$ **6.** $\dfrac{65}{97}$

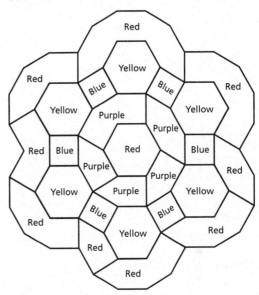

3.2 Puzzle Time
NEVER MIND I DON'T WANT TO SPREAD IT AROUND

3.3 Start Thinking!
For use before Activity 3.3

Sample answers:

stop: octagon

yield: equilateral triangle

no passing zone: isosceles triangle

speed limit: quadrilateral or rectangle

railroad crossing: 12-gon

school advance warning: pentagon

warning: quadrilateral or square

3.3 Warm Up
For use before Activity 3.3

1. −4 **2.** −13 **3.** 80

4. −26 **5.** −0.5 **6.** −3

Answers

3.3 Start Thinking!
For use before Lesson 3.3

Each angle is made up of a right angle $(90°)$ from a grid square, plus half a right angle $(45°)$ from half a grid square. So, the measure of each angle of the octagon is $90 + 45 + 135°$. The sum of the eight angles is $8(135) = 1080°$.

3.3 Warm Up
For use before Lesson 3.3

1. $360°$ 2. $1080°$ 3. $720°$
4. $360°$ 5. $540°$ 6. $180°$

3.3 Practice A

1. $720°$ 2. $540°$ 3. $1080°$ 4. $900°$

5. Yes, the sum of the angle measures is $1080°$.

6. $42°, 78°, 42°, 198°$

7. $120°, 120°, 120°, 120°, 120°, 120°$

8. $135°$ 9. $60°, 60°, 60°, 60°, 60°$

10. $86°, 86°, 82°, 36°, 70°$

3.3 Practice B

1. $900°$ 2. $1080°$ 3. $1440°$
4. $1260°$ 5. $110°$

6. $136°, 102°, 75°, 92°, 105°, 210°$

7. $99°, 95°, 145°, 101°, 100°$

8. 8 sides

9. a. concave b. not regular
   c. heptagon d. $900°$

3.3 Enrichment and Extension

1. 440 cm^2 2. 1254 mm^2
3. 14 in.^2 4. 480 yd^2

3.3 Puzzle Time

WHEN SHE GOT THERE THE CUPBOARD WAS BEAR

3.4 Start Thinking!
For use before Activity 3.4

B and C; D and G; They appear to have the same shape.

3.4 Warm Up
For use before Activity 3.4

1. $x = 2$ 2. $x = 16$

3.4 Start Thinking!
For use before Lesson 3.4

The sun's rays form congruent angles with the ground. When his shadow is equal to his height, then the sun is forming a $45°$ angle with the ground, making a $45°$-$45°$-$90°$ triangle. The triangle formed by the pyramid and its shadow is a similar $45°$-$45°$-$90°$ triangle. So, the height of the pyramid is the length of the shadow, plus half of the length of the base (to measure the height from the center of the pyramid).

3.4 Warm Up
For use before Lesson 3.4

1–2. Answers will vary. Check students' drawings and ratios.

3.4 Practice A

1. not similar; Corresponding angles are not congruent.

2. similar; Corresponding angles are congruent.

3. $x = 52$

4. a. $\angle B$ is congruent to itself. $\angle A$ and $\angle D$ have the same line of sight, and so they are congruent. Because two angles are congruent, the third angles are congruent. Because the triangles have the same angle measures, they are similar.

   b. $\dfrac{5}{x} = \dfrac{7}{42}$; $7x = 210$; $x = 30$ ft;
   $30 \text{ ft} + 5 \text{ ft} = 35 \text{ ft}$;
   The height of the building is 35 feet.

5. a. $\angle B$ and $\angle E$ are right angles, and thus congruent. $\angle BCA$ and $\angle ECD$ are vertical angles, and so they are congruent. Because two angles are congruent, the third angles are congruent. Because the triangles have the same angle measures, they are similar.

   b. $\dfrac{x}{8} = \dfrac{9}{3}$; $3x = 72$; $x = 24$ yd

3.4 Practice B

1. not similar; Corresponding angles are not congruent.

2. similar; Corresponding angles are congruent.

Answers

3. $x = 76$

4. a. $\angle B$ is congruent to itself. $\angle A$ and $\angle D$ have the same line of sight, and so they are congruent. Because two angles are congruent, the third angles are congruent. Because the triangles have the same angle measures, they are similar.

b. $\dfrac{3}{x} = \dfrac{5}{22}$; $5x = 66$; $x = 13.2$ ft;
$13.2 + 4.5 = 17.7$ ft; The height of the flag pole is 17.7 feet.

5. a. $\angle B$ and $\angle E$ are right angles, and thus congruent. $\angle BCA$ and $\angle ECD$ are vertical angles, and so they are congruent. Because two angles are congruent, the third angles are congruent. Because the triangles have the same angle measures, they are similar.

b. $\dfrac{0.2}{x} = \dfrac{0.1}{0.3}$; $0.1x = 0.06$; $x = 0.6$ mi

3.4 Enrichment and Extension

1. yes; The pattern repeats across the entire plane with no gaps or overlap.

2. triangles and hexagons

3. $60°$ **4.** $120°$

5. Check students' work.

6. triangle, triangle, triangle, triangle, hexagon

7. $360°$

8. *Sample answer:* floor tiles, quilts

9. *Sampler answer:* rectangles

3.4 Puzzle Time
SEA WEED

Technology Connection

1. *Sample answer:*

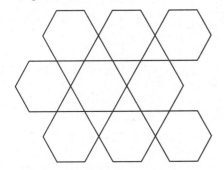

2. *Sample answer:*

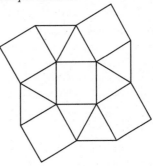

or

3. *Sample answer:*

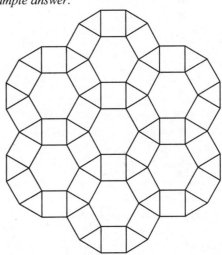

Chapter 4

4.1 Start Thinking!
For use before Activity 4.1

A and C; the graphs are lines.

4.1 Warm Up
For use before Activity 4.1

1.

x	−1	0	1	2
y	−5	−3	−1	1

2.

x	−1	0	1	2
y	2	1	0	−1

3.

x	−1	0	1	2
y	4	5	6	7

4.

x	−1	0	1	2
y	1.5	2	2.5	3

Answers

4.1 Start Thinking!
For use before Lesson 4.1

Answers will vary. Check students' graphs.

4.1 Warm Up
For use before Lesson 4.1

1–2. Answers will vary. Sample answers are given.

1.

x	0	2
$y = 4x - 2$	-2	6

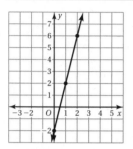

A different solution point on the line is $(1, 2)$.

2.

x	0	5
$y = -x + 5$	5	0

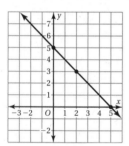

A different solution point on the line is $(2, 3)$.

4.1 Practice A

1–2. Sample answers are given.

1. $(-1, -1)$

x	0	1
$y = 4x + 3$	3	7

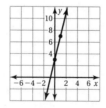

2. $(4, 5)$

x	0	2
$y = \dfrac{3}{2}x - 1$	-1	2

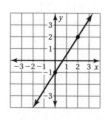

3.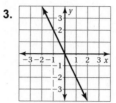

4.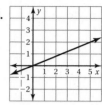

5.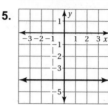

6.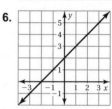

7.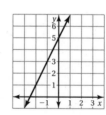

8.

9. a.

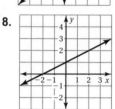

b. *Sample answer:* about $5.30   **c.** $5.33

10. $y = 2x + 5$

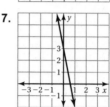

11. $y = -\dfrac{6}{5}x + 3$

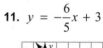

12. a. $y = 110 - 2.75x$

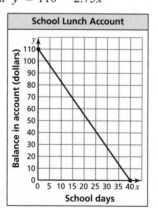

b. 40 school days

Answers

4.1 Practice B

1.

2.

3.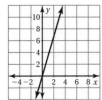

4.

5.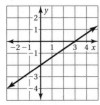

6.

7. a.

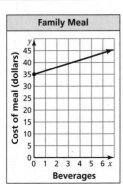

Family Meal

b. *Sample answer:* about $42   **c.** $42.50

8. $y = -\dfrac{3}{2}x - 3$

9. $y = -4x + 6$

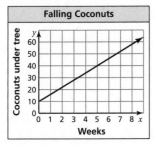

10. a. $y = 10 + 6x$

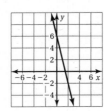

Falling Coconuts

b. after 7 weeks

11.

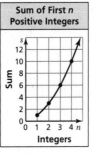

Sum of First n Positive Integers

not a line

4.1 Enrichment and Extension

1.

x	y
-2	7
-1	5
0	3
1	1
2	-1

2.

x	y
-2	11
-1	2
0	-1
1	2
2	11

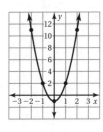

3.

x	y
-2	0
-1	1
0	2
1	1
2	0

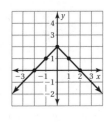

4. $y = -2x + 3$

5. $y = 3x^2 - 1$; The graph of the quadratic equation is shaped like a U.

6. $y = -|x| + 2$; The graph of the absolute value equation is shaped like an upside-down V, or mountain peak.

7. *Sample answer:* They all have different shapes.

8. The y-intercept would change and the graph would shift up or down.

Answers

4.1 Puzzle Time

A CREAM PUFFIN

4.2 Start Thinking!
For use before Activity 4.2

Sample answer: A ski slope is a natural incline, usually a mountain or hill. The mathematical term slope refers to how steep an incline is.

4.2 Warm Up
For use before Activity 4.2

1. 3   **2.** $\dfrac{2}{7}$ **3.** $\dfrac{2}{5}$

4. $\dfrac{5}{4}$ **5.** $\dfrac{2}{3}$ **6.** $\dfrac{4}{3}$

4.2 Start Thinking!
For use before Lesson 4.2

Monitor students during activity.

4.2 Warm Up
For use before Lesson 4.2

1. The lines are parallel.   **2.** The lines are parallel.

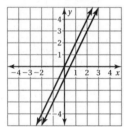

4.2 Practice A

1. a. lines A and C **b.** line B

   c. lines A and C; Both have a slope of $-\dfrac{1}{3}$.

2. The lines are parallel.   **3.** The lines are parallel.

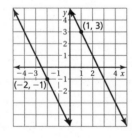

4. slope $= \dfrac{3}{2}$ **5.** slope $= -1$ **6.** slope $= 4$

7. slope $= 0$ **8.** slope $= 2$

4.2 Practice B

1. slope $= \dfrac{1}{5}$ **2.** slope $= 0$

3. slope $= -6$ **4.** slope $= \dfrac{4}{3}$

5. slope $= \dfrac{3}{2}$ **6.** slope $= -1$

7. 10 feet

8. a. slope $= 0.1$

   b. The phone calls cost $0.10 per minute.

   c. $0.50   **d.** 30 minutes

4.2 Enrichment and Extension

1.

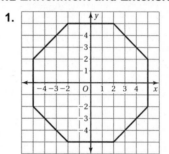

2. *Sample answer:* yes; The opposite sides appear to have the same slope. It looks like the pairs of opposite sides are slanted the same way.

3. From the top, going clockwise around the octagon, the slopes are 0, −1, undefined, 1, 0, −1, undefined, and 1. *Sample answer:* yes; The predictions were correct.

4. yes; The opposite sides have the same slope, so opposite sides are parallel.

5. *Sample answer:* yes; There are three sets of line segments that look like they have the same slope– the horizontal segments, the segments slanted up to the right, and the segments slanted up to the left.

6. From the top, going clockwise around the shape, the slopes are $-\dfrac{4}{3}$, 0, $\dfrac{4}{3}$, $-\dfrac{4}{3}$, 0, $\dfrac{4}{3}$, $-\dfrac{4}{3}$, 0, $\dfrac{4}{3}$, $-\dfrac{4}{3}$, 0, and $\dfrac{4}{3}$. *Sample answer:* yes; The predictions were correct.

7. no; None of the segments are perpendicular because $\dfrac{4}{3} \cdot 0 \neq -1$, $-\dfrac{4}{3} \cdot 0 \neq -1$, and $-\dfrac{4}{3} \cdot \dfrac{4}{3} \neq -1$.

Answers

4.2 Puzzle Time

I'M ON A ROLL

Extension 4.2 Start Thinking!
For use before Extension 4.2

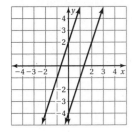 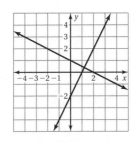

The two lines do not appear to intersect.

The graphs appear to intersect at right angles.

Extension 4.2 Warm Up
For use before Extension 4.2

1. slope of line B: 2; slope of line G: 2

2. slope of line B: 3; slope of line G: $-\dfrac{1}{3}$

Extension 4.2 Practice

1. A and B; They both have a slope of 3.

2. A and C; They both have a slope of $-\dfrac{1}{6}$.

3. no; $x = -1$ has an undefined slope and $y = 2$ has a slope of 0.

4. yes; Both lines are vertical and have an undefined slope.

5. yes; Both lines are horizontal and have a slope of 0.

6. yes; Opposite sides have the same slope.

7. B and C; Line B has a slope of 2. Line C has a slope of $-\dfrac{1}{2}$. The product of their slopes is $2 \bullet \left(-\dfrac{1}{2}\right) = -1$.

8. A and C; Line A has a slope of $\dfrac{1}{3}$. Line C has a slope of -3. The product of their slopes is $\dfrac{1}{3} \bullet (-3) = -1$.

9. yes; Line $x = 1$ is vertical. Line $y = 0$ is horizontal. A vertical line is perpendicular to a horizontal line.

10. no; Both lines are horizontal and have a slope of 0.

11. yes; Line $x = -2$ is vertical. Line $y = 2$ is horizontal. A vertical line is perpendicular to a horizontal line.

12. no; Adjacent sides are not perpendicular.

4.3 Start Thinking!
For use before Activity 4.3

Sample answer:

x	-1	0	1
y	0	2	4

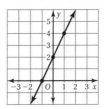

4.3 Warm Up
For use before Activity 4.3

1. $x = 12$ 2. $x = 18$ 3. $x = 6$

4. $x = 2$ 5. $x = 7$ 6. $x = 10$

4.3 Start Thinking!
For use before Lesson 4.3

Check student's sketches; The line that passes through the origin will have an equation of the form $y = mx$.

4.3 Warm Up
For use before Lesson 4.3

1. no; The graph of the equation does not pass through the origin.

2. yes; $y = 5x$; The graph is a line that passes through the origin.

3. yes; $y = \dfrac{1}{2}x$; The rate of change in the table is constant.

4. no; The rate of change in the table is not constant.

4.3 Practice A

1. yes; $y = 3x$; The graph is a line that passes through the origin.

2. no; The graph does not pass through the origin.

3. no; The rate of change in the table is not constant.

4. yes; $y = \dfrac{1}{4}x$; The rate of change in the table is constant.

Answers

5. a.

Your friend runs 7.5 miles in 1 hour.

b. *Sample answer:* 8 min

6. a. hamburgers; *Sample answer:* Hamburgers sell at a rate of about 2.67 per minute and wraps sell at a rate of 2.5 per minute.

b.

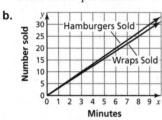

Sample answer: The graph of the hamburgers sold is steeper. Hamburgers are selling at a faster rate than wraps.

4.3 Practice B

1. no; The graph does not pass through the origin.

2. yes; $y = 12x$; The graph is a line that passes through the origin.

3. yes; $y = 4x$; The rate of change in the table is constant.

4. yes; $y = \frac{2}{3}x$; The rate of change in the table is constant.

5. a. $y = 9x$

b. It costs $9 to rent the lane for 1 hour.

c. $27

6. a. yes; The graph is a line that passes through the origin.

b. $y = \frac{1}{20}x$; The height of the water in the tank rises $\frac{1}{20}$ inch per gallon of water.

c. 12.5 in.

4.3 Enrichment and Extension

1. a. decrease **b.** increase **c.** It equals 1.

2. No, it does not have a constant rate of change.

3. direct variation **4.** inverse variation

5. neither **6.** neither

7. direct variation **8.** inverse variation

9. inverse variation; $c = \dfrac{200}{n}$

10. direct variation; $p = 20r$

4.3 Puzzle Time

CHEERIOS

4.4 Start Thinking!
For use before Activity 4.4

Sample answer: The point (4, 290) means that about 290 people attended the book fair on the 4th day. The graph is approximately linear. The approximate slope is 2.8. So, the book fair attendance increased by about 2.8 people each day.

4.4 Warm Up
For use before Activity 4.4

1.

x	0	1	2	3
y	−1	0	1	2

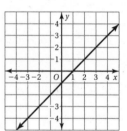

2.

x	−2	0	2	4
y	1	2	3	4

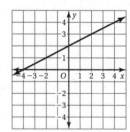

4.4 Start Thinking!
For use before Lesson 4.4

Sample answer: You buy x pairs of socks for $2.50 each and pay $5 for shipping. The slope is $2.50 per pair and the y-intercept is $5.

Answers

4.4 Warm Up
For use before Lesson 4.4

1. B; slope $= 2$, y-intercept $= -1$

2. A; slope $= -1$, y-intercept $= 2$

3. C; slope $= -2$, y-intercept $= -1$

4.4 Practice A

1. C; $-\dfrac{1}{2}$; 5

2. A; -3; -1

3. B; $\dfrac{2}{3}$; 2

4. $m = 1$; $b = 4$

5. $m = -8$; $b = 3$

6. $m = -\dfrac{5}{7}$; $b = -2$

7. $m = 1.75$; $b = -1$

8. $m = 6$; $b = 2$

9. $m = \dfrac{1}{9}$; $b = -7$

10. a.

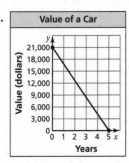

b. The value of the car decreases $4200 per year.

c. $21,000 is the initial cost of the car.

d. The value of the car is $0 after 5 years.

11. 2

12. 48

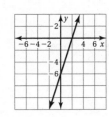

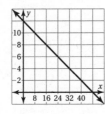

13. -3

14. $-\dfrac{2}{5}$

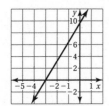

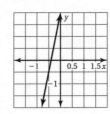

15. a.

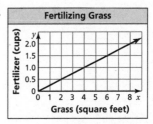

b. $\dfrac{1}{4}$ cup of fertilizer is needed per square foot of grass.

4.4 Practice B

1. $m = -\dfrac{3}{8}$; $b = 10$

2. $m = 4.5$; $b = 7$

3. $m = -\dfrac{4}{5}$; $b = -\dfrac{1}{5}$

4. $m = 5.5$; $b = -2.5$

5. $m = 4$; $b = \dfrac{2}{7}$

6. $m = \dfrac{2}{3}$; $b = -5$

7. $\dfrac{6}{5}$

8. 7.5

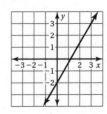

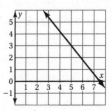

9. -6

10. $-\dfrac{7}{2}$

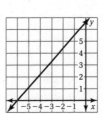

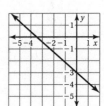

11. a. $y = 0.50x + 10$

b.

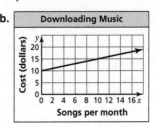

c. $17.50

Answers

12. a. $y = 6x$

b.

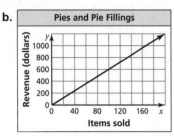
Pies and Pie Fillings

c. 184 items per month   **d.** 46 items per week

4.4 Enrichment and Extension

1. 1   **2.** 4   **3.** $-1\dfrac{3}{5}$ **4.** -4

5. 3   **6.** -2 **7.** $-2\dfrac{2}{3}$

4.4 Puzzle Time

THE LADY WHO GOT STOPPED FOR SPEEDING SO MANY TIMES THE POLICE GAVE HER SEASON TICKETS

4.5 Start Thinking!

For use before Activity 4.5

$2x + 5y = 10$; *Sample answer:* The graphs are the same. Multiplying the original equation by 5 and then adding $2x$ to each side yields $2x + 5y = 10$.

4.5 Warm Up

For use before Activity 4.5

1. $y = -x + 4$ **2.** $y = -2x + 10$

3. $y = -\dfrac{3}{4}x + 3$ **4.** $y = \dfrac{1}{2}x + \dfrac{4}{5}$

5. $y = 2x + 5$ **6.** $y = \dfrac{1}{2}x + 2$

4.5 Start Thinking!

For use before Lesson 4.5

Sample answer: It is easier to write in standard form because of the information you are given. You know that the sum of the two costs is $40, or $10x + 6y = 40$.

4.5 Warm Up

For use before Lesson 4.5

1. Let x represent non-highway hours and let y represent highway hours; $y = -\dfrac{5}{12}x + 4$

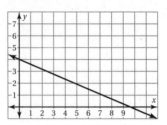

2. Let x represent number of hats and let y represent number of T-shirts; $y = -\dfrac{1}{2}x + 3$

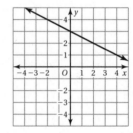

4.5 Practice A

1. $y = -4x + 10$ **2.** $y = 3x - 7$

3.

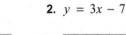

4.

5. $3; -2$ **6.** $-2; 5$

7.

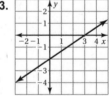

8.

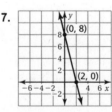

9. a. 11; 11 oranges and 0 apples contain 110 grams of fiber.

b. 22; 22 apples and 0 oranges contain 110 grams of fiber.

c. 10 g   **d.** 5 g

e. no; There cannot be 3.5 oranges in the package.

Answers

10. a. $8x + 6y = 144$ **b.** 18; 24

c.

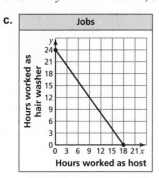

Jobs

d. 10.5 h

4.5 Practice B

1. $y = -\dfrac{2}{3}x + 4$ **2.** $y = 2x - 5$

3.

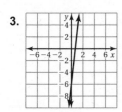

4.

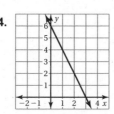

5. 0; 0   **6.** no x-intercept; 5

7.

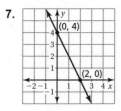

8.

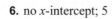
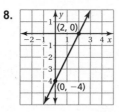

9. a. $80x + 40y = 480$ **b.** 6; 12

c.

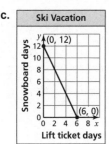

Ski Vacation

d. 5 days

10. a. $y = 80 + 32x$ **b.** -2.5; 80

c.

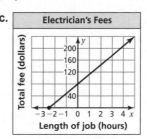

d. no; The visit cannot last a negative number of hours.

4.5 Enrichment and Extension

1. no; The graph is not a straight line.

2. 40

3. The trapeze artist starts 40 feet right of center.

4. 8

5. The trapeze artist swings back and forth past center more than once.

6. 16 seconds   **7.** 80 feet

8. no; The peaks and valleys on the graph do not vary. Realistically, the trapeze artist would not always swing to the same horizontal position.

9. no; It does not make sense to include negative numbers for time in this situation.

4.5 Puzzle Time

THEY JUMP SHIP

4.6 Start Thinking!
For use before Activity 4.6

The graph shows the temperature of an oven while it is preheating. The y-intercept, 70, represents the temperature of the stove before it was turned on. The slope, 35 degrees per minute, represents the heating rate.

4.6 Warm Up
For use before Activity 4.6

1. $-\dfrac{2}{3}$ **2.** 2

4.6 Start Thinking!
For use before Lesson 4.6

$y = 40x + 20$; the slope represents the monthly cost; the y-intercept represents the enrollment fee.

Answers

For use before Lesson 4.6

1. $y = \frac{1}{2}x$, $y = \frac{1}{2}x + 3$, $y = 2x + 6$, $y = 2x$

2. $y = x + 1$, $y = x - 5$, $y = -x + 5$,
$y = -x + 1$

4.6 Practice A

1. $y = 3x + 1$, $y = 4$, $y = 3x - 11$, $y = -2$

2. $y = -\frac{3}{2}x + 1$ **3.** $y = \frac{3}{5}x + 2$

4. $y = 2x + 3$ **5.** $y = -\frac{1}{2}x$

6. $y = -\frac{3}{2}x + 3$

7. a.

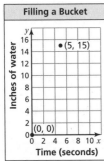

Filling a Bucket

b. There are 0 inches of water at 0 seconds. There are 15 inches of water after 5 seconds.

c.

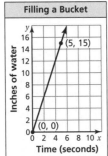

Filling a Bucket

d. The inches of water y in the bucket after x seconds.

e. $y = 3x$

4.6 Practice B

1. $y = 1$, $y = 3x - 5$, $y = -2$, $y = -3x - 5$

2. $y = -\frac{1}{4}x - 1$ **3.** $y = \frac{7}{5}x + 4$

4. a. 5.7 inches per year

   b. $y = 5.7x + 6$ **c.** 28.8 inches

5. $y = \frac{3}{2}x + 5$ **6.** $y = -2x - 3$

7. a.

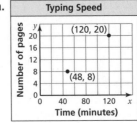

Typing Speed

b. $\dfrac{1 \text{ page}}{6 \text{ minutes}}$ or $\dfrac{1}{6}$ page per minute

c. $y = \frac{1}{6}x$

4.6 Enrichment and Extension

The equations match up with the graph in the corresponding position.

4.6 Puzzle Time

MORE THAN THE LION

4.7 Start Thinking!

For use before Activity 4.7

Sample answer: yes; You can plot the point and use the slope to graph the line. From the graph, you can write the equation.

4.7 Warm Up

For use before Activity 4.7

1. 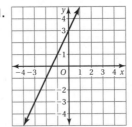   **2.**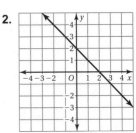

3. 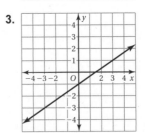   **4.**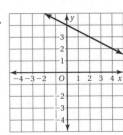

Answers

5. 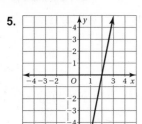   **6.**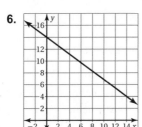

4.7 Start Thinking!
For use before Lesson 4.7

Sample answer: If you need to write the equation of a line given the slope and a point on the line, you can find the *y*-intercept (either graphically or algebraically). Then you follow the steps for writing an equation given the slope and *y*-intercept.

4.7 Warm Up
For use before Lesson 4.7

1. $y = 2x - 1$ **2.** $y = -x + 1$

3. $y = -\dfrac{1}{2}x - 2$ **4.** $y = \dfrac{2}{3}x - 1$

4.7 Practice A

1. $y = 3x + 4$ **2.** $y = -\dfrac{2}{3}x + 2$

3. $y = \dfrac{1}{4}x - 3$ **4.** $y = -\dfrac{4}{3}x + 1$

5. $y = -x + 4$ **6.** $y = 4x - 1$

7. $y = \dfrac{1}{3}x - 3$ **8.** $y = -\dfrac{5}{2}x + 2$

9. $y = -2x - 4$ **10.** $y = 5x + 1$

11. a. $V = -150x + 900$ **b.** \$900   **c.** \$150

4.7 Practice B

1. $y = \dfrac{5}{4}x - 2$ **2.** $y = -4x + 3$

3. $y = \dfrac{1}{3}x + 5$ **4.** $y = -\dfrac{3}{4}x - 1$

5. $y = 2x - 3$ **6.** $y = -3x + 2$

7. $y = 4x - 5$ **8.** $y = \dfrac{4}{5}x - 4$

9. $y = -\dfrac{1}{3}x + 2$ **10.** $y = \dfrac{5}{2}x - 1$

11. a. $y = -2x + 24$

   b. 24 feet   **c.** after 12 seconds

4.7 Enrichment and Extension

1. The slope is the negative of the grade, written as a fraction or decimal.

2. Bunny Slope: $-\dfrac{1}{25}$, Medium Trail: $-\dfrac{3}{20}$,

   Expert Trail: $-\dfrac{3}{10}$

3. $y = -\dfrac{1}{25}x + 58$

4. 58; The starting height of the trail is 58 meters.

5. 1450; The length of the trail is 1450 meters.

6. $y = -\dfrac{3}{20}x + 1530$ **7.** $y = -\dfrac{3}{10}x + 6000$

8. no; It has a grade of 8%.

4.7 Puzzle Time

THE TEAM SPIRIT

Technology Connection

1. 1.5

2. a. -1.5

   b. The sign changed.

   c. *Sample answer:* Visualize the points and determine whether the slope should be positive or negative to check your answer.

3. a. 0.667

   b. The are reciprocals.

   c. *Sample answer:* Compare the change in *y* to the change in *x* to determine whether the slope is steeper (magnitude greater than 1) or shallower (magnitude less than 1) to check your answer.

4. -0.57 **5.** 3.33   **6.** 0   **7.** 5

Chapter 5

5.1 Start Thinking!
For use before Activity 5.1

The only solution is (3, 2). Methods may vary. *Sample answer:* Trial and error, to find two numbers where one number is 1 greater than the other and whose sum is 5. Other methods are substitution and graphing.

Answers

5.1 Warm Up
For use before Activity 5.1

1.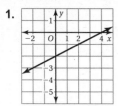

2.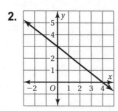

3.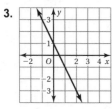

4.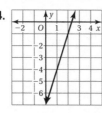

5.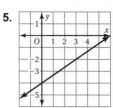

6.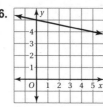

5.1 Start Thinking!
For use before Lesson 5.1

The solution is $(-1, -4)$. *Sample answer:* It's easier to see from the graph since you can see where the two lines intersect. With the table, you have to look at all of the values to see the ones in which the y-values are equal. In general, a graph is easier to use than a table because the solution may be excluded from the table.

5.1 Warm Up
For use before Lesson 5.1

1. $(2, 130)$ **2.** $(5, 80)$ **3.** $(4, 180)$

4. $(3, 45)$ **5.** $(6, 72)$ **6.** $(4, 50)$

5.1 Practice A

1. B   **2.** A   **3.** C

4. $(-2, 2)$ **5.** $(2, -5)$ **6.** $(5, -6)$

7. a. $R = 34x$ **b.** 6 bracelets

8. a. $x + y = 21$

       $x = y + 3$

   b. 12 pens, 9 pencils

5.1 Practice B

1. $(3, 15)$ **2.** $(-2, -13)$ **3.** $(8, -2)$

4. a. $R = 16x$ **b.** 250 tickets

5. $(4, 7)$ **6.** $(1, -2)$ **7.** $(-3, 0)$

8. $x + y = 60$

     $x = 2y$

40 one-bedroom apartments, 20 two-bedroom apartments

9. yes; The two lines could be parallel.

10. a. 25 min   **b.** 50 min   **c.** the tortoise

5.1 Enrichment and Extension

The solutions of the systems reading across are:

$(0, 0)$; $(3, 4)$; $(-7, 13)$; $\left(\dfrac{2}{3}, \dfrac{13}{3}\right)$; $(-2, 2)$; $(4, 6)$;

$(5, -2)$; $(2, 2)$; $\left(-\dfrac{1}{7}, \dfrac{8}{7}\right)$; no solution; $(1, 3)$; $(3, 0)$

5.1 Puzzle Time

THE TEACHER TOLD HIM IT WAS A PIECE OF CAKE

5.2 Start Thinking!
For use before Activity 5.2

$A = 3 + (2 + 0.5A)$

$A = 5 + 0.5A$

$0.5A = 5$

$2(0.5A) = 2(5)$

$A = 10$

$C = 2 + 0.5(10) = 2 + 5 = 7$

Amelia is 10 and Caleb is 7.

5.2 Warm Up
For use before Activity 5.2

1. $y = -2x + 5$ **2.** $b = a - 3$

3. $x = 5y - 12$ **4.** $c = \dfrac{7}{3}d + 4$

5. $y = -\dfrac{4}{3}x + 8$ **6.** $x = -\dfrac{3}{2}y + 2$

Answers

5.2 Start Thinking!
For use before Lesson 5.2

Check students' solutions. The solutions are $(1, 3)$ and $(-4, 1)$. The second system is easier to solve by graphing because the equations are in a form that is easy to graph. Also solving it by substitution involves fraction operations, which can be tricky. The first system is easier to solve by substitution. Graphing the second equation in the first system can be tough because the y-intercept is 3.6.

5.2 Warm Up
For use before Lesson 5.2

For Exercises 1–6, answers will vary. Sample answers are given.

1. $x + y = 2$
$x = y$

2. $y = x + 1$
$2x - 3 = y$

3. $x = 3y$
$2x - y = 10$

4. $y = 2x$
$x + y = 6$

5. $x + y = 11$
$x - y = -1$

6. $2x + y = 7$
$x = 3y$

5.2 Practice A

1. $y = 5x - 2$; It is already solved for y.

2. $3x - 12y = 6$; Every term is divisible by 3, so you can easily solve for x.

3. $\frac{1}{5}x + y = 8$; Can easily solve for y.

4. $(2, 5)$　　**5.** $(-3, -10)$　　**6.** $(17, 3)$

7. a. $x + y = 25$
$y = x + 7$

b. 9 treadmills　**c.** 16 stationary bikes

8. $(7, -2)$　　**9.** $(5, 5)$　　**10.** $\left(0, -\frac{1}{3}\right)$

11. a. $x + y = 24$
$x = 3y$

b. 18 spoons　**c.** 6 forks

12. $2x + 2y = 34$
$y = 2x + 2$

length: 12 cm; width: 5 cm

13. 42 cars; 18 trucks

5.2 Practice B

1. $(-5, 1)$　　**2.** $(3, -2)$　　**3.** $\left(4, \frac{1}{2}\right)$

4. a. $208x + 52y = 5460$
$y = x + 10$

b. \$19　**c.** \$29

5. $(7, 8)$　**6.** $(-6, 2)$　**7.** $\left(\frac{3}{2}, 1\right)$　**8.** 83

9. a. $x + y = 98$
$5x = 9y$

b. 63 food tents　**c.** 35 retail tents

10. a. 9 two-year-olds　**b.** 18 three-year-olds
c. 18 four-year-olds

5.2 Enrichment and Extension

1. *Sample answer:* $y = x, y = 2x$

2. $y = 2x, x = -2$

3. *Sample answer:* $y = x, y = 6$

4. $y = -x + 12, x = -2$

5. *Sample answer:* $y = -x + 6, y = 2x$

6. $y = x, y = -x + 6$

7. $x = -2, y = x + 2$

8. $y = -x + 12, y = x + 2$

9. $y = x + 2, x = 1$

10. $y = 2x, y = -x + 12$

11. $y = 3x + 4, y = 4x + 1$

12. *Sample answer:* $y = -x + 6, y = 4x + 1$

13. *Sample answer:*
$x + 2y = -16$
$y = x + 172$

5.2 Puzzle Time

IN A POLE VAULT

Answers

5.3 Start Thinking!
For use before Activity 5.3

Operation 1:
$$\begin{array}{r} 3 + 7 = 10 \\ 2 + 4 = 6 \\ \hline 1 + 3 = 4 \end{array}$$

Operation 2:
$$\begin{array}{r} 6 + 14 = 20 \\ 2 + 4 = 6 \\ \hline 8 + 18 = 26 \end{array}$$

Yes, after completing the operations, the statements are true. You can use the method of adding the equations together to solve the system:

$$\begin{array}{r} x + y = 10 \\ x - y = 4 \\ \hline 2x = 14 \\ x = 7 \end{array}$$

$x = 7$, so $7 + y = 10$, and $y = 3$.

The solution of the system is $(7, 3)$.

5.3 Warm Up
For use before Activity 5.3

1. $y = 15$ 2. $x = -6$ 3. $x = -16$

4. $y = 19$ 5. $x = -4$ 6. $y = 7$

5.3 Start Thinking!
For use before Lesson 5.3

Both students used elimination to correctly solve the system. Maddie multiplied the second equation by -2, added the new equation to the first equation, and solved for y. Sophie multiplied the second equation by -3, added the new equation to the first equation, and solved for x. Each student used substitution to correctly solve for the second variable.

5.3 Warm Up
For use before Lesson 5.3

1. $(8.5, 1.5)$ 2. $(-6, 7)$

3. $(8.5, 1)$ 4. $(1, -8)$

5.3 Practice A

1. $(3, -1)$ 2. $(2, 1)$ 3. $(3, 5)$

4. a. $5x + 2y = 9$
   $5x + 6y = 17$

   b. $1 per pound   c. $2 per pound

5. $(-4, 2)$ 6. $(1, 0)$ 7. $(-2, -3)$

8. a. $x + y = 20$
   $3x + 8y = 100$

   b. 12 multiple choice

   c. 8 short response

   d. 4 multiple choice, 11 short response

9. a. yes

   b. You added the equations instead of subtracting them.

5.3 Practice B

1. $(0, 0)$ 2. $(-5, -2)$ 3. $(8, 3)$

4. a. $x + y = 42$
   $x = y - 8$

   b. 17 magazine subscriptions

   c. 25 magazine subscriptions

5. $(6, -3)$ 6. $(-1, 1)$ 7. $(-3, -3)$

8. a. *Sample answer:* $a = -5$

   b. *Sample answer:* $b = 4$

9. $390

10. a. $a = -3$ b. $b = -1$ c. $c = 1$

5.3 Enrichment and Extension

1. *Sample answer:* It is best to use graphing when both equations are in a form that is easy to graph and the solution has integer values. It is best to use substitution when one or both of the equations are already solved for one of the variables. It is best to use elimination if it is difficult to solve for one of the variables in one of the equations.

2. *Sample answer:* The advantage to graphing is that you can visualize the solution and how the lines intersect. The disadvantages are that it can take more time to graph, and if the answer is not at a point where the grid squares cross, you cannot find the solution by graphing.

   The advantage to substitution is that you can always find the correct answer. The disadvantage is that sometimes solving for one of the variables is tricky, especially if it involves a lot of fractions.

   The advantage to elimination is that you can always use the method. It is quicker than the other methods if the equations are hard to solve for one of the variables. The disadvantage is that there are often more steps, thus more places to make calculation errors.

Answers

3. *Sample answer:* I prefer elimination because it works in all situations and I don't have to bother to solve one of the equations for one of the variables.

4. graphing; $(-1, 3)$ 5. elimination; $(4, 6)$

6. substitution; $(-2, 18)$ 7. graphing; $(3, 3)$

8. elimination; $(-3, 4)$ 9. elimination; $(-3, -7)$

10. substitution; $(-7, -4)$ 11. substitution; $(0, 1)$

5.3 Puzzle Time

SECOND BASE TO THIRD BASE BECAUSE THERE IS A SHORTSTOP

5.4 Start Thinking!

For use before Activity 5.4

Sample answer: No, a pair of numbers cannot add up to two different numbers. The system has no solution. Another system with no solution is:

$y = 2x - 6$

$y = 2x + 1$

5.4 Warm Up

For use before Activity 5.4

1. parallel   2. coincide

3. intersect at one point   4. coinside

5. intersect at one point   6. parallel

5.4 Start Thinking!

For use before Lesson 5.4

Sample answer: In both instances with no solution, you go through all of the steps of solving and end up with a false statement, such $10 = 6$. The two processes are different because solving a system first involves eliminating one of the variables to get an equation in one variable. In solving an equation with a solution of all real numbers or solving a system with infinitely many solutions, you go through all of the steps of solving and end up with a statement that is always true, such as $3 = 3$. The two processes are different because solving a system first involves eliminating one of the variables to get an equation in one variable.

5.4 Warm Up

For use before Lesson 5.4

1. no solution   2. $x = -0.5, y = 2.5$

3. $x = 10, y = 0$ 4. no solution

5.4 Practice A

1. infinitely many solutions; The lines are identical.

2. no solution; The lines have the same slope and different y-intercepts.

3. one solution; The lines have different slopes.

4. no solution   5. $(3, -7)$

6. infinitely many solutions

7. no

8. a. yes; If the slopes are different, then the y-intercept is the one solution.

   b. no; The y-intercept is a solution to the system.

   c. yes; If both equations have the same slope, then they are the same line.

9. There is no such two-digit number. The system has no solution.

10. $a = 18, b = 6$

5.4 Practice B

1. no solution   2. $(-3, 5)$ 3. no solution

4. infinitely many solutions

5. $(0, 0)$

6. infinitely many solutions

7. infinitely many solutions

8. Yes, if the y-intercepts are the same. If the y-intercepts are different, then the system has no solution.

9. a. $y = 4x + 13$

   $y = 4x$

   b. no; The system has no solution.

10. *Sample answer:*   11. *Sample answer:*
    $x + y = 3$ $2x - y = 3$
    $2x + 2y = 6$ $x + y = 3$

12. *Sample answer:*
    $y = 3x + 2$
    $y = 3x - 5$

13. $a = 15, b$ is any number except 3.

Answers

5.4 Enrichment and Extension

1. $a = 1, b = -1$

2. $a = \dfrac{1}{2}, b = -2$

3. $a = -1, b = 6$

4. $a = 1, b = 2$

5. $a = 3, b$ is any number except 1.

6. $a = \dfrac{1}{3}, b = 3$

7. $a = -2, b = 11$

8. $a = 12, b = -4$

9. Check students' work.

5.4 Puzzle Time

PAY HIM

Extension 5.4 Start Thinking!
For use before Extension 5.4

Sample answer: The graph shows the linear equations related to each side of the equation. The x-coordinate of the point of intersection is the solution of the equation.

Extension 5.4 Warm Up
For use before Extension 5.4

1. $m = -8$

2. $x = 6$

3. $p = 3$

4. $x = 7$

5. $r = 3$

6. $x = -5$

Extension 5.4 Practice

1. $x = 4$ **2.** $x = -3$ **3.** $x = 1$ **4.** $x = -1$

5. no; You cannot have -38 CDs.

6. $x = 8$

7. $x = -2.5$

8. no; The graph of the system $y = 50 - 6x$ and $y = 75 - 6x$ is a pair of parallel lines.

9. a. $\dfrac{1}{3}x = x - 20$

   b. \$30   **c.** \$10

   d. *Sample answer:* the cost of the lemonade

Technology Connection

1. $(3, 7)$

2. $(2.5, -3)$

3. $(-1, 0)$

4. $(-12, -4)$

Chapter 6

6.1 Start Thinking!
For use before Activity 6.1

Answers will vary depending on the cost of milk. For example, if one milk costs \$0.25, then the entries in the mapping diagram would be \$0.25, \$0.50, \$0.75, and \$1.00. A mapping diagram maps one value to another.

6.1 Warm Up
For use before Activity 6.1

1. $x = 11.4$

2. $x = -11\dfrac{1}{4}$

3. $x = 7.34$

4. $x = -7\dfrac{1}{4}$

5. $x = -26\dfrac{1}{4}$

6. $x = -\dfrac{3}{5}$

6.1 Start Thinking!
For use before Lesson 6.1

The output is 15. Observe students playing the Guess the Function Game.

6.1 Warm Up
For use before Lesson 6.1

1. Add 4; missing entries are 8, 9, and 10.

2. Multiply by 5; missing entries are 20, 25, and 30.

6.1 Practice A

1. As each input increases by 1, the output increases by 3.

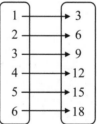

2. As each input increases by 1, the output increases by 2.

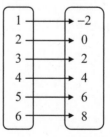

Answers

3. $(0, 1), (2, 2), (4, 3), (6, 4)$

4. $(1, 9), (4, 4), (7, -1), (10, -6)$

5.

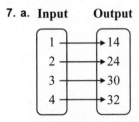

6.

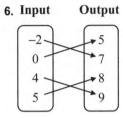

7. a.

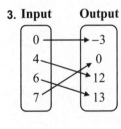

b. Every input has exactly one output. So, the relation is a function.

c. For each additional ticket purchased, the price per ticket decreases $2.

d. $30

e. The cost is the same, you should invite two more friends and get 5 tickets rather than 3 tickets.

f. If the pattern continued, the cost for 8 tickets would be $0.

6.1 Practice B

1. $(1, 2), (5, 6), (9, 4), (13, 8)$

2. $(3, 1), (4, -1), (5, 1), (6, -1)$

3.

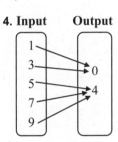

4.

5.

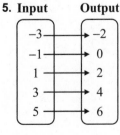

As each input increases by 2, the output increases by 2 (or each output is 1 more than the input).

6.

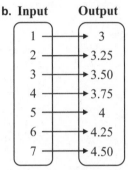

As each input increases by 3, the output decreases by 5.

7. a. $3.75, $4.00, $4.25, $4.50

b.

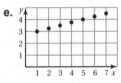

c. Every input has exactly one output. So, the relation is a function.

d. $(1, 3), (2, 3.25), (3, 3.50), (4, 3.75), (5, 4),$ $(6, 4.25), (7, 4.50)$

e.

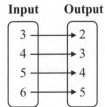

f. The cost is $3 for the first minute and $0.25 for every additional minute.

6.1 Enrichment and Extension

1. function; Each input is paired with exactly one output.

2. function; Each input is paired with exactly one output.

3. not a function; The input 1 has two outputs, 2 and 4.

4. not a function; The input 3 has two outputs, 1 and 5.

5. a. *Sample answer:* **b.** *Sample answer:*

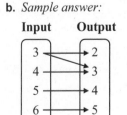

Answers

6. a. *Sample answer:*

Input Output

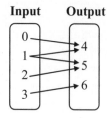

b. *Sample answer:*

Input Output

7. a. *Sample answer:* $(3, 3)$

b. *Sample answer:* $(2, 3)$

8. a. *Sample answer:* $(7, 10)$

b. *Sample answer:* $(4, 1)$

9. a. *Sample answer:* $(0, 0)$

b. *Sample answer:* $(5, 0)$

6.1 Puzzle Time

TULIPS

6.2 Start Thinking!

For use before Activity 6.2

$y = 7x$; If the length is 7 meters and the width is x meters, then the area y is the product of the length and width.

6.2 Warm Up

For use before Activity 6.2

1. $(4, 1)$ **2.** $(1, 3)$

6.2 Start Thinking!

For use before Lesson 6.2

Sample answer: The cost y of buying x apples at $0.59 per apple can be represented by the equation $y = 0.59x$.

The variable x represents the number of apples and y represents the total cost.

Input, x	Output, y

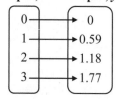

6.2 Warm Up

For use before Lesson 6.2

1. $y = 10x$ **2.** $y = x + 16$

3. $y = \dfrac{x}{2}$ **4.** $y = x - 10$

6.2 Practice A

1. $y = x + 10$ **2.** $y = 3x$

3. $y = x - 8$ **4.** $y = 2x$

5. $y = -3$ **6.** $y = 24$

7. $y = 39$ **8.** $y = 3$

9.   **10.**

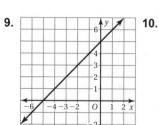

11.   **12.**

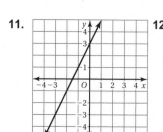

13. a. $d = 6h$ **b.** $d = 12$ miles

14. a. $s = a - 4$ **b.** $s = \$3.50$ **c.** $a = \$6$

6.2 Practice B

1. $y = x + 4$ **2.** $y = -\dfrac{x}{2}$ **3.** $y = 5x$

4. $y = x - 2$ **5.** $y = 2$ **6.** $y = -3$

7.   **8.**

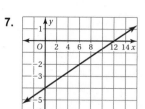
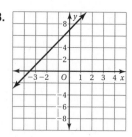

9. a. $d = 70h$ **b.** $d = 245$ miles

10. $x = 4$ **11.** $x = -4$

12. a. $P = 1.50b - 90$ **b.** $b = 60$ bags

13. $A = \left(\dfrac{P}{4}\right)^2$

Answers

6.2 Enrichment and Extension

1. $f(x) = 2x$

2. $f(x) = x - 1$

3. $f(x) = 4x + 7$

4. $f(x) = \dfrac{3}{4}x + 5$

5. $f(0) = 0, f(2) = 16, f(4) = 32$

6. $f(0) = 7, f(2) = 9, f(4) = 11$

7. $f(0) = 5, f(2) = 3, f(4) = 1$

8. $f(0) = 8, f(2) = 14, f(4) = 20$

9. $f(0) = 9, f(2) = 5, f(4) = 1$

10. $f(0) = 0, f(2) = 1, f(4) = 2$

11. $f(0) = 6, f(2) = \dfrac{13}{2}, \text{ or } 6\dfrac{1}{2}, f(4) = 7$

12. $f(0) = 3, f(2) = 6.2, f(4) = 9.4$

13. $f(0) = 1, f(2) = 5, f(4) = 17$

14. *Sample answer:* $f(x) = 2$

6.2 Puzzle Time

YOU DON'T HAVE TO TELL ME IT IS ALL OVER TOWN

6.3 Start Thinking!

For use before Activity 6.3

Answers will vary. Check students' sketches, tables, and graphs.

6.3 Warm Up

For use before Activity 6.3

1. $y = \dfrac{1}{3}x + 2$

2. $y = -3x + 7$

6.3 Start Thinking!

For use before Lesson 6.3

Sample answer: A linear function has a graph in which the points fall on a line. The function $y = x - 2$ is an example of a linear function.

6.3 Warm Up

For use before Lesson 6.3

1. $y = 4x$

2. The variable x represents the side length of a square; the variable y represents the perimeter.

3.

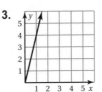

6.3 Practice A

1. $y = -2x + 1$

2. $y = \dfrac{3}{2}x$

3. $y = -3x$

4. $y = \dfrac{x}{5}$

5. a. independent variable: x

dependent variable: y

b. $y = \dfrac{1}{16}x$; It costs about \$0.06 for 1 fluid ounce of brewed coffee.

c.

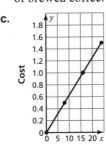

d. \$2

6. a. independent variable: x

dependent variable: y

b. $y = 3x$

c.

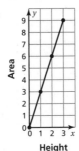

d. 6 ft

6.3 Practice B

1. $y = -\dfrac{1}{4}x - 1$

2. $y = -1$

3. $y = -2x$

4. $y = \dfrac{2}{5}x + 3$

Answers

5. a. independent variable: x

dependent variable: y

b. $y = 0.75x$; It takes 0.75 minute to make 1 burrito.

c.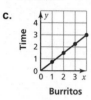

Burritos

d. 5.25 min

6. a. independent variable: x

dependent variable: y

b. $y = 64x$

c.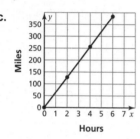

Hours

d. 320 mi

e. $r = 64$ mi/h   **f.** $6\frac{1}{4}$ h

6.3 Enrichment and Extension

1. At iteration 0, you have a completely shaded box. To go from iteration 0 to iteration 1, you split the box into 9 smaller blocks, keep the box in the upper left corner, and delete every other box thereafter.

2. Each of the smaller boxes in iteration 1 is similar to the original box in iteration 0.

3.

Iteration	Number of Squares
0	1
1	5
2	25
3	125
4	625

4. At each iteration, the number of squares multiplies by 5; After the first iteration, the iteration number tells you how many factors of 5 to multiply together to determine the number of squares.

5. no; There is no number that can be added to the number of squares each time to produce the next amount of squares.

6. The pattern will repeat an infinite number of times. Part of the area of the original box will always remain. So, you can keep applying the procedure of deleting some boxes and keeping others.

6.3 Puzzle Time

FROSTBITE

6.4 Start Thinking!

For use before Activity 6.4

The height of a plane during take-off is linear. The others are nonlinear. Check students' graphs.

6.4 Warm Up

For use before Activity 6.4

1. 20 cm; 24 cm^2 **2.** 24 cm; 20 cm^2

3. 56 ft; 192 ft^2 **4.** 40 in.; 91 in.^{2}

6.4 Start Thinking!

For use before Lesson 6.4

Sample answer: The cost of admission for x people is linear. The length of time you wait in line at each ride is nonlinear.

6.4 Warm Up

For use before Lesson 6.4

1.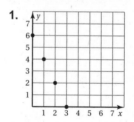

linear

2.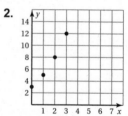

nonlinear

3.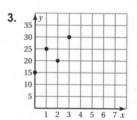

nonlinear

4.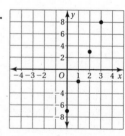

linear

Answers

6.4 Practice A

1. linear

2. nonlinear

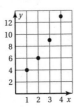

3. nonlinear; The graph is not a line.

4. linear; The graph is a line.

5. nonlinear; The rate of change is not constant.

6. linear; The rate of change is constant.

7. nonlinear; The rate of change is not constant.

8. a. *Sample answer:* 1

   b. 1.5

   c. $y = 0.25x - 0.5$; It costs $0.25 for 1 ounce of cereal.

6.4 Practice B

1. nonlinear

2. linear

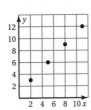

3. linear; The graph is a line.

4. nonlinear; The graph is not a line.

5. nonlinear; The equation cannot be written in slope-intercept form.

6. linear; The equation can be written in slope-intercept form.

7. linear; The rate of change is constant.

8. a. nonlinear; Commission does not show constant change.

   b. $600

9. nonlinear; The equation cannot be written in slope-intercept form.

6.4 Enrichment and Extension

1. *Sample answer:* Taylor earns $10 for allowance each week. The amount of money she earns in x weeks is a linear function.

   Aiden earns $1 per chore that he completes each week. Some weeks he does all of his chores, but other weeks he does not. The amount of money he earns in x weeks is a nonlinear function.

2. *Sample answer:* The cost of buying one song is $0.99. The cost of buying x songs is a linear function.

   The length of each song on a CD is different. If you graph the song length versus the track number, it is likely a nonlinear function.

3. *Sample answer:* Maddie is allowed to watch one hour of television per day. The amount of time she is allowed to watch television in x days is a linear function.

   Hayden is allowed to watch television each day after he finishes his homework. Assuming that his homework takes different amounts of time to finish each day, the amount of time he spends watching television is a nonlinear function.

4. *Sample answer:* The cost of a plane ticket is $350. The cost for x people is a linear function.

   An airplane's altitude versus time during a flight is a nonlinear function.

5. *Sample answer:* The perimeter of a square with side length x is a linear function.

   The area of a square with side length x is a nonlinear function.

6. *Sample answer:* The cost of a medium drink at the food court is $2. The cost of x medium drinks is a linear function.

   The number of cars parked at a shopping mall throughout the day is a nonlinear function.

7. nonlinear

8. *Sample answer:* The initial temperature is room temperature, about 70 degrees. After 1 minute, the oven is turned on and takes about 9 minutes to preheat. The oven door is opened around minute 12 and again at minute 22. So the cookies took 10 minutes to bake. The oven was turned off around minute 23.

9. *Sample answer:* Once the oven reaches the desired temperature, the heating element shuts off. When it cools a certain amount, about 25 degrees, the heating element turns on again, and so on.

10. 400; 13

Answers

6.4 Puzzle Time

YOUR NAME

6.5 Start Thinking!
For use before Activity 6.5

Sample answer: The graph of a linear function shows a constant rate of change. For example, $y = 2x + 1$.

The graph of a nonlinear function does *not* have a constant rate of change. For example, $y = 2x^2 + 1$.

6.5 Warm Up
For use before Activity 6.5

1. 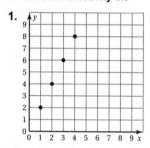 **2.**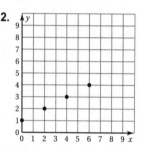

3.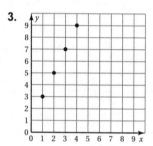

6.5 Start Thinking!
For use before Lesson 6.5

6.5 Warm Up
For use before Lesson 6.5

1. The speed of the car accelerates for a while, then is at a constant rate, then accelerates again, then is at a constant rate before slowing to a stop.

2. Sales increase for a period of time, then they level out for a while before increasing again.

6.5 Practice A

1. *Sample answer:* The speed of the wind increases at an increasing rate, then decreases at a constant rate, increases at an increasing rate, decreases at a constant rate, and then increases at an increasing rate.

2. *Sample answer:* The grass grows at a constant rate, then is cut (thus decreasing the height). This is repeated.

3. *Sample answer:* The height of the airplane decreases at an increasing rate and then decreases at a decreasing rate.

4. *Sample answer:* The number of gallons of gasoline in the tank increases at a constant rate.

5. **a.** *Sample answer:* The number of cars in the parking lot is increasing at an increasing rate.

   b. *Sample answer:* The number of cars in the parking lot is decreasing at an increasing rate.

6. 7.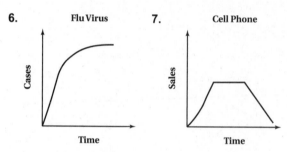

8.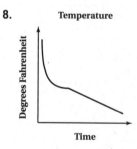

6.5 Practice B

1. *Sample answer:* The number of customers increases at a constant rate and then decreases at a constant rate.

2. *Sample answer:* The height increases at an increasing rate and then increases at a decreasing rate.

3. *Sample answer:* The cost of the postage remains constant, then jumps, remains constant, then jumps, and repeats this pattern.

Answers

4. *Sample answer:* The height of the water decreases at a constant rate, remains the same, decreases at a constant rate, remains the same, and then decreases at a constant rate.

5. a. *Sample answer:* The Demand curve remains constant. The Supply curve decreases at an increasing rate.

   b. The left side represents a surplus. The right side represents a shortage. *Sample answer:* On the left side supply is greater than the demand. On the right side demand is greater than the supply.

   c. *Sample answer:* The equilibrium point moves up and left, so a shortage occurs sooner.

6.5 Enrichment and Extension

1–6. Sample answers are given.

1. discrete data; Only integers between 1 and 31 make sense.

2. discrete data; There will be one fixed amount of money each year.

3. discrete data; Only positive integers make sense.

4. continuous data; It makes sense to use any number for the weight of people.

5. continuous data; It makes sense to use any number for the distance.

6.5 Puzzle Time

PIANO

Technology Connection

1–2. *Sample answer:* Yes, the point $(4, 7)$ disappears and is replaced by the point $(4, 8)$.

3. *Sample answer:* Yes, the point $(4, 8)$ disappears and is replaced by the point $(4, 12)$.

4. *Sample answer:* The graph does not add the new value. You must make a new graph to incorporate the new data point.

5. *Sample answer:* no; You must select the data you want for a new graph.

6. *Sample answer:* A scatter plot using 1 color for (x, y) and another for $(x, y2)$. The second set of points is 2 units above the first set.

7. *Sample answer:* Scatter plots that connect the points with smooth curves or straight lines are a good choice of *xy*-plots.

Chapter 7

7.1 Start Thinking!
For use before Activity 7.1

Sample answer: no; The lengths of the sides can be any two lengths that have the given product; Yes; because the sides of a square are the same length, the area is the square of the side length. For example, if the area is 64 square meters, then the length of each side would be 8 meters.

7.1 Warm Up
For use before Activity 7.1

  1. 144   **2.** 81   **3.** 324

  4. 2.56   **5.** 6.25   **6.** $\dfrac{4}{9}$

7.1 Start Thinking!
For use before Lesson 7.1

Shelley; the solutions are 20 and -20.

7.1 Warm Up
For use before Lesson 7.1

  1. 9 in.   **2.** 13 cm   **3.** 1 yd   **4.** 1.5 m

7.1 Practice A

  1. $s = 14$ in.   **2.** $r = 6$ m   **3.** ± 4

  4. 0   **5.** 11   **6.** $-\dfrac{1}{6}$

  7. $\pm\dfrac{17}{7}$ **8.** -0.8 **9.** 13

  10. 3   **11.** $\sqrt{64} > 5$

  12. $0.6 < \sqrt{0.49}$ **13.** $r = 4$ ft

  14. $x = 11$ widgets   **15.** $s = 10$ in.

7.1 Practice B

  1. $s = \dfrac{13}{15}$ cm   **2.** $r = 11$ yd   **3.** ± 15

  4. ± 20 **5.** -22 **6.** $\pm\dfrac{5}{8}$ **7.** 2.5

  8. ± 1.3 **9.** 4.8   **10.** 6

  11. $\sqrt{\dfrac{49}{9}} > 2$ **12.** $\dfrac{2}{5} = \sqrt{\dfrac{12}{75}}$ **13.** $r = 12$ m

  14. $s = 24$ m

Answers

7.1 Enrichment and Extension

1. $p = \pm 7$ **2.** $a = \pm 10$ **3.** $r = \pm 4$

4. $j = \pm 2$ **5.** $d = \pm 4$ **6.** $y = \pm 2$

7. $x = \pm 5$ **8.** $s = \pm 1$ **9.** $t = \pm 5$

10. $p = \pm 3$ **11.** $r = 5$ ft

7.1 Puzzle Time

EATING SWORDFISH

7.2 Start Thinking!
For use before Activity 7.2

$\sqrt{169} = 13$; *Sample answer:* Square roots are positive unless there is a negative in front of the radical sign.

7.2 Warm Up
For use before Activity 7.2

1. 6   **2.** -8 **3.** $\dfrac{7}{9}$

4. -15 **5.** 11   **6.** $\dfrac{12}{13}$

7.2 Start Thinking!
For use before Lesson 7.2

Sample answer: To find the square root of a number, you are determining what number when multiplied by itself, equals the given number. For example, $\sqrt{4} = 2$. To find the cube root of a number, you are determining what number when multiplied by itself, and multiplied by itself again, equals a given number. For example, $\sqrt[3]{8} = 2$.

7.2 Warm Up
For use before Lesson 7.2

1. 40   **2.** $\dfrac{1}{6}$

7.2 Practice A

1. $s = 30$ cm   **2.** $s = \dfrac{1}{2}$ in.   **3.** 5

4. -1 **5.** -2 **6.** -10

7. 20   **8.** 8   **9.** $-\dfrac{1}{4}$

10. 0.1   **11.** $-\sqrt[3]{27} > -4$

12. $\sqrt[3]{64} > \sqrt{16}$ **13.** $6\pi \approx 18.8$ in.

14. $8\pi \approx 25.1$ m   **15.** cube B; 1 ft

7.2 Practice B

1. 7   **2.** -11 **3.** -20 **4.** 15

5. $\dfrac{1}{4}$ **6.** $-\dfrac{5}{3}$ **7.** 138   **8.** $2\dfrac{17}{27}$

9. -976 **10.** 168   **11.** $-\dfrac{25}{2}$

12. a. 12 ft   **b.** 864 ft^2 **c.** 144 ft^2

13. $>$ **14.** $>$

15. *Sample answer:* 8 and -8; 27 and -27

16. 3 m   **17.** $x = 2$ **18.** $x = 1$

7.2 Enrichment and Extension

1.

r	n	$x = r^n$	$\sqrt[n]{x}$	Check
1	7	1	1	$1 \bullet 1 \bullet 1 \bullet 1 \bullet\ 1 \bullet 1 \bullet 1 = 1$
2	6	64	2	$2 \bullet 2 \bullet 2 \bullet 2 \bullet 2 \bullet 2 = 64$
3	5	243	3	$3 \bullet 3 \bullet 3 \bullet 3 \bullet 3 = 243$
4	4	256	4	$4 \bullet 4 \bullet 4 \bullet 4 = 256$

2. 2   **3.** 3   **4.** 5   **5.** 3

6. 3; 27,000 is the least multiple of 9000 that is a perfect cube.

7. 6; 512 is the greatest factor of 3072 that is a perfect cube.

7.2 Puzzle Time

COAT OF PAINT

7.3 Start Thinking!
For use before Activity 7.3

right triangle; yes, any lengths a, b, and c such that $a^2 + b^2 = c^2$

7.3 Warm Up
For use before Activity 7.3

1. 1.2   **2.** ± 30 **3.** $\dfrac{2}{3}$

4. -21 **5.** ± 22 **6.** -50

Answers

7.3 Start Thinking!
For use before Lesson 7.3

Sample answer: In a gymnastics floor routine, the gymnasts must stay within a 12-meter-by-12-meter square. Often they perform tumbling passes in which they start in one corner of the square and end up in the opposite corner. You can use the Pythagorean Theorem to find how far they traveled from one corner to the other. Also, in baseball, the bases form a square with 90-foot sides. You can use the Pythagorean Theorem to find how far the catcher must throw the ball to throw out a runner at second base.

7.3 Warm Up
For use before Lesson 7.3

1. $c = 10$ cm
2. $c = 13$ in.
3. $c = 6$ m
4. $c = 17$ ft

7.3 Practice A

1. $c = 10$ ft
2. $b = 12$ cm
3. $a = 2$ m
4. $b = 20$ yd
5. 6 in.
6. $x = 29$ yd
7. $x = 6.5$ cm
8. no; The other leg would be 0 meters long, which is impossible.
9. $x = 7$

7.3 Practice B

1. $c = 37$ mm
2. $a = 3$ ft
3. $b = 2$ in.
4. $a = 5$ cm
5. 26 in.
6. 9 in.
7. $x = 6$ cm
8. 8 fewer blocks

7.3 Enrichment and Extension

1. 3248 mi
2. 1624 mi
3. 615, 574, 435
4. 249,380,384,400
5. 499,380 mi^2
6. 360 m^2

7.3 Puzzle Time

STOP HOUNDING ME

7.4 Start Thinking!
For use before Activity 7.4

Sample answer: π, some square roots, like $\sqrt{2}$ and $\sqrt{3}$

7.4 Warm Up
For use before Activity 7.4

1. 50
2. 26
3. 34
4. 41
5. 90
6. 6.5

7.4 Start Thinking!
For use before Lesson 7.4

Sample answer: First find the area, 93.5 in.^2. Ask yourself, "What number times itself is 93.5?" Because $9^2 = 81$ and $10^2 = 100$, you know that the number must be between 9 and 10. Try squaring values between 9 and 10 to find the number that produces the value closest to 93.5. A square with sides of about 9.7 inches has the same area as an 8.5-inch-by-11-inch sheet of paper.

7.4 Warm Up
For use before Lesson 7.4

1. yes
2. no
3. no
4. yes
5. yes
6. no

7.4 Practice A

1. yes
2. no
3. irrational
4. rational
5. rational
6. rational
7. irrational; The area is 4π square feet and π is irrational.
8. a. 6   b. 5.7
9. a. 25   b. 25.1
10. a. -3 b. -2.8
11. a. 2   b. 1.9
12. 18 ft
13. $\sqrt{70}$; $8 = \sqrt{64} < \sqrt{70}$
14. 3; A positive number is greater than a negative number.
15. $16\frac{1}{4}$; $\sqrt{210} < \sqrt{225} = 15$
16. $\sqrt{\frac{4}{25}}$; $\sqrt{\frac{4}{25}} = \frac{2}{5} = \frac{4}{10}$
17. $4 < a < 9$; *Sample answer:* $a = 6$.
18. yes; $\sqrt{\frac{1}{9}} = \frac{1}{3}$
19. no; 5 is not a perfect square.

Answers

20. yes; $\sqrt{\dfrac{2}{18}} = \sqrt{\dfrac{1}{9}} = \dfrac{1}{3}$

7.4 Practice B

1. no   **2.** yes

3. rational   **4.** rational   **5.** rational   **6.** irrational

7. irrational; The circumference is 10π meters and π is irrational.

8. a. -5 **b.** -5.3 **9. a.** 20   **b.** 19.9

10. a. 1   **b.** 0.9   **11. a.** 1   **b.** 1.2

12. a. $c = \sqrt{2450}$

    b. $\left(49^2 = 2401\right) < 2450 < \left(50^2 = 2500\right)$

    c. 49.5 ft

13. $\sqrt{220}$; $14.75^2 = 217.5625$

14. $-\sqrt{135}$; $-145 < -135$, so $-\sqrt{145} < -\sqrt{135}$

15. $\dfrac{3}{8}$; $\left(\dfrac{3}{8}\right)^2 = \dfrac{9}{64} > \dfrac{7}{64}$

16. -0.25; $-\sqrt{\dfrac{1}{4}} = -0.5$

17. $49 < a < b < 64$; *Sample answer:* $a = 50$, $b = 60$

7.4 Enrichment and Extension

1. 36 and 49   **2.** 7

3. 6.71   **4.** 6.855

5. 46.99; The numbers are very close.

6. 5.4775; The square of the estimate is about 30.003, which is very close to 30.

7.4 Puzzle Time

THE LOBSTER THAT BECAME A POLICEMAN BECAUSE HE BELIEVED IN CLAW AND ORDER

Extension 7.4 Start Thinking!
For use before Extension 7.4

Sample answer: You determine a decimal is a repeating decimal if a given set of numbers repeats itself consistently.

Extension 7.4 Warm Up
For use before Extension 7.4

1. terminating   **2.** repeating

3. repeating   **4.** terminating

5. repeating   **6.** repeating

Extension 7.4 Practice

1. $\dfrac{2}{9}$ **2.** $-\dfrac{7}{9}$ **3.** $-2\dfrac{1}{3}$

4. $8\dfrac{7}{9}$ **5.** $-10\dfrac{5}{9}$ **6.** $24\dfrac{8}{9}$

7. $\dfrac{26}{45}$ **8.** $-1\dfrac{41}{90}$ **9.** $-3\dfrac{13}{15}$

10. $-\dfrac{32}{99}$ **11.** $6\dfrac{13}{99}$ **12.** $7\dfrac{10}{11}$

7.5 Start Thinking!
For use before Activity 7.5

$a^2 + b^2 = c^2$; *Sample answer:* 3, 4, and 5; No, the lengths must form a right triangle.

7.5 Warm Up
For use before Activity 7.5

1. 2.5 in.   **2.** $3\sqrt{2}$ cm

3. 48 ft   **4.** $\sqrt{33}$ m

7.5 Start Thinking!
For use before Lesson 7.5

Answers will vary. Check students' problems and sketches.

7.5 Warm Up
For use before Lesson 7.5

1. If $|a| = -a$, then a is a negative number; false; $a = 0$

2. If two lines are perpendicular, then one line is vertical and the other line is horizontal; false; $y = 2x$ is perpendicular to $y = -\dfrac{1}{2}x$ and the lines are not vertical or horizontal.

3. If a^2 is a positive number, then a is a negative number; false; $a^2 = 4$ and $a = 2$

4. If $a - 1$ is an even number, then a is an odd number; true; Adding 1 to an even number creates an odd number.

Answers

5. If a triangle is a right triangle, then the side lengths of the triangle are 3, 4, and 5; false; A right triangle can have side lengths 5, 12, and 13.

6. If the y-intercept of a graph is -3, then the line is given by the equation $y = 2x - 3$; false; $y = x - 3$ has a y-intercept of -3.

7.5 Practice A

1. If $2a$ is an even number, then a is an odd number; false; $2a = 8$ is an even number and a equals 4.

2. If $\dfrac{1}{a}$ is negative, then a is negative; true; Reciprocals have the same sign.

3. not a right triangle   **4.** right triangle

5. $\sqrt{10}$ **6.** 5   **7.** $\sqrt{53}$

8. yes   **9.** yes   **10.** no   **11.** yes

12. a. 8.8 ft   **b.** 8.6 ft   **c.** your friend

13. 204.9 ft

7.5 Practice B

1. right triangle   **2.** not a right triangle

3. $\sqrt{13}$ **4.** $\sqrt{97}$ **5.** $\sqrt{146}$

6. The x-coordinate -1 was incorrectly substituted into the distance formula.

$$d = \sqrt{\left[-5 - (-1)\right]^2 + (-2 - 4)^2}$$
$$= \sqrt{16 + 36}$$
$$= \sqrt{52}$$

7. no   **8.** yes   **9.** no

10. a. $\sqrt{73}$

b. $\sqrt{73}$

c. yes; The square of a positive value is the same as the square of its negative.

d. *Sample answer:*

$(3, -2)$ and $(-6, 5)$; distance $= \sqrt{130}$

$(-3, 2)$ and $(6, -5)$; distance $= \sqrt{130}$

11. $159

7.5 Enrichment and Extension

1. right   **2.** obtuse   **3.** obtuse

4. right   **5.** acute   **6.** acute

7. obtuse   **8.** right   **9.** acute

10. right   **11.** acute   **12.** obtuse

7.5 Puzzle Time

A D-HORSE

Technology Connection

1. $c = 37$ **2.** $c = 69.7$

3. $b = 5.5$ **4.** $b = 0.51$

Chapter 8

8.1 Start Thinking!
For use before Activity 8.1

Sample answer: filling cylindrical jars with homemade jam

8.1 Warm Up
For use before Activity 8.1

1. 64   **2.** 196   **3.** 400

4. 324   **5.** 625   **6.** 441

8.1 Start Thinking!
For use before Lesson 8.1

Sample answer: Find the area of the base by finding the radius and squaring it, then multiplying that number by π. Find the measure of the height and multiply that number by the area of the base.

8.1 Warm Up
For use before Lesson 8.1

1. $54\pi \approx 169.6$ in.^{3} **2.** $1600\pi \approx 5026.5$ ft^3

3. $162\pi \approx 508.9$ m^3 **4.** $192\pi \approx 603.2$ in.^{3}

8.1 Practice A

1. $147\pi \approx 461.8$ in.^{3} **2.** $36\pi \approx 113.1$ m^3

3. $\pi \approx 3.1$ cm^3 **4.** $600\pi \approx 1885.0$ ft^3

5. $32\pi \approx 100.5$ in.^{3} **6.** $288\pi \approx 904.8$ mm^3

7. 32,987 gal   **8.** $108\pi \approx 339$ cm^3

9. 4 times more volume

Answers

8.1 Practice B

1. $243\pi \approx 763.4$ mm^3
2. $126\pi \approx 395.8$ ft^3
3. $1200\pi \approx 3769.9$ in.^{3}
4. $729\pi \approx 2290.2$ m^3
5. 7 in.
6. 47 ft
7. **a.** 1000 ft^3 **b.** 5 ft **c.** 754 gal

8.1 Enrichment and Extension

1. **a.** 48.9% **b.** 16.1 in.^{2}

2. **a.** 92.4%

   b. The smallest diameter is 1 inch because the cherries have a 1-inch diameter. The smallest height is 10 inches because the 10 cherries will be stacked on top of each other. The smallest volume is about 7.85 cubic inches. They would save 77.27 square inches because the surface area of the prism is 110.26 square inches and the surface area of the cylinder is about 32.99 square inches.

3. *Sample answer:* Extra cardboard and plastic and other packaging materials are used to make the package. This means wasted trees and other resources. It also means that more energy is spent making the packaging products. The extra packaging also takes up more space in a landfill. Because the packaging is bigger, it will take up more space when being transported, so fewer items can fit in a shipment. This will lead to more energy being wasted and more money being spent in transportation.

4. *Answer should include, but is not limited to:* Make sure students mention how much of the volume of the packaging is wasted, a new packaging design, how much packaging is saved, and some of the environmental consequences from Exercise 3.

8.1 Puzzle Time

THE SAILORS WHO COULDN'T PLAY CARDS BECAUSE THE CAPTAIN WAS STANDING ON THE DECK

8.2 Start Thinking!
For use before Activity 8.2

square: $A = s^2$; rectangle: $A = bh$

triangle: $A = \frac{1}{2}bh$; circle: $A = \pi r^2$

8.2 Warm Up
For use before Activity 8.2

1. $169\pi \approx 530.9$ m^2
2. $400\pi \approx 1256.6$ cm^2
3. $81\pi \approx 254.5$ in.^{2}
4. $\frac{625}{4}\pi \approx 490.9$ ft^2

8.2 Start Thinking!
For use before Lesson 8.2

Sugar cone 1 has a volume of about 131.9 cubic centimeters and sugar cone 2 has a volume of about 166.7 cubic centimeters. Because the volume of sugar cone 2 is greater it can hold more ice cream.

8.2 Warm Up
For use before Lesson 8.2

1. $432\pi \approx 1357.2$ m^3
2. $64\pi \approx 201.1$ in.^{3}
3. $\frac{640}{3}\pi \approx 670.2$ cm^3
4. $\frac{847}{6}\pi \approx 443.5$ yd^3

8.2 Practice A

1. $12\pi \approx 37.7$ ft^3
2. $\frac{28}{3}\pi \approx 29.3$ cm^3
3. $\frac{5}{3}\pi \approx 5.2$ in.^{3}
4. $15\pi \approx 47.1$ m^3
5. $\frac{\pi}{3} \approx 1.0$ mm^3
6. $324\pi \approx 1017.9$ ft^3
7. 8π ft^3
8. **a.** $\frac{160}{3}\pi \approx 167.6$ in.^{3} **b.** 2.9 qt

8.2 Practice B

1. $\frac{640}{3}\pi \approx 670.2$ mm^3
2. $84\pi \approx 263.9$ ft^3
3. $\frac{243}{4}\pi \approx 190.9$ in.^{3}
4. $\frac{125}{3}\pi \approx 130.9$ cm^3
5. 6.0 in.
6. 5.0 m
7. **a.** $\frac{5}{3}\pi \approx 5.2$ cm^3 **b.** 3.5 sec **8.** 1 : 2

8.2 Enrichment and Extension

1. *Sample answer:* The cake cone will hold more because the dimensions are close and cylinders hold more.

2. cake cone: 100.5 cm^3; sugar cone: 48.2 cm^3

Answers

3. *Sample answer:* The prediction was correct.

4. *Sample answer:* You will probably get more if you order the cake cone because you can fit more in the cake cone. Two scoops of hard ice cream has a fixed volume, so it doesn't matter which cone you choose.

5. 24 cm   **6.** about 2 batches

7. a. The regular size cake cone holds about 67 cubic centimeters, which is more than what the sugar cone holds.

   b. about 5.3 cm

8.2 Puzzle Time

THE PUNY EXPRESS

8.3 Start Thinking!
For use before Activity 8.3

volume of a cylinder: $V = Bh$; volume of a cone:

$V = \frac{1}{3}Bh$; *Sample answer:* Both formulas multiply

the area of the base and the height. Both objects have a base that is a circle. The volume of the cone is

multiplied by $\frac{1}{3}$.

8.3 Warm Up
For use before Activity 8.3

1. 50.3 cm^2 **2.** 113.1 m^2

3. 153.9 ft^2 **4.** 615.8 in.^{2}

8.3 Start Thinking!
For use before Lesson 8.3

Sample answer: A coach inflates a ball with air.

8.3 Warm Up
For use before Lesson 8.3

1. $\frac{256}{3}\pi \approx 268.1$ ft^3 **2.** $\frac{4000}{3}\pi \approx 4188.8$ cm^3

3. $288\pi \approx 904.8$ m^3 **4.** $\frac{5324}{3}\pi \approx 5575.3$ yd^3

8.3 Practice A

1. $\frac{2048}{3}\pi \approx 2144.7$ cm^3 **2.** $36\pi \approx 113.1$ ft^3

3. $4500\pi \approx 14{,}137.2$ in.^{3} **4.** $972\pi \approx 3053.6$ mm^3

5. 6 in.   **6.** 7.5 cm

7. 0.5 in.^{3} **8.** 33.5 ft^3 **9.** 1523.6 cm^3

8.3 Practice B

1. $\frac{10{,}976}{3}\pi \approx 11{,}494.0$ m^3

2. $\frac{243}{2}\pi \approx 381.7$ mi^3

3. $\frac{62{,}500}{3}\pi \approx 65{,}449.8$ ft^3

4. $\frac{4}{3}\pi \approx 4.2$ cm^3 **5.** 12 yd

6. 10.5 mm   **7.** 14.1 in.^{3}

8. 65.4 ft^3 **9.** 572.6 m^3

8.3 Enrichment and Extension

1. *Sample answer:* 6 in.

2–3. Answers will vary. Check students' measurement and ratios.

4. *Sample answer*: 18 in.

5. *Sample answer*: During a game of dodgeball, you want to avoid throwing balls that are too large for your hand.

6. *Sample answer*: A ratio greater than 1 indicates the ball is smaller than your hand size.

7. *Sample answer*: When the ball is squeezed, the circumference is lessened, allowing you to grip it better.

8.3 Puzzle Time

THE DOORBELL

8.4 Start Thinking!
For use before Activity 8.4

Sample answer: A juice factory uses volume to figure out how much juice to put into different sizes of bottles.

8.4 Warm Up
For use before Activity 8.4

1. yes   **2.** no   **3.** no

4. yes   **5.** no   **6.** yes

8.4 Start Thinking!
For use before Lesson 8.4

Sample answer: Two figures are similar if corresponding sides are proportional and corresponding angles are equal.

Answers

8.4 Warm Up
For use before Lesson 8.4

1. a. $\dfrac{25}{16}$ because $\left(\dfrac{5}{4}\right)^2 = \dfrac{25}{16}$.

   b. $\dfrac{125}{64}$ because $\left(\dfrac{5}{4}\right)^3 = \dfrac{125}{64}$.

8.4 Practice A

1. no   **2.** yes

3. $h = 6$ ft   **4.** $\ell = 3$ m; $h = 24$ m

5. 592.6 mm^3 **6.** 361.1 ft^2

7. a. 56.3 in.^{2} **b.** 63.3 in.^{3}

8.4 Practice B

1. $r = \dfrac{4}{3}$ ft

2. $h = 37.5$ cm; $w = 8$ cm

3. 150.4 m^2 **4.** 227.6 cm^3 **5.** 25.0 in.^{3}

6. a. 1559.3 cm^3 **b.** 7219.0 cm^3

   c. $\ell \approx 18.3$ cm; $w = 17.5$ cm; $h = 22.5$ cm

8.4 Enrichment and Extension

1. Step 1: Fill the 3-cup container. Pour all of it into the 4-cup container.

   Step 2: Refill the 3-cup container and pour it into the 4-cup container until it is full. Because there are already 3 cups in the 4-cup container, there are exactly two cups left in the 3-cup container.

2. Step 1: Fill the 9-cup container. Pour it into the 4-cup container until it is full and there are 5 cups left in the 9-cup container.

   Step 2: Empty the 4-cup container. Pour the remaining water in the 9-cup container into the 4-cup container until it is full and there is exactly 1 cup left in the 9-cup container.

   Step 3: Empty the 4-cup container. Pour the 1 cup from the 9-cup container into the 4-cup container.

   Step 4: Refill the 9-cup container. Pour it into the 4-cup container until it is full. Because there is already 1 cup in the 4-cup container, there are exactly 6 cups left in the 9-cup container.

3. Step 1: Fill the 4-cup container. Pour all of it into the 7-cup container.

   Step 2: Refill the 4-cup container. Pour it into the 7-cup container until it is full and there is exactly 1 cup left in the 4-cup container.

   Step 3: Empty the 7-cup container. Pour the 1 cup from the 4-cup container into the 7-cup container.

   Step 4: Refill the 4-cup container. Pour it into the 7-cup container. Because there is already 1 cup in the 7-cup container, there are now exactly 5 cups in the 7-cup container.

4. Method 1: Step 1: Fill the 5-cup container. Pour it into the 3-cup container until it is full and there are exactly 2 cups left in the 5-cup container.

   Step 2: Empty the 3-cup container. Pour the 2 cups from the 5-cup container into the 3-cup container.

   Step 3: Refill the 5-cup container. Pour it into the 3-cup container until it is full. Because there are already 2 cups in the 3-cup container, there are exactly 4 cups left in the 5-cup container.

   Method 2: Step 1: Fill the 3-cup container. Pour all of it into the 5-cup container.

   Step 2: Refill the 3-cup container. Pour it into the 5-cup container until it is full and there is exactly 1 cup left in the 3-cup container.

   Step 3: Empty the 5-cup container. Pour the 1 cup from the 3-cup container into the 5-cup container.

   Step 4: Refill the 3-cup container. Pour it into the 5-cup container until it is full. Because there is already 1 cup in the 5-cup container, there are now exactly 4 cups in the 5-cup container.

   Method 2 wastes 5 cups of water, but method 1 wastes 6 cups of water.

5. Step 1: Pour the 8-cup container into the 5-cup container until it is full and there are exactly 3 cups left in the 8-cup container.

   Step 2: Pour the 5-cup container into the 3-cup container until it is full and there are exactly 2 cups left in the 5-cup container.

   Step 3: Pour all of the 3-cup container into the 8-cup container. There should be a total of 6 cups in the 8-cup container.

   Step 4: Pour the 2 cups from the 5-cup container into the 3-cup container.

   Step 5: Pour the 8-cup container into the 5-cup container until it is full and there is exactly 1 cup left in the 8-cup container.

   Step 6: Pour the 5-cup container into the 3-cup container until it is full and there are exactly 4 cups left in the 5-cup container.

   Step 7: Pour the 3-cup container into the 8-cup container. Because there is already 1 cup in the 8-cup container, there are exactly 4 cups in the 8-cup container. Also, there are 4 cups in the 5-cup container.

Answers

8.4 Puzzle Time
MUSSELS

Technology Connection
1. 8 **2.** −7.5 **3.** 12 **4.** 0.3 in.

Chapter 9
9.1 Start Thinking!
For use before Activity 9.1

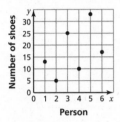

9.1 Warm Up
For use before Activity 9.1

1–6.

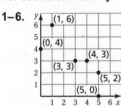

9.1 Start Thinking!
For use before Lesson 9.1

Sample answer: In general, if a scatter plot has a *positive* relationship, as the value of *x* increases so does the value of *y*. The points lie close to a line. In general, if a scatter plot is *nonlinear*, the points lie in the shape of a curve.

9.1 Warm Up
For use before Lesson 9.1

1. a.

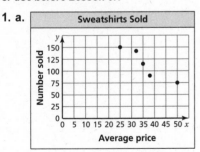

b. As the average price of the sweatshirts increases, the number of sweatshirts sold decreases.

9.1 Practice A

1. positive linear relationship; As the age of the automobile increases, the odometer reading increases.

2. negative linear relationship; As time spent fishing increases, the amount of bait in the bucket decreases.

3. no relationship; The number of passengers in a car is not related to the number of traffic lights.

4. a. $(3, 24)$, $(6, 61)$, $(5, 56)$, $(1, 15)$

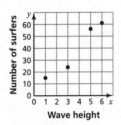

b. positive linear relationship

5. a. about 4 days

b. about 12 lawns

c. positive linear relationship

6. positive linear relationship; gap between *y*-values of 5 to 9

7. positive linear relationship; gap between *x*-values of 9 to 13 and 16 to 20, outlier at $(24, 1150)$, clusters around 12 and around 15

9.1 Practice B

1. a. $(56, 0)$, $(45, 5)$, $(39, 9)$, $(24, 15)$, $(17, 23)$, $(6, 26)$, $(0, 32)$;

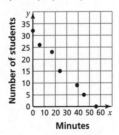

b. negative linear relationship

2. a. about 16 bushels

b. about 175 apples

c. positive linear relationship

3. *Sample answer*: the number of items in a cart and the total cost

Answers

4. a. 0 yard sales; 18 yard sales

   b. January, February, and December

   c. nonlinear relationship

   d. *Sample answer*: a snowy climate

   e. gap between *y*-values of 4 to 12

9.1 Enrichment and Extension

1. *Sample answer:* yes; A person's hand size and foot size will usually be proportional. As a person's foot size gets larger, so does the hand size and vice-versa.

2. *Answer should include, but is not limited to:* The student should have two measurements (one for hand size, one for foot size) for each student in the class.

3. *Answer should include, but is not limited to:* The student should have a scatter plot labeled with foot size on the *x*-axis and hand size on the *y*-axis. All student data from Exercise 2 should be correctly plotted.

4. *Sample answer*: The hypothesis from Exercise 1 was correct. The data shows that a larger foot size indicates a larger hand size usually.

5. *Sample answer*: about 32 cm

6. *Sample answer*: yes; This measurement is close to the approximation. Because most humans share this type of proportionality, the scatter plot is a good predictor.

7. *Sample answer*: about 26 cm

9.1 Puzzle Time

SANDCRAB

9.2 Start Thinking!

For use before Activity 9.2

Answers will vary. Check students' graphs and predictions.

9.2 Warm Up

For use before Activity 9.2

1. $y = -\dfrac{1}{5}x + 4$ **2.** $y = -3x + 6$

3. $y = -\dfrac{1}{2}x + 7$ **4.** $y = x + 1$

5. $y = \dfrac{1}{3}x$ **6.** $y = 2x + 8$

9.2 Start Thinking!

For use before Lesson 9.2

B; the line best follows the trend shown by the points. There are approximately the same number of points above and below the line.

9.2 Warm Up

For use before Lesson 9.2

1–2.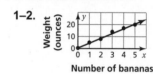

3. *Sample answer:* $y = 4x + 0.5$

4. *Sample answer:* 40.5 lb

9.2 Practice A

1. a. 3 months   **b.** 7 lb

   c.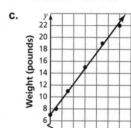

   d. *Sample answer:* $y = 1.3x + 7$

   e. *Sample answer:* 30.4 lb

   f. positive linear relationship

2. a–b.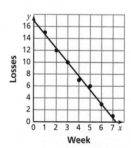

   c. *Sample answer:* $y = -2.3x + 17$

   d. negative linear relationship

   e. There are fewer losses each week.

3. a. no relationship

   b. no; Many possible lines could be drawn, but no best fit.

   c. no; There is no relationship, so you are unable to predict.

Answers

9.2 Practice B

1. a. $12   **b.** 20 fl oz

c.
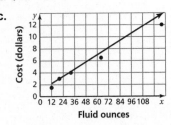

d. *Sample answer:* $y = 0.1x + 1$

e. *Sample answer:* $26.60

f. positive linear relationship

2. a–b.
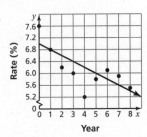

c. *Sample answer:* $y = -0.2x + 7$

d. *Sample answer:* 5%

e. negative linear relationship

f. Mortgage interest rates are dropping about 0.2% per year.

3. a. constant relationship

b.
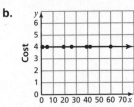

c. $y = 4$

d. Everyone pays $4 to see the show.

9.2 Enrichment and Extension

1.
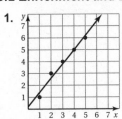

2. $n = 5$

3.

x	y	xy	x^2	y^2
1	1	1	1	1
2	3	6	4	9
3	4	12	9	16
4	5	20	16	25
5	6	30	25	36

$A = 15$ $B = 19$ $C = 69$ $D = 55$ $F = 87$

4. $r \approx 0.986$

5. Because r is very close to 1, the data has a strong positive relationship. The scatter plot supports the conclusion because the data is very linear and has a positive slope.

9.2 Puzzle Time

BEEBOP

9.3 Start Thinking!
For use before Activity 9.3

	Boys	Girls
6th grade	50	35
7th grade	75	45
8th grade	60	60

9.3 Warm Up
For use before Activity 9.3

1. 16   **2.** 16   **3.** 18

9.3 Start Thinking!
For use before Lesson 9.3

Answers will vary.

9.3 Warm Up
For use before Lesson 9.3

1. 18   **2.** 28

9.3 Practice A

1. a. 32 games

b. 0 games

c. 32 home games were won; 8 home games were lost; 33 home games were played with an open roof; 7 home games were played with a closed roof.

d. 62.5%

Answers

2.

		Pet Preference		
		Dogs	Cats	Total
Gender	Male	17	8	25
	Female	14	20	34
	Total	31	28	59

3. a.

		Age			
		20–29	30–39	40–49	Total
Texts Regularly?	Yes	25	11	2	38
	No	7	13	10	30
	Total	32	24	12	68

b.

		Age		
		20–29	30–39	40–49
Texts Regularly?	Yes	78%	46%	17%
	No	22%	54%	83%

Sample answer: About 78% of the people in the survey who are 20–29 years old text regularly.

c. yes; People who are 20–29 years old are more likely to text regularly than people who are 40–49 years old.

9.3 Practice B

1. 91 cars have 2 doors; 109 cars have 4 doors; 79 cars have 4 cylinders; 121 cars have 6 cylinders.

2. a. 26

b. 87 students chose watching television; 84 students chose playing video games; 58 students chose going online; 75 students are in 10th grade; 74 students are in 11th grade; 80 students are in 12th grade.

c. $\frac{30}{229} \approx 13.1\%$

3. a.

		Hair Color			
		Red	Blonde	Brunette	Black
Gender	Female	3	15	41	33
	Male	4	21	30	27

b. 7 classmates have red hair; 36 classmates have blonde hair; 71 classmates have brunette hair; 60 classmates have black hair; 92 students are female; 82 students are male.

c.

		Hair Color			
		Red	Blonde	Brunette	Black
Gender	Female	43%	42%	58%	55%
	Male	57%	58%	42%	45%

9.3 Enrichment and Extension

1. a. 46

b. 62

c. 53

d. *Sample answer:* Claire will win because the current totals are 53 for Owen and 73 for Claire.

2. a.

	Own dog	Do not own dog
Own cat	3	5
Do not own cat	7	5

b. 10

c. 5

3. a. The missing value is 21. **b.** 172 **c.** 39%

4. 7 boys play soccer.

	Play soccer	Do not play soccer
Girls	10	4
Boys	7	4

9.3 Puzzle Time

JUMP ROPE

Answers

9.4 Start Thinking!
For use before Activity 9.4

Sample answer: pictograph, bar graph, circle graph, line graph, histogram, stem-and-leaf plot, box-and-whisker plot, dot plot, scatter plot; line graphs, stem-and-leaf plots, dot plots, and scatter plots can be used to display a list of values. Pictographs, bar graphs, and circle graphs can be used to display information divided into categories. Line graphs and scatter plots can be used to display the relationship between two sets of data.

9.4 Warm Up
For use before Activity 9.4

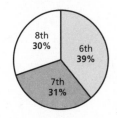

1. **Students by Grade**
   - 8th 30%
   - 6th 39%
   - 7th 31%

2. **Favorite Color**
   - Pink 10%
   - Other 20%
   - Green 15%
   - Blue 35%
   - Red 20%

9.4 Start Thinking!
For use before Lesson 9.4

Sample answer: Both a bar graph and a histogram have bars that represent data, but the bar graph has distinct categories and the histogram uses equal intervals.

Both a line graph and a dot plot use a number line to display data. A line graph uses line segments to show how data changes over time. A dot plot uses ●'s to show the number of times a value occurs in a data set.

Both a stem-and-leaf plot and box-and-whisker plot display one-variable data and show the variability and distribution of data. A stem-and-leaf plot organizes the data numerically. A box-and-whisker plot divides the data into quarters.

9.4 Warm Up
For use before Lesson 9.4

1. Answers will vary. Sample displays are a bar graph, a line graph, a stem-and-leaf plot, and a box-and-whisker plot.

9.4 Practice A

1. *Sample answer:* line graph; shows data over time

2. *Sample answer:* bar graph; shows data in categories

3. *Sample answer:* histogram; shows frequency in intervals of same size

4. *Sample answer:* scatter plot; shows the relationship between two data sets

5. The break in vertical axis makes it appear that many more apples were sold.

6. The size of the age intervals is not the same.

7. *Sample answer:* scatter plot; shows a relationship between two data set

8. line graph

9. *Sample answer:* box-and-whisker plot; shows variability of data

10. *Sample answer:* pictograph; shows data in specific categories

11. *Sample answer:* stem-and-leaf plot; orders the data and shows the distribution

9.4 Practice B

1. *Sample answer:* bar graph; shows data in categories

2. *Sample answer:* histogram; shows frequency in intervals of same size

3. *Sample answer:* scatter plot; shows the relationship between two data sets

4. *Sample answer:* circle graph; shows data as parts of a whole

5. It looks like equal amounts of fruit were consumed, until you look at the key.

6. Unequal spacing on the vertical axis does not show the larger number of occurrence in the older age groups.

7. *Sample answer:* dot plot; shows the number of times each value occurs

8. stem-and-leaf plot

9. *Sample answer:* scatter plot; shows the relationship between two data sets

10. *Sample answer:* circle graph; shows data as parts of a whole

11. a. A pictograph does not show the kind of precise data a Board of Directors would need.

    b. *Sample answer:* line graph

9.4 Enrichment and Extension

1. mean: $15, median: $13.50, mode: $12

2. a. mean

   b. It is the highest of the three and makes it appear that the company offers a high hourly wage to its workers.

Answers

3. a. The competitor is using the mode. The newspaper is using the median.

b. The competitor picked the mode because it is lowest and they want to make it look like their competitor does not offer a good hourly wage. The newspaper picked the median because it represents the data well.

4. median

5. no; The people that have been with the company the longest will probably have the highest pay rates of anyone in the company.

9.4 Puzzle Time

STICK

Technology Connection

1. $y = 0.71x + 0.8603$ **2.** 10.8, or 11 points

3. 22.16, or 22 points

Chapter 10

10.1 Start Thinking!

For use before Activity 10.1

Sample answer: area and volume formulas, Pythagorean Theorem; x squared; the area of a square is the side length raised to the second power; x cubed; the volume of a cube is the edge length raised to the third power.

10.1 Warm Up

For use before Activity 10.1

1. 125   **2.** 1000   **3.** -27

4. 100,000   **5.** 256   **6.** 16

10.1 Start Thinking!

For use before Lesson 10.1

Answers will vary. Check students' poems.

10.1 Warm Up

For use before Lesson 10.1

1. 2^3 **2.** $(-7)^2$ **3.** $\left(\dfrac{2}{3}\right)^5$

4. $\left(-\dfrac{1}{6}\right)^3$ **5.** 11^7 **6.** $\left(-\dfrac{1}{4}\right)^4$

10.1 Practice A

1. 6^5 **2.** $(-2)^3$ **3.** $\left(\dfrac{2}{3}\right)^4$

4. $(-1.2)^3$ **5.** $\left(\dfrac{1}{5}\right)^2 x^3$ **6.** $10^2(-n)^3$

7. $(-5)^4 y^5$ **8.** 81   **9.** -625

10. 81   **11.** $\dfrac{1}{64}$ **12.** $2^2 \bullet 5^3$

13. -11 **14.** 29   **15.** 4   **16.** 42

17. a. $3 \bullet \left(\dfrac{5}{6}\right)^4$ **b.** $\dfrac{625}{432} \approx 1.4$ ft

18. a. $4 \bullet \left(\dfrac{1}{2}\right)^3$ **b.** $\dfrac{1}{2}$ mi

10.1 Practice B

1. 4^6 **2.** $(-12)^5$ **3.** $-\left(\dfrac{3}{7}\right)^3$

4. $\left(-\dfrac{3}{7}\right)^3$ **5.** $(-9)^4 x^3$ **6.** $25^4(-p)^5$

7. $(-2)^2 x^3 y^4$ **8.** 343   **9.** -256

10. 256   **11.** $\dfrac{8}{125}$ **12.** $3^3 \bullet 7^2$

13. -95 **14.** -83 **15.** -22 **16.** 0

17. a. $7 \bullet \left(\dfrac{7}{8}\right)^3$ **b.** $\dfrac{2401}{512} \approx 4.7$ ft

10.1 Enrichment and Extension

1. An upside-down gray triangle is drawn in the middle of every white triangle.

2.

3.

Step	White Triangles	Gray Triangles
0	1	0
1	3	1
2	9	4
3	27	13
4	81	40

4. Each one is a power of 3.

Answers

5. Each one is the sum of the white and gray triangles in the previous step.

6. 3^9

10.1 Puzzle Time

WITH HIS HONEYCOMB

10.2 Start Thinking!
For use before Activity 10.2

Sample answer: Without exponents, to write an expression like x^{50}, you would need to write out x fifty times. It's easier to write the expression using exponents.

10.2 Warm Up
For use before Activity 10.2

1. 243　　　　**2.** 625　　　　**3.** 1,000,000

4. −64　　　　**5.** 9　　　　**6.** −32

10.2 Start Thinking!
For use before Lesson 10.2

$2^6 \cdot 2^7$, $(-2)^2 \cdot (-2)^{12}$, $c^3 \cdot c^4$

10.2 Warm Up
For use before Lesson 10.2

1. 2^7　　　**2.** 7^{12}　　　**3.** $\left(\dfrac{1}{2}\right)^7$

4. $\left(-\dfrac{3}{5}\right)^6$　　**5.** x^{16}　　**6.** y^4

10.2 Practice A

1. 2^5　　　**2.** 9^{14}　　　**3.** $(-7)^8$

4. $\left(\dfrac{5}{8}\right)^{12}$　　**5.** c^6　　**6.** q^8

7. $\left(-\dfrac{4}{9}\right)^7$　　**8.** $(4.7)^5$　　**9.** 3^6

10. k^{50}　　**11.** $\left(\dfrac{1}{2}\right)^{12}$　　**12.** $(9.2)^{18}$

13. $16n^2$　　**14.** $-32w^5$　　**15.** $\dfrac{1}{81}p^4$

16. $15.625\,j^3$　　**17.** $a^{18}b^{18}$　　**18.** 2187

19. no; $3^2 \cdot 4^2 = 144$ and $12^4 = 20,736$

20. a. $V = \dfrac{4}{3}\pi\left(\dfrac{d}{2}\right)^3$; $V = \dfrac{1}{6}\pi d^3$　　**b.** $V = \dfrac{4}{81}\pi$ cm^3

10.2 Practice B

1. 8^{10}　　　**2.** $(-16)^{26}$　　　**3.** $\left(-\dfrac{5}{9}\right)^{10}$

4. $\left(\dfrac{1}{15}\right)^{13}$　　**5.** q^{16}　　**6.** $(13.2)^8$

7. $(-7.4)^{21}$　　**8.** 9^9　　**9.** d^{12}

10. $(2.9)^{18}$　　**11.** $\left(\dfrac{5}{8}\right)^6$　　**12.** $\left(-\dfrac{2}{9}\right)^{15}$

13. $16p^4$　　**14.** $\dfrac{1}{125}k^3$　　**15.** $2.744c^3$

16. m^8n^8　　**17.** 5832　　**18.** $\dfrac{2}{25}v^3$

19. a. $V = \pi\left(\dfrac{2}{3}h\right)^2 h$; $V = \dfrac{4}{9}\pi h^3$　　**b.** $V = \dfrac{3}{16}\pi$ in.^{3}

20. $x = 10$　　　　**21.** $x = 6$

10.2 Enrichment and Extension

1. x^{64}　　**2.** y^{81}　　**3.** a^{121}　　**4.** b^{729}

5.

n	2^n	2^{2^n}	Fermat number
1	2	4	5
2	4	16	17
3	8	256	257
4	16	65,536	65,537

6. Each term is the square of the previous term.

7. yes; Because the exponent 2^n increases by a power of two each time.

8. 2^{2^n}; Because 2^n grows faster than n^2.

10.2 Puzzle Time

THE PIANO TEACHER WHO CALLED THE LOCKSMITH BECAUSE ONE OF HER KEYS GOT STUCK

Answers

The Product of Powers Property states that
$a^m \cdot a^n = a^{m+n}$; Check students' conjectures.

10.3 Warm Up
For use before Activity 10.3

1. $5 \cdot 5 \cdot 5 \cdot 5$ 2. $7 \cdot 7 \cdot 7$

3. $6 \cdot 6 \cdot 6 \cdot 6 \cdot 6 \cdot 6 \cdot 6$

4. $(-4) \cdot (-4) \cdot (-4)$

5. $(-3) \cdot (-3) \cdot (-3) \cdot (-3) \cdot (-3)$

6. $(-1) \cdot (-1) \cdot (-1)$

10.3 Start Thinking!
For use before Lesson 10.3

Sample answer: disagree; Scott's calculation has three
steps while using the Quotient of Powers Property has
only two steps: subtract $5 - 2$ to get 3, and then raise
2 to the third power to get 8. Also, if you are trying to
simplify a variable expression, you often cannot do
calculations in the numerator and denominator.

10.3 Warm Up
For use before Lesson 10.3

1. 5^3 2. 4^4 3. 2.5^3

4. 10.1^4 5. $(-5)^2$ 6. -2

10.3 Practice A

1. 3^2 2. 10^8 3. -4 4. $(5.6)^6$

5. p^2 6. $(-0.7)^{13}$ 7. s^{21} 8. π^5

9. $\dfrac{2^{30}}{2^{18}} = 2^{12}$ times more bytes of memory

10. 6^6 11. 3^6 12. $(-0.5)^5$ 13. m^7

14. $25n^4$ 15. x^3z^2 16. $8c^6d^5$ 17. a^2b^3

18. $x = 5$ 19. $x = 1$

10.3 Practice B

1. 12^{11} 2. 7.6^{10} 3. $(-9)^{12}$ 4. -8.5

5. u^{22} 6. π^5 7. $(-1000)^5$ 8. t^2

9. $\dfrac{10^{12}}{10^3} = 10^9$ 10. 11^{11} 11. 2.5^6

12. $(-7.9)^5$ 13. b^{20} 14. $64m^5n^4$

15. $r^3s^4t^9$ 16. p^8q^3 17. $3a^2b^9$

18. $x = 4$ 19. $x = 3$

10.3 Enrichment and Extension

1. 770   2. 436   3. 9124   4. 943

5. 1412   6. 85   7. 346   8. 875

9. 989   10. 607   11. 7825   12. 57,425

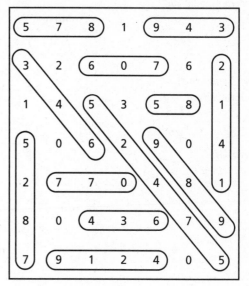

about 1 in $26^{130,000}$

10.3 Puzzle Time
DOGGY DISKETTES

10.4 Start Thinking!
For use before Activity 10.4
Answers will vary.

10.4 Warm Up
For use before Activity 10.4

1. 5^3 2. 2^3 3. 4^6

4. a^{12} 5. c^4 6. n^{10}

Answers

10.4 Start Thinking!
For use before Lesson 10.4

Sample answer: yes; $\left(\dfrac{1}{2}\right)^{-2} = 4$, which is greater than 1.

yes; $(-2)^{-1} = -\dfrac{1}{2}$, which is less than 0.

10.4 Warm Up
For use before Lesson 10.4

1. 1   **2.** 49   **3.** 1

4. 1   **5.** 729   **6.** 1

10.4 Practice A

1. $\dfrac{1}{81}$ **2.** 1   **3.** $\dfrac{1}{64}$ **4.** $-\dfrac{1}{729}$

5. 1   **6.** $\dfrac{1}{64}$ **7.** $\dfrac{1}{216}$ **8.** 16

9. a. 10^6 **b.** 10^{18} **c.** 10^3 **d.** 10^{21}

    e. $\dfrac{1}{10^{21}}$ **f.** $\dfrac{1}{10^3}$ **g.** $\dfrac{1}{10^{15}}$

10. $\dfrac{8}{x^3}$ **11.** $\dfrac{m^6}{125}$ **12.** $7p^6$

13. $\dfrac{10}{t^3}$ **14.** $\dfrac{5}{d^5}$ **15.** 24

10.4 Practice B

1. $\dfrac{1}{125}$ **2.** 1   **3.** 36   **4.** 1

5. $\dfrac{1}{1000}$ **6.** $\dfrac{1}{9}$ **7.** 1   **8.** $\dfrac{1}{256}$

9. a. $\dfrac{1}{10^{15}}$ **b.** $\dfrac{1}{10^9}$ **c.** $\dfrac{1}{10^{18}}$ **d.** $\dfrac{1}{10^3}$

    e. 10^3 **f.** 10^{12} **g.** $\dfrac{1}{10^{27}}$

10. $\dfrac{2}{u^{12}}$ **11.** $\dfrac{18}{w^3}$ **12.** $\dfrac{y^5}{z^3}$ **13.** $\dfrac{b^9}{8}$

10.4 Enrichment and Extension

1. no; The graph is not a straight line.

2. 1   **3.** no

4.

x	y
-3	8
-2	4
-1	2
0	1
1	$\dfrac{1}{2}$
2	$\dfrac{1}{4}$
3	$\dfrac{1}{8}$

It is the same graph reflected across the y-axis.

5. 1

6. yes; Because a is positive, the value of a^0 is always 1.

7. 1

10.4 Puzzle Time
IT WAS PETRIFIED

10.5 Start Thinking!
For use before Activity 10.5

Sample answer: A scientist may use negative exponents for measurements that are smaller than one. For example measurement of human hair or blood cells.

10.5 Warm Up
For use before Activity 10.5

1. 1000   **2.** $\dfrac{1}{10,000}$

3. 100,000   **4.** $\dfrac{1}{100}$

5. 10,000,000,000   **6.** $\dfrac{1}{100,000}$

Answers

10.5 Start Thinking!
For use before Lesson 10.5

Expectations may vary. The mass of an electron is about $9.10938188 \times 10^{-31}$ kilogram and the mass of Earth is about 5.9742×10^{24} kilograms.

10.5 Warm Up
For use before Lesson 10.5

1. 43,000,000,000

2. 0.0012

3. 7,330,000,000,000,000,000

4. 0.00000000000009365

10.5 Practice A

1. 62,100,000,000

2. 51,700,000,000,000,000

3. yes; The factor is at least 1 and less than 10. The power of 10 has an integer exponent.

4. no; The factor is greater than 10.

5. yes; The factor is at least 1 and less than 10. The power of 10 has an integer exponent.

6. no; The factor is less than 1.

7. no; The factor is greater than 10.

8. yes; The factor is at least 1 and less than 10. The power of 10 has an integer exponent.

9. 8,000,000   10. 0.09   11. 2000

12. 0.00053   13. 120,000,000   14. 786,000

15. a. 150,000,000,000 m   b. 384,000,000 m
    c. Moon

16. a. 432,000 sec   b. 2,592,000 sec
    c. 31,536,000 sec   d. 31,622,400 sec
    e. 86,400 sec $= 8.64 \times 10^4$ sec

10.5 Practice B

1. 0.00000000086

2. 4,390,000,000,000

3. no; The factor is greater than 10.

4. yes; The factor is at least 1 and less than 10. The power of 10 has an integer exponent.

5. yes; The factor is at least 1 and less than 10. The power of 10 has an integer exponent.

6. no; The factor is less than 1.

7. no; The factor is greater than 10.

8. yes; The factor is at least 1 and less than 10. The power of 10 has an integer exponent.

9. 0.0005   10. 154,000   11. 0.00000178

12. 0.0009876   13. 20,800,000   14. 355,500,000

15. a. Sun   b. Moon   c. 6,380,000 m
    d. 1,740,000 m   e. 700,000,000 m

16. a. 157,800,000 sec   b. 15,780,000 sec
    c. 2,630,000 sec

10.5 Enrichment and Extension

1. $3 \bullet 10^4 + 0 \bullet 10^3 + 2 \bullet 10^2 + 7 \bullet 10^1 + 5 \bullet 10^0$

2. $1 \bullet 2^6 + 0 \bullet 2^5 + 0 \bullet 2^4 + 1 \bullet 2^3 + 0 \bullet 2^2$
   $+ 1 \bullet 2^1 + 0 \bullet 2^0$

3. 74

4. a. 4   b. 3   c. $3 \bullet 4^2 + 3 \bullet 4^1 + 1 \bullet 4^0 = 61$

5. a. $2 \bullet 3^4 + 2 \bullet 3^3 + 0 \bullet 3^2 + 1 \bullet 3^1 + 2 \bullet 3^0$
      $= 221$
   b. $3 \bullet 8^3 + 0 \bullet 8^2 + 0 \bullet 8^1 + 4 \bullet 8^0 = 1540$
   c. $5 \bullet 6^2 + 0 \bullet 6^1 + 1 \bullet 6^0 = 181$
   d. $3 \bullet 16^2 + 1 \bullet 16^1 + 2 \bullet 16^0 = 786$

6. 101001

10.5 Puzzle Time

GHOULIE

10.6 Start Thinking!
For use before Activity 10.6

Sample steps for a large number: Move the decimal point to the right of the first nonzero digit. Count the number of places you moved the decimal point. This becomes the exponent of the power of 10. *Sample steps for a small number:* Move the decimal point to the right of the first nonzero digit. Count the number of places you moved the decimal point. Put a negative sign in front of it. This becomes the exponent of the power of 10.

Answers

10.6 Warm Up
For use before Activity 10.6

1. 6000   **2.** 0.0004

3. 200,000   **4.** 0.026

5. 52,500,000,000   **6.** 0.0000852

10.6 Start Thinking!
For use before Lesson 10.6

Students' estimates will vary. *Sample answer:* about 7.1×10^9 people

10.6 Warm Up
For use before Lesson 10.6

1. 3.4×10^{-4} **2.** 6.75×10^6 **3.** 7.0×10^{-8}

4. 1.25×10^5 **5.** 1.52×10^{10} **6.** 9.17×10^{-10}

10.6 Practice A

1. 3.5×10^5 **2.** 4×10^{-4} **3.** 5.27×10^{-13}

4. 1.25×10^7 **5.** 1.9×10^9 **6.** 1.0×10^{-7}

7. 5.0×10^{12} **8.** 6.524×10^{-5}

9. $3.26 \times 10^8, 3.6 \times 10^8, 6.3 \times 10^8$

10. $5.05 \times 10^{-13}, 9.8 \times 10^{-12}, 1.23 \times 10^{-11}$

11. $5.6 \times 10^{-7}, 6.18 \times 10^7, 6.8 \times 10^7$

12. $4.27 \times 10^{-5}, 4.7 \times 10^{-5}, 4.81 \times 10^{-5}$

13. $2.0 \times 10^{11}; 4.0 \times 10^{11}$ **14.** 1.0×10^{-10} m

15. a. 5.9×10^{10} **b.** 2.8×10^{10} **c.** 1.01×10^{11}

16. a. 1.0×10^{-6} **b.** 1.0×10^{-3}

17. $3.2\%, \dfrac{16}{5}, 3.2 \times 10^2, 322$

18. $0.58, \dfrac{589}{1000}, 5.89 \times 10^3$

10.6 Practice B

1. 8.5×10^{-5} **2.** 4.1×10^8 **3.** 1.43×10^{-2}

4. 1.3475×10^{11} **5.** 7.0×10^{15} **6.** 1.99×10^{-12}

7. 5.24×10^{13} **8.** 6.133×10^{-8}

9. $4.15 \times 10^{14}, 4.5 \times 10^{14}, 5.4 \times 10^{14}$

10. $7.22 \times 10^{-22}, 2.8 \times 10^{-20}, 3.11 \times 10^{-19}$

11. $4.1 \times 10^{-5}, 4.181 \times 10^{-5}, 4.118 \times 10^{-3}$

12. $6.17 \times 10^{-32}, 6.7 \times 10^{-32}, 3.72 \times 10^{32}$

13. 1.992×10^{-23} kg   **14.** 400

15. a. 1.07×10^3 **b.** 1.89×10^{11}

16. a. 6.94×10^6 **b.** 402 mi^2

17. $0.53\%, 0.00538, \dfrac{538}{1000}, 5\dfrac{3}{8}$

18. $0.0082, 8.19 \times 10^{-2}, \dfrac{270}{330}$

10.6 Enrichment and Extension

1.

Element	Chemical Symbol	Mass (amu)	Mass (g)
Silver	Ag	1.26×10^{25}	21
Oxygen	O	1.69×10^{25}	28
Platinum	Pt	9.64×10^{24}	16
Helium	He	3.01×10^{22}	0.05
Nitrogen	N	2.05×10^{25}	34

2. heptagon

10.6 Puzzle Time

MAJAMAS

10.7 Start Thinking!
For use before Activity 10.7

Sample answer: Students will likely say that it is easier to copy the second number; some benefits are that you are less likely to introduce errors when copying the number and that you can easily see the magnitude of a number in scientific notation by looking at the exponent.

10.7 Warm Up
For use before Activity 10.7

1. yes; The factor is at least 1 and less than 10. The power of 10 has an integer exponent. So, the number is written in scientific notation.

2. no; The factor is less than 1. So, the number is not written in scientific notation.

Answers

3. no; The power of 10 is not an integer exponent. So, the number is not written in scientific notation.

4. no; The factor is greater than 10. So, the number is not written in scientific notation.

10.7 Start Thinking!
For use before Lesson 10.7

To write a number in scientific notation, move the decimal point to the right of the first nonzero digit. Then, count the number of places you moved the decimal point. This determines the exponent of the power of 10. Use a positive exponent when you move the decimal place to the left, and a negative exponent when you move the decimal to the right. *Sample answer:* Scientific notation is used to write very small numbers and very large numbers.

10.7 Warm Up
For use before Lesson 10.7

1. 5.4×10^4 **2.** 4.17×10^6

3. 3×10^{15} **4.** 3.3×10^8

10.7 Practice A

1. 7×10^4 **2.** 4.5×10^{-3} **3.** 3.9×10^{-5}

4. 1.4×10^9 **5.** 1.24×10^{-5} **6.** 1.517×10^{13}

7. 4.0×10^7 **8.** 2×10^0 **9.** 6×10^3

10. 3×10^5 **11.** 4.2×10^{-20} **12.** 6.4×10^{11}

13. 2.2×10^{-1} **14.** 2.25×10^{-3}

15. $1.6 \times 10^{-15} \text{ m}^2$ **16.** $5.6 \times 10^{10} \text{ ft}^2$

17. General Sherman; $4.65 \times 10^3 \text{ ft}^3$ greater than Washington; $5.9 \times 10^3 \text{ ft}^3$ greater than General Grant

10.7 Practice B

1. 3×10^1 **2.** 6.2×10^{-5} **3.** 6.87×10^{-2}

4. 5.89×10^{14} **5.** 2.4×10^4 **6.** 4×10^2

7. 2.5×10^{-2} **8.** 2.7×10^{12} **9.** 6.5×10^3

10. 5×10^{14} **11.** 8×10^{-25} **12.** 1.83×10^{-6}

13. 1.86×10^5 **14.** 1×10^{14}

15. $7.02 \times 10^{12} \text{ m}^2$ **16.** $2.652 \times 10^{-9} \text{ ft}^2$

17. about 50 times greater

10.7 Enrichment and Extension

1. 20.5×10^6 **2.** 48×10^{-9} **3.** 341×10^3

4. 815×10^{-9} **5.** 272×10^{12} **6.** 800×10^6

7. 55×10^{-6} **8.** 81.5×10^6 **9.** 331.2×10^6

10. 5.244×10^9 **11.** 1.92×10^{-3} **12.** 450×10^9

13. *Sample answer:* It is easier to compare numbers.

14. *Sample answer:* It is more difficult to determine the factor of the number.

10.7 Puzzle Time

IT QUACKED UP

Technology Connection

1. 1.736×10^{13} **2.** 1.8×10^{-4}

3. 56,066,000 **4.** 7.9×10^{-5}

5. 1.725 **6.** 5.02×10^{10}

7. 2.98×10^{-9} **8.** 3,062,500,000

9. Answers may vary depending on type of calculator. For TI-83 Plus: Answers that have 10 or fewer digits are displayed using standard notation. Answers that have more than 10 digits are displayed using scientific notation.